Tom Tullett was formerly the Chief of the *Daily Mirror*'s Crime Bureau and the only journalist to have been a member of the Criminal Investigation Department at Scotland Yard. Since the war he has covered every major crime in this country and many in other parts of the world. He has an intimate knowledge of London's underworld and of police work.

In addition to being one of the best-known crime reporters in Fleet Street, he has written the following books: *Portrait of a Bad Man*, *Inside Interpol*, *Inside Dartmoor*, *Bernard Spilsbury: His Life and Cases* (with Douglas G. Browne) and *No Answer from Foxtrot Eleven*.

By the same author

TOM TULLETT

Clues to Murder

Famous Forensic Murder Cases of Professor J. M. Cameron

GRAFTON BOOKS

A Division of the Collins Publishing Group

LONDON GLASGOW
TORONTO SYDNEY AUCKLAND

Grafton Books
A Division of the Collins Publishing Group
8 Grafton Street, London W1X 3LA

Published by Grafton Books 1987
Reprinted 1989

First published in Great Britain by
The Bodley Head Ltd 1986

Copyright © Tom Tullett and J. M. Cameron 1986

ISBN 0-586-06930-5

Printed and bound in Great Britain by
Collins, Glasgow

Set in Times

Contents

Acknowledgements

Clues to Murder is about criminal investigation and, in particular, how forensic science helps the detective to find the murderer and prove the case.

The close and friendly co-operation of Professor Cameron and his staff at the London Hospital has been an essential factor in the writing of this book. The exclusive material they have furnished is highly authoritative.

My sincere thanks are due to Sir Kenneth Newman, QPM, Commissioner of the Metropolitan Police, for permission to look into criminal records and to talk to detectives who have intimate knowledge of murder investigation.

Many policemen, now retired, have given immense assistance. They are: Roy Habershon, MBE, H. D. Walton, QPM, John Lynch, Frank Cater, Patrick Sugrue, John Grant and Fred Narborough. Many other detectives in the Home Counties, including Ray Farrant, John McConnell, Peter Blythe, Jack Reece and George Harris have helped by recalling their investigations in fine detail, and Miss Plank and the staff of the New Scotland Yard Reference Library have been wonderfully helpful.

Many friends and former colleagues in Fleet Street, including Edward Vale, Brian McConnell, QGM, George Hollingbury, James Reid, Percy Hoskins and Albert Foster have given great assistance.

My thanks are due to the Medico Legal Society for permission to use Professor Cameron's address on the Dingo Baby Case, and the publishers Mayhew-

McCrimmon Ltd for permission to use the chapter from the book entitled *Face to Face with the Turin Shroud*. Thanks are also due to the following for permission to reproduce photographs: The Commissioner of the Metropolitan Police, pages 4, 5, 11, 12; the *Daily Mirror*, pages 5 (top), 8 (top), 10 (top), 13, 16; Kent Constabulary, pages 1, 2, 6; Thames Valley Police, page 3; Hertfordshire Constabulary, page 7 (top); Essex Police, page 9; Bedfordshire Police, page 10. Professor Cameron supplied the photographs from Hong Kong and from Singapore.

Introduction

The fact of James Malcolm Cameron's birth was in no way remarkable, but the place of his birth was personally far-reaching in that this outstanding forensic scientist is usually addressed by those who know and work with him as 'Taffy'.

It happened when he was playing rugby for the High School of Glasgow Former Pupils and other representative sides like the West of Scotland. At that time the games were being reported on radio and the commentators found that there were so many players called Cameron that some method of distinguishing each one was required. One commentator decided to inquire into the birthplaces of the various Camerons and when he heard that James Malcolm was born in Wales the fast-running wing-threequarter was henceforth referred to as 'Taffy'. The name has stuck and today he is known all over Britain, and in many other countries where sudden death is investigated, as 'Taffy' Cameron.

He was born on 29 April, 1930, in Swansea, the only child of the late James Cameron and Doris Mary Robertson from Glasgow. His father was a professional footballer who played centre-forward for Clyde, and a Powderhall sprinter. By trade he was a drapery salesman.

At school Taffy displayed his father's sporting prowess in rugby and athletics. He was also in the school debating team, and in one contest, in 1947, against the Glasgow High School for Girls, he first met Primrose Miller McKerrell. Later he went to Glasgow University to study law. However, after a losing battle with Latin, he studied medicine and soon developed an enthusiasm for orthopaedics.

He qualified as a doctor in 1953, when he was twenty-three years old. From there, after doing general surgery, he began to specialize in orthopaedic surgery, and developed a bent for pathology. In 1956 he married Primrose McKerrell, the girl from his school days, and his career made rapid strides. He made a special study of Perkes Disease, a deformity of the head of the femur which causes osteochondrosis of the hip.

By the time he was thirty Cameron was Senior Registrar in Pathology at the Southern General Hospital, Glasgow, and Lecturer in Pathology at Glasgow Royal Infirmary, and in 1961 he was awarded the Western Regional Hospital Board prize in original research for his work on Perkes Disease. His prize was a trip to London to continue his research.

At that time Professor Francis Camps, the renowned pathologist, was holding a course for the Diploma of Medical Jurisprudence. Dr Cameron attended and was asked to give a paper on phosphorus poisoning. Afterwards he was invited to dine with Professor Camps, who suggested he might like to join his Forensic Department at the London Hospital Medical College in Whitechapel, East London.

After Cameron had returned to Glasgow he received two letters. One was from Professor Camps offering him a lectureship at the London Hospital; the other said he had won a prize offered by the Arthritis and Rheumatism Foundation. That prize was a travelling fellowship to Wisconsin, USA, to continue his study for a Ph.D. in bone pathology. Cameron chose the former and, three months later, was installed at the London Hospital.

In the late 1960s Professor Camps went to the Sudan to advise on forensic medicine and most of the important work of the department fell to Dr Cameron. This continued until 1972 when Professor Camps retired, and shortly afterwards he fell ill and died. The pressure of work was such at that time that Cameron, only just past forty, suffered a heart attack. When he recovered he was promoted to his present title of professor.

Today he is Professor of Forensic Medicine at the University of London and Director of the Department of Forensic Medicine at the London Hospital, and for many years he has been one of the experts who advise the Home Office on criminal cases and, in particular, on murder. In addition he is Lecturer in Forensic Medicine at St Bartholomew's Hospital, at the Royal Free Hospital, at University College Hospital and to the Metropolitan Police Detective Training School. He also lectures to many police forces, to the Royal Military Police and to barristers, and he is Honorary Consultant in Forensic Medicine to the Royal Navy and the Army. His cases have taken him all over the world.

His office has an ever-open door and many people visit him for advice, which he gives unfailingly. The visitors are younger pathologists, doctors and detectives needing help in their own pursuit of how a death occurred. I have known the Professor for many years and he has always been prepared to discuss a case and give the benefit of his own thorough investigation. If he did not know, or was not sure, he would admit it. Everyone who sees much of him speaks of him with genuine affection. He is courteous but stern in the mortuary or when working at the scene of a crime, but when work is over he has an infectious sense of humour.

His work load is prodigious. On most days he is conducting post-mortem examinations from eight to ten o'clock in the morning and he lectures several times a week. He agrees that his job of performing about 1,300 autopsies a year is punishing and macabre. And while he is respectful of the dead and their families, his defence against the never-ending stream of human agonies is an ability to see, sometimes, the humorous side.

He still laughs about the time he was called at short notice to fly to Durban on a murder case. The urgency was such that the detective superintendent who was to accompany him sent a car and two police motor cyclists to rush him to the airport. On the way one of the motor cyclists was in a collision and Taffy Cameron went to attend to the unconscious policeman. He diagnosed a broken collar bone and strapped it up. As he finished the policeman recovered consciousness and Cameron introduced himself. Recognition dawned and the police-man said, 'I don't want you. You only deal with the dead. Bugger off.'

Later he told the story to Superintendent Pat Sugrue, who was fretting at the airport, and said, 'I couldn't blame him. Who wants to see me when he's alive?'

As detectives always carry the Murder Bag, full of aids to investigation, Professor Cameron carries his own sturdy and rather battered case which contains sketch pads, gloves, sponges, surgical instruments, dungarees, pots and small bags, a thermometer, a trowel, chalk, tape and note pads. If there is time he takes a team consisting of his secretary, a photographer, one or two technicians and a junior lecturer. He is always assisted by the police, who usually send a photographer, plus a Scenes of Crime Officer to look for clues and to collect them. Once the scene of the crime is dealt with, the rest of the pathol-ogist's work is done in the mortuary or the laboratory.

The attendance to sudden death is a hard taskmaster for it is totally unpredictable, as frequently happening at night and at weekends as during a nine-to-five, five-day week. There are times when a full night's sleep is impossible.

Although he is known to the world as a forensic scientist delving into the mysteries of death, Cameron finds time to work in the treatment of the living. He has a passionate interest in battered babies, a problem in which he became involved in 1964, when he performed post-mortems on the bodies of more than twenty babies who had died as a result of violent attacks. He made a detailed report, assisted by colleagues, to the Director of Public Prosecutions. He also advises on the treatment of ortho-paedic complaints.

Until 1985 he was Secretary General for the British Academy of Forensic Sciences and still remains the Editor of its magazine, *Medicine, Science and the Law*. The Society was founded by Professor Camps, who was its first President. He also serves on the Standing Committee of 'Justice', which investigates cases in which justice may have miscarried.

Taffy Cameron refers to the mortuary as 'The Temple of Truth', which is not an original description, but dates back to famous pathologists of the past, people like John Glaister, Bernard Spilsbury and Francis Camps. It means that in the finding out of the time and cause of death there is no subterfuge. There is a naked body exposed to the expert to yield all the secrets of death in all its forms. And his findings have to be exact.

The pathologist is the expert witness whose career resembles an iceberg, nine-tenths of which is hidden. Out of the 25,000 post-mortem examinations Cameron has made, only a small proportion have had to do with murder, but his findings have often not only pointed the police in the right direction to find the murderer but have been vital evidence at trials.

Professor Cameron's headquarters are at the London Hospital where he has his office. On the wall behind his desk hangs a plaque in a wooden frame, surrounded by crests of the many police forces he has assisted, all gifts from the detectives. Within the wooden frame is written the maxim of Giovanni Battista Morgagni, the father of morbid anatomy. It reads: 'Those who have dissected or inspected many bodies have at least learned to doubt, while those who are ignorant of anatomy and do not take the trouble to attend to it, are in no doubt at all.'

That is the creed of all pathologists.

In this book reference is made to 'the team', the people who work with Professor Cameron both at the scenes of crime and in the forensic laboratory. These eight people are an integral part of many of his investigations.

PATHOLOGISTS
Dr Peter Vanezis
Dr Peter Jerreat
Dr Michael Heath

FORENSIC ODONTOLOGIST
Bernard Sims

TECHNICIANS
Ron Grounsell
Tom West

PHOTOGRAPHER
Ray Ruddick

SECRETARY
Mrs Jenny Hunnisett

1
The Early Years

On New Year's Eve, 1962, Dr Cameron joined the staff of the Department of Forensic Medicine, University of London, at The London Hospital Medical College in Whitechapel. He was then thirty-two years old and appointed Lecturer, a similar post to the one he had previously held at Glasgow University. For a man destined to become one of the world's foremost experts on murder it was fitting that he went to work in the area of East London where Jack the Ripper had roamed the streets years before, killing prostitutes and on each occasion removing one of the body organs by rough surgery before he left the scene. There had been many other murders in the area, including the killing of policemen by anarchists in the Sidney Street Siege and also the interesting medical case of the Elephant Man, the human freak who was a permanent side-show in a shop opposite the London Hospital.

Head of the department was Professor Francis Camps, one of the Home Office pathologists, permanently on call to assist the Criminal Investigation Department of the police in cases of murder. In the early years, while Professor Camps was very much in charge, Cameron dealt with many murders, but few that made newspaper headlines. One in which he played a minor but important part was in March 1963, the murder of a twenty-two-year-old prostitute, Veronica Walsh, also known as Vicki Pender.

Hers was a world of cheap thrills and pep pills; of seedy clubs and brief encounters. The slim, attractive

woman with flaming red hair was found murdered in her
flat in Adolphus Road, Finsbury Park, in North London.
She was half-naked and had been strangled. Bruises on
her face and head suggested she had put up a struggle
with her murderer.

Vicki Pender was one of the prostitutes who could no
longer solicit for custom in the streets due to the new
Street Offences Act of 1958, which had provided sterner
penalties for the offence and had driven prostitution
underground. She worked from a £4-a-week bed-sitting-
room.

The police discovered that the murdered woman was
well known in Soho clubs and on the day she died had
taken a quantity of drugs known as purple hearts and had
smoked marijuana. She was also being propositioned to
act in blue films and, police believed, had already made
some.

Detective Superintendent Ernest Sims of the Yard's
Murder Squad took charge of the case and called in
Professor Camps. After the post-mortem examination
Camps asked Cameron to assess the injuries to the dead
woman's face, in particular a vicious blow to her chin.
Cameron was able to prove that the blow to the chin of
the dead woman had been inflicted with a blunt instrument with a patterned surface, possibly from a knitted
glove covering the butt of a gun or a cosh.

In due course Superintendent Sims arrested and
charged a thirty-three-year-old salesman, Colin Welt
Fisher, with Vicki Pender's murder. Fisher was a married
man living at St Margaret's Way, Leverstock Green,
Hemel Hempstead, and had left home in March to spend
the weekend in London. In fact he spent the next few
days with Vicki Pender and they had both indulged in
drugs and sex. Fisher was remembered and later identified
by a number of night-club employees and when seen by

the police confessed to the killing. Some other club hostesses had been propositioned by Fisher and they had told Superintendent Sims.

Fisher was tried for murder, found guilty and sentenced to life imprisonment. His appeal against the verdict was dismissed.

Finding the cause of death is one of the prime functions of the pathologist and like many other doctors Cameron takes the view that murders can be committed and not be recognized by general practitioners. He wrote a paper in 1964 entitled 'Things are not always what they seem!'

In it he remarked that although in fiction a hat-pin stuck into the heart is often a favourite method of murder, this type of injury is, fortunately, rare or, more correctly, seldom reported. He then instanced two cases with which he had been concerned where the real cause of death was only found during routine autopsies after deaths that had merely been reported to the coroner as unexpected and sudden. Both were initially diagnosed by unsuspicious doctors as death from natural disease.

The first case concerned a sixty-three-year-old man, Mr Thomas, who was in good health but on whose chest Cameron found the minute marks of a pin which had penetrated the left ventricle of the heart. Cameron's findings were that the man himself had pushed an instrument, possibly a hat-pin, twice into his body and then withdrawn it completely. At the inquest evidence was given of a drunken family quarrel the evening before the death. As a result of Dr Cameron's evidence an open verdict was returned.

The second case was that of a woman of eighty-five who was first thought to have died from a heart attack. On closer examination Dr Cameron saw a metal hat-pin protruding from her chest. He found that there were nine tentative pinpricks over the mid-line of the chest made

with the pin and there were pinpricks on the thumb side
of her right index finger. The hat-pin had been pushed
into her heart and, in that case, a verdict of suicide was
recorded. In the first case, the fact that a hat-pin had
been used could not be confirmed, though in retrospect,
the suggestion appears to be upheld. In the second case
there was no doubt.

Those last two examples illustrate the thin line between
the discovery of a crime and the easy assumption of
natural causes. An equally essential part of the pathologist's job is establishing the identity of a victim. In one
of Cameron's earliest cases in 1963 a unique identification
was made in the St Pancras mortuary by most of the
publicans in the King's Cross area of North London.

The police had found a man bludgeoned to death and
hanging by telephone wire from a beam in a bus garage.
The victim had the appearance of a heavy drinker, but
there was nothing in his pockets to identify him. Dr
Cameron cut down the body and had it removed to the
mortuary and after examination was able to tell Detective
Chief Superintendent Roy Habershon that the man had
been drinking most of the day, probably in local public
houses, since he appeared to be of the vagrant type who
lived locally in fairly rough style. Habershon, later to be
in charge of the Scotland Yard's Bomb Squad, was a
forthright detective. He sent a police van to every local
public house and requested each publican to attend the
mortuary. Within the hour, no fewer than thirty-six men
were ushered into the chilly atmosphere of white marble
slabs.

They all knew the dead man, but could only identify
him as the man they called 'Old Street', so named because
he lived in the Salvation Army hostel in Old Street, less
than a mile from where he was found dead. It was then
easy to identify him properly through the hostel records.

It was to prove almost as easy to arrest and convict his killers. The murder was the result of a drunken brawl at pub closing time, a common affair at that time in that part of London, where main-line railway stations attracted late-night itinerant thieves and vagabonds with an eye to picking up anything from travellers or stealing from the unwary. One witness who was helpful was a man who had a habit of whistling through his teeth when he talked. Habershon noticed that the nearer he got to the truth the more he whistled. In the end, when the whistle was almost continuous, he gave the names of the people who had taken part in the drunken brawl, which had been intended to frighten and gone too far. The six men were all convicted of manslaughter and sent to prison.

A warm day in August 1963 found Cameron in an office block in Cold Blow Lane, New Cross, in South-East London, where he had been called to the scene of a murder. The victim was a twenty-two-year-old married woman and she had been stabbed to death. Her body was lying beside her chair and her note book was still on her desk by her typewriter. It was a murder which presented no problems but it was a sad case, for the husband, Alan Kenneth Hall, a twenty-eight-year-old house painter, was suffering from acute mental depression after the victim, his wife, Joyce, had left him.

On that morning he had waited outside the office until his wife had arrived for her secretarial job. He accompanied her to the manager's office where she worked and other employees heard raised voices and then saw 'flailing arms' through the frosted glass. One of the clerks ran into the room and saw Hall standing over his wife, who was screaming, 'He has stabbed me.' Hall was held and the police called.

In a statement he said that for about two months he and his wife had been having rows about her going to

work. Hall claimed that she appeared to be more inter-
ested in her job than the home and her four-year-old son,
Joey. She had left home and refused to return, leaving
Hall to look after the child.

Dr Cameron gave evidence as to the several stab
wounds at the trial, when Hall pleaded not guilty to
murder but guilty to manslaughter and was sentenced to
five years imprisonment.

Hall had experienced a miserable childhood. His father
had died when he was very young and his mother had
become an alcoholic. As a child he was beset with fear
and anxiety and he had joined the army to get away from
his background. His marriage was a great turning-point
for him and his only interest was to make it a success.
But, soon after the baby was born, his wife left him for
three months. Twice she returned to him and then went
away again and he suspected she was associating with
another man.

It was another small human tragedy of a type which
Cameron was to become used to, and yet wonder about
as he learnt the weaknesses, the wild decisions and the
motivations of people that lead them to murder.

The life of a pathologist is not always concerned with
murder. In August 1964 Dr Cameron was called to the
Bexley Mental Hospital, in Kent, where a body had been
found in a cornfield nearby. The skeletized remains had
been disturbed by a combine harvester.

The body was lying on its right side and fully dressed.
Nearby lay a small, empty, brown tablet bottle, an empty
vodka bottle and four full cans of bitter lemon and one
empty one. This was no case of murder, and Dr Cameron
reported that the cause of death was unascertainable, but
that foul play did not appear to have played any part in
it.

In fact, the dead man had been a patient in the

nearby mental hospital, because Cameron was able to find enough clues in the skeletized body and the clothes to point to a man named James Reginald Powditch, a patient who had gone for a walk and never returned.

Here again, it was the clues to identity which were important. First the teeth and the jaws were proved to be identical with those of the missing man. In addition the dead man had a deformity of the ring finger of the right hand, which also could be proved. But, most importantly, the frontal sinuses were identical with those of James Powditch.

It had been known for a long time that frontal sinuses are as surely identifiable as fingerprints if an exact match can be made. But often bodies are found that are completely unknown and therefore uncharted. In this case, because the man had been a patient in the hospital, there had been an X-ray recorded of his head. With the X-ray print superimposed on those taken by Dr Cameron he was able to write: 'My opinion is that with all these similarities there can be little doubt that the skeleton found in the grounds of Bexley Mental Hospital on Saturday, 8 August 1964, is none other than that of James Reginald Powditch.'

The presumption was that the man had gone to the field to take drugs and to drink the vodka, perhaps to commit suicide. But Cameron could not go as far as that. He found no traces of drugs in the little brown bottle and the minute remaining concentration of alcohol in the vodka bottle was normal. Nobody knew whether the bottle had been full or, indeed, when it had been emptied, and the skeletized body could not reveal such fine points.

The case, however, was another milestone in pathology in proving that when more ordinary methods of identification, like fingerprints, photography, scars and marks, fail the comparison of sinuses can be proof positive.

It was in 1965 that the name of Dr Cameron, Home Office pathologist, began to be noticed. Inevitably until this time he had been overshadowed by his senior, Professor Camps, but as the older man neared retirement the younger one was increasingly on call for cases of murder.

On 22 August 1965 Dr Cameron was asked by the Kent police to go to Margate, where the body of a young woman had been found by a road-sweeper. On the way to work the road-sweeper walked through Dane Park and there he had seen the naked body and called the police.

Later that day Dr Cameron wrote this report:

Scene: The body of a slim young girl lying on her back beneath a tree with well established rigor, congestion of face and marks around the neck. There was congealed blood around the left nostril and mouth with slight deformity of the left lower jaw. A brown suede jacket and white woollen cardigan both completely undone in front had been pulled off the left shoulder and up under her back. Apart from that clothing and a pair of blue ankle socks, the body was naked.

Some distance from the body, about seventy-five feet away, were other articles of clothing including two black casual shoes, a white brassière with a torn strap and navy-blue knickers. Some distance away from that group of articles was a pair of jeans, with the zip undone, folded on top of a white handbag inside which were four tablets similar in colour and appearance to Drinamyl.

It appeared that the body had been dragged over the ground and there were scratch marks on the back of the calves, heels, thighs and buttocks, and there were leaves and grass sticking to the back of the body.

There was evidence of a fractured jaw and bruising of the neck. No definite evidence of rape but evidence suggesting recent intercourse.

My opinion is that death was caused by asphyxia and constriction of the neck.

The dead girl was identified as red-haired Shona Margaret Berry who was known locally as 'Toni', a local 'Mod'

teenager who lived with her parents only a few hundred
yards from where she was killed.

Squads of detectives under Detective Superintendent
Arthur Hall rounded up hundreds of teenagers for questioning, and under the impact of the girl's violent death
their tongues were unlocked. It was then that the police
found out about the widespread traffic in 'purple hearts'
and Drinamyl tablets and blatant promiscuity in a prosaic
and, apparently, respectable boarding-house in Addington Road, Margate, known locally as the 'Madhouse'.

Its correct name was the Croydon Guest House and its
landlady was eminently respectable Mrs Ellen Wilson,
who liked young people and liked to give her lodgers a
homely atmosphere. What she did not know was that the
pep-pill menace had hit the younger generation and that
many of her visitors were drug addicts and also heavy
drinkers. Many of the people who used the 'Madhouse'
came from the provinces, from the Midlands and Birmingham and some came from local towns and Margate
itself.

According to various teenage witnesses, two months
after her sixteenth birthday Toni Berry, who worked
locally as a waitress, spent a Friday night with drug-
taking teenagers in the 'Madhouse'. She had been there
many times, but that night she had sexual intercourse
with a man called 'John' and got home at 9.30 A.M. on
the following day. She went back to the 'Madhouse'
during the Saturday afternoon and in the evening went to
the Tahiti Club, a sea-front coffee bar where this clique
of adolescents used to gather. Friends noticed that she
was distressed and seemed to be suffering from what they
called a 'count-down', their term for the drug effects
wearing off.

When the Tahiti closed at 11 P.M. she went to the
Excel bowling alley and then to a cafeteria with a group

of other girls. She swallowed a number of drug tablets there and then met a man called Alan Michael Houchin, a twenty-seven-year-old mechanic from Bell Green Lane, Sydenham, London. The couple were seen by a thirteen-year-old schoolgirl to leave at 1.40 A.M., their arms around each other.

Police traced Alan Houchin to his home on the following day and he was taken back to Margate where he made a statement. He said that he had arrived in Margate on the Friday night with a man called Constable. Together they went to the boarding-house and in one room there were about twenty people, including three girls. One of the girls was Shona Berry and they were all under the influence of drugs. Houchin said he spent that night in a chair and after lunch next day he went back to the house with a girl called Judy, who was also under the influence of drugs. He had intercourse with her four times that afternoon.

In the evening he went to a public house where he had four pints of beer and fifteen brown and white drug tablets. Then he went to the cafeteria and met Shona Berry. She told him she had had a bad 'count-down' and that she wanted some more pills, so he bought her ten brown and white tablets for one shilling each. Then he said he took the girl back to the boarding-house and then drove home to London.

Chief Detective Inspector Edward Jenvey, who had taken the statement, told Houchin that he believed his story up to the time of going to the bowling alley but that he was not satisfied with the truth of Houchin's version after that.

After a pause the Chief Inspector asked Houchin to explain certain bloodstains on his clothing. Then came the truth:

'She was on about sex all the time and egged me on. She teased me and I lost my rag and hit her. She asked me to take her back to the "Madhouse" and when the landlord disturbed us she said, "Let's go over to the park." In the park we started snogging and I suggested we move to a bench.

'She said "What's wrong here?" I suggested we move further into the park in case anyone walked through. We lay down still snogging and messing about. She was teasing and talking. I thought she was having me on. I slapped her face and called her a bitch. I went to walk away but she dragged me back.

'We started snogging again and she was again teasing me. I then hit her again on the face and she said, "Come on, little boy, be a man." She seemed to be really enjoying it.

'I grabbed her by the throat and pulled my thumbs back and shook her. As I let go she wheezed once. I tried to feel her heart. I ripped her brassière off but could not feel anything. I tried to make her heart beat. I rubbed her rib cage but nothing happened. I half dragged and half carried her a few yards and again tried to make her breathe but nothing happened.

'I then realized what had happened. I went back to the "Madhouse" but my room was locked. I got into my van and drove home. I don't know why this happened, but it might have been the drugs or the beer.'

At Kent Assizes, Maidstone, Alan Michael Houchin was found guilty of murdering Shona 'Toni' Berry and sentenced to life imprisonment. The all-male jury took only fifty-five minutes to reach this verdict.

In his summing up Mr Justice Sachs said, 'This is a case of grave importance to the community. In the last four days we have traversed much ground, some of it strange and distasteful. You may have been revolted at the picture we got of the place known as 5 Addington Road, the Croydon Guest House, or, more often, the "Madhouse". There teenagers congregated in numbers to indulge in sex and drugs. There, there was no such thing as shame. They copulated in front of others and drug-taking was accepted as normal. That place was a shameful place – an absolute disgrace to the town in which it lay. It is now closed but too late for the girl who died.'

The boarding-house was closed, the traffickers in amphetamine drugs and their derivatives rounded up and the teenage drugs scene in Margate faded away. But the 'Madhouse Killer' was recalled again when Alan Houchin was released from jail on licence eleven years later. He raped a nineteen-year-old girl and was sentenced to nine years further imprisonment. In passing sentence Mr Justice Purchase said, 'You raped this girl in a most base and brutal fashion. Bearing in mind what you did in 1965 I have no doubt that the circumstances she has described were not exaggerated.'

2
A Difficult Identification

In August 1965 a thirty-year-old woodcutter, Isaiah Jackson, was walking where he worked in Queensdown Warren, Chestnut Plantation, in Hartlip Woods, near Sittingbourne in Kent, when he saw some torn and tattered baby clothes lying in a heap on the ground. He raked the bundle over with a stick and saw something fleshy in it, which he thought might have been the body of a baby. But it was so decayed he could not be certain and eventually he left it and went home.

That same evening his employer called on Isaiah Jackson to pay him his wages, and Jackson told him what he had found. As it was still light the two men walked to the wood to look and they agreed that the bundle of clothes and flesh could have been the body of a baby. Both men went home without reporting the matter but Jackson was uneasy and he decided, two days later, to tell the police of his discovery.

On Monday, 13 August, he telephoned the local police. A constable picked him up by car and took him back to the wood and he pointed out what he had found. The remains were covered and Detective Chief Superintendent Arthur Hall called Dr Cameron at the London Hospital. Next day Dr Cameron went to the wood and looked at the decomposed body of what appeared to be a baby girl of about eighteen or twenty-four months old. The body was 'in a state of decomposition, with adipocere formation* and larval infestation. Fragments of skull bone

* Adipocere formation is a fatty, waxy substance generated in dead bodies buried in moist places.

were lying separately in the base of a shallow hollow together with three strands of knotted string or cord. Both hands and one foot were missing. The hollow appeared to have been lined with a plastic bag and a piece of cardboard. Various items of clothing were also found and placed in polythene bags.'

The local coroner, Mr Harris, authorized that the body could be removed from the area and it was taken to the London Hospital where Dr Cameron began his detailed examination after the body had been X-rayed. There were three other pathologists present, including Professor Francis Camps, and five other members of the forensic department. The small body was clothed in a manufac-tured woollen cardigan with buttons, with the top three done up; a pink knitted coat; a yellow nylon dress with a button at the back of the neck, done up, with a nylon lace overskirt with a small pocket; a white petticoat; a woollen vest with short sleeves; and a nappy, folded in half, with a blue-topped 'Safety-pop' safety pin over the right hip and a white-topped 'Safety-pop' safety-pin lying free over the left hip. Under the body was a piece of flat, thin wood, tapering from one inch to a point, approximately seven inches in length.

An examination of the skull fragments found at the scene revealed that the skull had been fractured in several places from three separate blows.

Dr Barbara Dodd, the senior lecturer in serology (the science of blood grouping) made an examination of the muscle from the thigh and was able to say that the blood group of the body was consistent with Group A. Mr Bernard Sims, lecturer in Forensic Odontology, was able, by examination of the teeth, to say that the dead child was more likely to have been nearer twelve months old. He could deduce this by the amount of dentine and the amount of enamel formed after birth, calculated by the daily rate of growth. Mr L. J. Rae, consultant radiologist, put the age of the child between nine and thirty months.

The articles of clothing were taken by Dr Cameron to a trade buyer of children's clothing. He reported that although they were not of top quality they showed no indication of source.

The clothing, which had been photographed where it was found in the weeds, was now cleaned and photographed again on a model doll. The string was washed and sent to an expert to trace its source. And an analysis of the soil where the body was found and the larval infestation combined with weather factors suggested that the body had been exposed to the elements for approximately eight weeks.

Detective Chief Superintendent Arthur Hall of the Kent police had as many clues as he was likely to get at this stage. Now he needed publicity, and he called in the press. On 24 August this story appeared in the London *Evening News*:

Police in Kent today appealed for help in identifying a baby girl aged eighteen months to two years, whose body was found on 20 August partially buried in a wood at Queensdown Warren, Hartlip, near Sittingbourne.

They issued photographs of the baby's clothes including this picture of a pink cardigan and pink coat with a fawn border.

The police said: 'It is urgently desired to ascertain the identity of this child.'

The baby was dressed in a nappy secured over each hip by a safety-pin, Golden Baby plastic pants, white woollen vest, white flannel petticoat, yellow nylon dress patterned with orange flowers with green centres, a knitted pink woollen cardigan with a blue hooped strip and the pink coat with border.

That story was published in newspapers all over the country, but there was no immediate response. Chief Superintendent Brown then asked ATV to run the story and picture on 'Police Five', their special programme which gives details of unsolved crimes, and shortly afterwards Kent police headquarters received an urgent telephone call from the police at Birmingham. A woman who recognized the coat and the hooped cardigan had told them that she thought she could identify the child because she had been its foster-parent. She knew every detail of that child's clothing because she had helped knit some of it herself.

A detective went to see Mrs Laura Violet Kempton, at Handsworth New Road, Birmingham. She told the officer that she was a married woman with four children and that in 1964 she had answered an advertisement in the *Birmingham Mail* asking for short-term foster-parents for the Birmingham Diocesan Moral Welfare Society. She was interviewed and found suitable and collected a mother, a baby and a crib on 6 August 1964 from Little Moor Hill Home, Smethwick, and took them to her home. She gave the mother's name as Lois M. Lord, a New Zealander living at an address in London Road, Sittingbourne. She thought she was a schoolteacher. She described Lois Lord as aged about twenty to twenty-five, good-looking with a nice figure and smartly dressed. She left the same day to go to Sittingbourne. Mrs Kempton said that Miss Lord took the baby away from the house on Thursday, 18 May 1965 at about 4 P.M. in a green Mini car, saying the baby was being taken by BOAC to New Zealand on 26 May.

The baby's name was Denise Mary Lord and she had been born on 4 July 1964. Mrs Kempton said:

'When she left us she was dressed in a pink set. The bonnet was pink with white edging round the front and a white ribbon. The coat was pink. Owing to the coat being too small I knitted a white edging to the coat but only to the collar and front and not round the bottom . . . I had to work an extra buttonhole in so there were four pink buttons on the coat. Under this was a pink and blue-hooped cardigan. Under the cardigan was a lemon dress . . . the dress was patterned in some way . . . under the dress was a winceyette petticoat . . . she had a white nappy and she had "Golden Baby" rubber panties around it. The nappy had two odd pins.'

Everything began to fit together and when Mrs Kempton was shown the clothes she positively identified them as those being worn by Denise Lord on the day she last saw her alive.

At a house in London Road, Sittingbourne, police found a Mrs Maylum who agreed that Lois Lord had been a paying guest there. Mrs Maylum told the detective that sometime in May she found a brown paper bag which Lois Lord had put out for burning and saw sticking out of the top a brooch in the shape of a guitar. Mrs Maylum had said, 'Don't burn the brooch, a child might like it.'

Miss Lord replied, 'Go through the bag and you may find the photograph of the "Beatle" which belongs to the brooch,' and then left the house to go to school.

Mrs Maylum looked through the bag for the photograph and came across a half-torn letter which she read. It was from the Kemptons to Lois Lord and said, 'What have you done with Denise? We rang BOAC on both dates you mentioned and on neither date was a baby booked for New Zealand.' Mrs Maylum burned the letter with the other rubbish, and thought no more about it.

The trail led on to a garage in Kingston, Surrey, where Lois Lord had hired a green Mini saloon at Easter time. One day she gave her landlady, Mrs Maylum, a lift to Rainham, a nearby village, and before they left Lois Lord asked to borrow a spade 'to dig up some plants from a friend's garden to take to school'. She returned the spade later that same day. That was on 23 April.

By mid-September the movements of Lois Lord had been traced completely, from the time she came to Britain, in about February 1964, to the time she left in September 1965. She must have been in the early stages of pregnancy when she arrived but had managed to conceal it so well that not a single person, including several men friends, ever noticed, and not one of the people police interviewed ever suspected. Only a welfare worker and the hospital and Mrs Kempton knew that she had given birth to a child in July of that year.

Interpol, the international police organization, was called in and they made inquiries about flights to New Zealand. Lois Lord was traced to that country and finally to Sydney, Australia, where she was working as a housekeeper. The local police, armed with all the details of the investigation from Sittingbourne, went to see her.

Lois Lord admitted killing her child, and the Sydney police sent a report back to Sittingbourne.

Lois Lord (*née* Aitken) was born on 27 July 1942, and was married in New Zealand on 17 April 1963. The marriage lasted only a few months, due to the cruelty of her husband, and she then apparently formed an association with a New Zealander of Maori strain, by whom she became pregnant. However, it is doubtful whether she could have known who was the father of the child, either her husband or the half-caste Maori, until its actual birth.

Much of the evidence collected by the police in England was corroborated by Lord.

'I had to go teaching . . . I had to . . . I had no money, I had to . . . Denise had to be adopted or sent back to New Zealand, or something. I was on my own, nobody in England except the welfare people knew I was having a baby . . .'
Lord also states that 'the Kemptons felt that something material should be done about Denise's future and kept pressing

me by letter to do something.' This also after the removal of the child. They wanted to know when the child's father was coming to England to take the child to New Zealand. In fact, following a telephone call at Christmas 1964, when Denise was six months old, Lord had had very little contact with and certainly no material help from the child's father. The Kemptons themselves hesitated to adopt Denise as they were too old.

Lord also said that she was in touch with the baby's father and had suggested that if he provided half the baby's fare to New Zealand she would provide the other half. The child was not available for adoption because of her mixed blood and also because the documents authorizing adoption signed by the offender's husband were thought to be inaccurate and forged. The child's father felt he could not afford half the fare to New Zealand on the pretext that he had just loaned a substantial sum of money to his own father.

Following Christmas 1964 Lord states that she realized that she had to do something about the child and 'It was my duty, as I had brought her into the world, to give her the best I could, and what better place than heaven . . . I had nothing to offer her. I thought about taking her life for some time. I can't remember now just how long, but I felt she was getting bigger all the time and it had to be done soon, because the bigger she got the more difficult it would have been to take her life.'

Lord then indicates that having left her friends in Forest Hill (London) on Easter Monday, she visited friends in Bournemouth and went to Birmingham on Thursday. It had been her intention to take the child's life en route to London – but she felt that she was at the disadvantage of not knowing the countryside and she therefore decided to go straight to Sittingbourne, the area she knew well. After a tiresome journey during which the baby cried most of the time Lord then took the child straight to the river where she drowned her in deep water around a pylon – she then wrapped the child in sheeting and struck it two or three blows from the car jack on the back and side of the child's head as she lay, probably dead by that time, on the floor of the car.

The following day Lord arranged to bury the child's body in the woods, for which, she agrees, she borrowed a spade from her landlady. She described saying a prayer before finally placing an old log over the grave.

Following the burial Lord went to a pub (it was lunchtime)

and had several brandies. She then met some friends in Maidstone with whom she had a few beers. She admits to keeping up the pretence with all those involved with the baby's welfare and admitted to wanting to tell her landlady of what she had done on one occasion.

'Then one Thursday, late in August, I read a little bit in the late news that a baby had been found in Hartlip Woods, and I knew, or guessed anyway, that it was Denise. I just wanted to go home then and see my parents.'

Then followed a small statement, exactly as she said it, without any prompting, and without being questioned. She said: 'I did bear a child on 4 July 1964, named Denise Mary. I passed judgement on my own child and tried to do what would be best for her without a father, home or love. I put her into a life of utter bliss, with God in heaven.

'I strongly feel that, being the bearer of the child, I had every right to do this and that it was God's will.

'I would never have taken her life could I have felt sure that there would be some happiness for her, but to be faced with the above circumstances, it just did not seem fair. I feel I gave her a true Christian burial.'

Lois Lord was held in custody, in Sydney, and eventually extradited to Britain where she was charged with murder at Sittingbourne in March 1966. Although she had co-operated fully with the police in Australia she now refused to co-operate at all, and the two police officers in Sydney who had taken her statement and asked her questions had to be called to England to establish proof under oath.

On 9 May 1966, Lois Lord appeared before Mr Justice Melford Stevenson at Maidstone Summer Assizes. She pleaded not guilty to murder and guilty to infanticide.*

* The Infanticide Act, 1922. This merciful statute created the offence of infanticide. It provided that a mother who, before she had fully recovered from the effects of childbirth, kills her newly born baby, shall be dealt with and punished 'as if she had been guilty of manslaughter'. Formerly in cases where the facts were proved, juries were obliged to find these unhappy women guilty of wilful murder, and judges to go through the distressing and empty form of passing sentence of death

Her plea of not guilty to murder was accepted by the court and Mr N. McKinnon, prosecuting, said the medical evidence was such that it was quite clear that at the time when the child was killed she was not fully responsible for her actions. The evidence was, he said, that in her distraught condition she drowned the child, hit it across the head with a motor tool, and buried it in a wood. Two doctors gave evidence on her behalf.

One testified that he found Lois Lord a strange mixture of naïvety and mild depression so that she was brought within the provisions of the Infanticide Act of 1938. The second told the court:

'There is a history of psychoneurosis and instability in childhood. This was aggravated by her unhappy marriage, by finding herself alone with an unwanted baby and, possibly, at that stage of the pregnancy, in a state of anxiety and depression which culminated in the killing of her child. Therefore I think at the material time she had abnormality of mind amounting to disease which substantially impaired her mental responsibility.'

Lois Lord was twenty-three years old and she sobbed bitterly as she stood in the dock and listened while Mr Justice Melford Stevenson gave her a discharge on the condition that she must return to New Zealand and live with her parents.

---

upon them, well knowing that it would never be carried out. In the seventeen years before the passing of the Act no fewer than sixty women were sentenced to death for killing their newly born children. With one exception, all were reprieved. It was to put an end to this anomaly that the 1922 Act was passed. Nowadays, The Infanticide Act of 1938 provides that when a woman by any wilful act or omission causes the death of her child being under the age of twelve months, but at the time of the act or omission the balance of her mind is disturbed by reason of her not having fully recovered from the effect of giving birth to the child or by reason of the effect of lactation consequent upon the birth of the child, then she may be dealt with and punished as though she had been guilty of the offence of manslaughter.

3
Murder at Mr Smith's Club

While Dr Cameron was still working in Glasgow a number of powerful gangs had developed in London that specialized in extortion. Their targets were successful and respectable social clubs, and the gangsters offered them their 'protection' against any violence in return for a large fee, sometimes as much as £500 a week. It was an idea borrowed from America, where it had been successful until the FBI had clamped down.

The gangs operated mostly in the East and West End areas of London and such was the violence used that most club owners were too frightened to resist. Many clubs had gone out of business after their premises had been smashed up. The Kray twins, Ronald and Reginald, operated in East London, an area they called their 'manor', and they resented intrusions by any member of an opposition gang from a different part of London. Retribution was swift if an intruder was found to have strayed into their 'manor'; the punishment was a savage beating and a slash across the face with a razor blade. It was this rule of fear that allowed the gang leaders to retain power in their own territory. It also allowed them to sell their 'protection'.

It was a simple operation. A gang would find a flourishing business – a public house, a club, a dance hall or a casino – and check that cash was flowing in regularly. They would send an emissary, praising the comfort and the success of the enterprise, and then would come the gentle, friendly warning, that it would be a pity 'if this place was ruined by thugs'.

There would follow a long and detailed explanation of how such a tragedy could be averted. The emissary knew of a firm which specialized in making sure that such premises would not be invaded. If the owner of the premises was sufficiently frightened and agreed, a contract was made. If he did not, a gang of hoodlums was sent in to wreck the place, followed by another approach.

The gang which operated on the south side of the River Thames were the Richardsons, a mob expert in making money by any kind of criminal activity, including theft, blackmail and fraud. They were also experts in the protection racket, and their eyes fell upon a new South London club at Catford, called 'Mr Smith's', which also included a gambling casino. It had opened in 1965 and the premises were expensively furnished and lush, like the new, family-type clubs which were flourishing in the North of England. It had been opened by the late Diana Dors, and at the inaugural party champagne flowed.

Mr Smith's Club had been running successfully for some months when in March 1966 two men entered the club. The clientele were too innocent to recognize either of them. One was Edward Richardson, who described himself officially as a company director with interests in a fruit-machine firm, a scrap-metal business and a wholesale chemists. His companion was the notorious 'Mad Frankie' Fraser, a thug with a long history of crime who wore a cut-throat razor in the top pocket of his well-cut suit as some people wear a handkerchief. Shortly after completing a three-year sentence for stealing large quantities of cigarettes, he took part in an attack on Jack 'Spot' Comer, at one time styled 'King of the Underworld'. Jack 'Spot' Comer's wounds needed seventy-eight stitches and Fraser went back to prison for another seven years. He had twice been certified insane and had been in the Broadmoor Criminal Lunatic Asylum.

In a quiet and well-mannered way the two men ordered drinks and asked to see the manager. The actual words were never recalled accurately but the meaning was plain: 'You have a nice and successful club and it would be a pity if the wrong people came here. There would be fighting, people would get hurt and the club would be ruined. We suggest that you employ us to keep the club in order.' The message was unmistakable and it was sufficient for the club's managing director to travel from Manchester to meet Richardson and Fraser. The result was that Richardson was asked to hire some suitable protectors for Mr Smith's Club.

The club carried on, but the atmosphere there was strangely quiet and uneasy. There were rumours that a rival gang had their eye on the place. A casual visitor would not have noticed it, but the habitués sensed trouble and in the early hours of the morning on 8 March 1966 the management suggested to several customers that it might be wise for them to go to their homes. Some of them did and several of the staff were sent home as well. Some twenty men had drifted into the club and they had formed themselves into two groups, one opposite the other. Nothing was said but the air was alive with bristling hostility. The scene was set for a showdown between rival gangs, one seeking to take from the other the prize of protection of Mr Smith's Club.

At five minutes to three Edward Richardson jumped from his chair and shouted that there would be no more drinks served without his permission. The silence was broken with shouts of defiance, curses and insults as the two mobs surged into battle. One customer ran to the street, followed by the rest of the staff. As the outside doors banged shut, revolver shots rang out and then the sound of a shotgun being fired. Some of the men inside collapsed, cursing and writhing in pain, and the luckier ones continued to do battle. It was described later as being 'like a scene from a Western film' in which tables and chairs were overturned and flung in all directions and fumes of cordite filled the room. The noise had wakened the neighbours from sleep, and they had left their beds and stood sheltering in their doorways. When they saw the gangsters erupting into the street they slammed shut their doors, bolted them and drew the curtains.

The shooting died away, car engines burst into urgent life and injured men were bundled in and driven to hospital. One of them was Edward Richardson, peppered with shot. The police arrived in force and found one man dead in the street and another, doubled-up with a broken leg, lying behind a hedge in a front garden. The dead man was Richard Hart, aged thirty, a married man with a small child. He was a drifter who had dabbled in crime and was content to live off the rich pickings of the extortion gangs. The second man was Frankie Fraser. A bullet had broken his leg and under his body was a gun, said to have been the weapon that killed Hart. Fraser had been dragged to the spot where he was found and an attempt had been made to hide him so that he could be removed later.

Detective Chief Superintendent John Cummings, who was in charge of the Catford area, took over the case. In the shambles of what had been a luxury club he found four more men wounded by bullets or shotgun pellets. Dr Cameron was called from his Bromley home and examined the scene at the club and Richard Hart's body before it was removed to the mortuary. He teamed up with an old friend and colleague, John McCafferty, the Scotland Yard expert on firearms. The two had worked together on many occasions and had had many triumphs.

Superintendent Cummings and his team rounded up all the people who had been in the club but found none of them willing to talk at that stage. He found the same reticence among those who had been injured in the fight and were undergoing hospital treatment. Gangsters all over the world, like the Mafia, practise the law of silence if it is the police asking the questions, not for altruistic reasons but for their own safety. Cummings and his men soon arrested a number of suspects but the exact truth of what had happened was slow in coming to the surface. He consulted John McCafferty and together they decided to reconstruct the bloody battle of Mr Smith's Club.

Superintendent Cummings sent his detectives to interview the people who had been present and find out exactly where they were sitting or standing when the shooting began. This was no easy task because many of those who had been in the club that night did not like being involved in police investigations. Many of them had criminal records. But Cummings and his detectives succeeded in placing all the tables and chairs in the positions they had occupied on the night of the battle. A master-plan was drawn and all the furniture marked with the appropriate names. Then McCafferty made a trajectory chart from the bullet and shotgun pellet holes in the walls and furniture, and was able to pin-point with accuracy the path and spread of the sawn-off .410 shotgun and to work out from which positions a revolver or pistol had been fired.

John Cummings and his detectives, McCafferty and Cameron then studied the statements made by all the witnesses and were able to reconstruct the events of that night, providing information which was the basis of the evidence given later at the Old Bailey.

The dead man, Richard Hart, was shot in the back and Dr Cameron said that the pistol was held at 'near touching range'. At that time his jacket had been pulled down over his elbows so that he was powerless to defend himself. The bullet track entered the chest cavity through the ribs and entered the left lung. There were also massive bruises all over the body, particularly around the face and head. Death was due to haemorrhage.

Francis Fraser, aged forty-two, was charged with the murder but found not guilty because not one of the people present gave evidence that they had actually seen the shooting and could not say who had fired the shot.

William Alfred Haward, twenty-four, was sentenced to eight years' imprisonment and William James Botton, forty-six, to five years for causing an affray; Fraser and Richardson were both sentenced to five years' imprisonment on the same charge. Two other men were found not guilty and discharged.

In fact the battle at the Catford club was the beginning of the end for the 'protection' gangs. Soon afterwards gang warfare broke out and, after a massive police investigation, many of the leaders and their henchmen went to prison.

4

The Red Mini Murder

Although Home Office pathologists usually work on the side of the police there are times when they are retained by the defence. Early in 1967 Dr Cameron was asked by the defence in a case known as 'The Red Mini Murder' to conduct a post-mortem on the victim, Mrs June Serina Cook, a schoolteacher who was, at first, thought to have been killed in a car accident. It had happened on the night of Thursday, 2 March, and the keen observation and suspicion of a village police constable called Sherlock had led to the discovery of a cruel murder plot.

Soon after 10 P.M. the constable, stationed at Nettlebed, near Henley-on-Thames, was patrolling in a radio police car. He was directed to go to the scene of an accident on the road through Rumerhedge Wood about three miles away. On a bend in the narrow road through forest he found two cars with their headlights lighting up a third, a red Morris Mini with its front bumper against a beech tree. Three men were standing by the Mini, who told the constable that they had not been involved in the accident and that an ambulance had already taken the two occupants of the car to hospital. They said the male passenger had been dazed but the woman driver unconscious. One of the three men was a nearby garage owner, who had been alerted to the crash and had brought blankets and hot water bottles and instructed his wife to telephone for the police and an ambulance. One of them mentioned that another man had been bending over the woman driver on the ground when he had arrived on the scene and then gone off to his car down the road and driven away.

Sherlock noted that there were no recent brake marks on the road, that there was only slight damage to the Mini and that the windscreen was unbroken. When he examined the interior he saw that the driver's side was very heavily bloodstained. However, because of the slight damage to the car he assumed the occupants had not been seriously injured and he asked the garage owner, Mr Johns, to drive it to his garage. Sherlock himself reversed the car on to the road, having straightened the bumper and wing away from the off-side front wheel.

Sherlock drove to his police house at Nettlebed, taking with him a woman's handbag he had found in the Mini and a pair of women's shoes he had found at the side of the car. It was midnight, and he telephoned the Battle Hospital, in Reading, to check on the condition of the passengers. He was told that the woman was dead and that the man was drunk.

He reported to his headquarters at Henley that the accident had been fatal and then drove to the hospital where he asked to see the dead woman. She had been heavily bandaged round the head and face and the surgeon on duty explained that apart from severe head injuries he had also had to perform a tracheotomy operation to help her breathe. He said the woman was near to death when she was admitted. The man who had been in the car with her was uninjured and when he saw him Sherlock noticed that he smelled of alcohol and was slightly incoherent, though at the time Sherlock concluded the man was still in shock rather than actually drunk. He gave his name as Raymond Sidney Cook and said he was thirty-two, a draughtsman working in Reading. The dead woman was his wife, June Serina Cook, a forty-one-year-old schoolteacher with two young sons. As Mr Cook required no further treatment at the hospital Sherlock offered to drive him home to Spencers Wood, on the Basingstoke road out of Reading. It was an unfamiliar area to Sherlock so he asked his passenger for directions. He was surprised that Cook responded with precise details, but whenever he mentioned the accident the replies relapsed into vague mumblings.

At Cook's house the constable called the family doctor and got the district nurse to relieve the baby-sitter. Then he discovered that Mrs Cook's parents lived next door and spoke to them. He got the firm impression that they did not approve of their son-in-law and that the Cooks had not been getting on well of late. Sherlock made one last effort to find out more from Cook about the circumstances of the accident but, again, he was offered only a jumble of words which made no sense.

When he left he drove straight to his headquarters and reported that there were a number of facts about the accident which he found unsatisfactory and that had not been explained. He thought the damage to the car did not explain the fatal injuries to Mrs Cook, and how was it that Mr Cook was not injured at all? He was not at all happy that whenever he mentioned the accident the answers he received from Mr Cook were incoherent.

The more Sherlock thought about the accident the less he liked it. He drove back to Rumerhedge Wood and looked again at the scene. He saw pieces of bark which the car had knocked off the tree and remembered that the windscreen was intact. He also remembered that when he sat in the car to reverse it he had had no need to adjust the rear-view mirror, although he was six inches taller than the dead woman. The ignition had been off and so were the lights but the handbrake was on. And who was the man who was said to have been bending over the woman as she lay on the ground and who had gone back to his car and driven away?

Before he went to bed that morning Constable Sherlock sent a message to his headquarters requesting the attendance of a Scenes of Crime Officer.

Later that day, although he was officially off duty, he went to see the Mini at Mr Johns's garage. The driver's seat had been washed clean of blood as had the steering wheel, the windscreen and the driver's window and door. Now, in daylight, he could see that the outside of the car was spattered with blood, a different colour red to that of the car's bodywork. And above the off-side rear wheel arch was a hair soaked in blood and sticking to the paint.

Thinking that Mr Cook would perhaps be sufficiently recovered to talk about the accident, Sherlock went to see him. Cook made a statement to him to the effect that the previous night he had been driving home with his wife after having dinner at an hotel in Pangbourne. He had felt sick and stopped the car so that his wife could take the wheel. Soon after she had done so, a car with dazzling headlights approached from the opposite direction and Cook could remember nothing more.

Cook signed the statement and Sherlock took it to the police station at Henley. While he was there he talked to his sergeant about the man who had been at the scene and then driven away. The witness who told that story was a fireman who had come upon the accident when he was driving a friend home, two of the men whom Sherlock had seen and spoken to on the previous night. The fireman had seen the sergeant that day and told him that before he got to the accident his headlights had picked out a car parked half across the narrow road facing them. Its sidelights were on and its boot open. His impression was that the car was a Cortina of a dark colour. When he rounded the next bend, a hundred yards on, he and his friend saw the Mini with the woman stretched out on the ground beside it and a man bending over her. The man had told them there was another person in the car – this was Mr Cook – who appeared to be dazed and, later, was rather difficult. The man who had been bending over the woman on the ground straightened up and said he would bring some towels from the boot of his car. He walked in that direction and they heard the slamming of the boot and the noise of the car being driven away.

That man had obviously arrived at the scene earlier than anyone else and might possibly have some knowledge of the cause of the accident. Next day a message was sent to all stations in the surrounding areas asking police to trace the driver of a Cortina who suddenly left the scene of the accident and might have been involved or been a witness.

The Scenes of Crime Officer, Sergeant McMiken, had been detained on another case. Now he arrived and was taken to Rumerhedge Wood, with Sherlock acting as guide. First he took photographs of the damaged tree and then moved back down the road to take a long shot showing the bend in the road. As he planted his tripod on the gravel surface he noticed a large, dark stain seven inches across that looked like dried blood. It was seventy-five yards from the scene of the accident and Sherlock had not spotted it. The sergeant took scrapings of the gravel. Then they drove to the garage where the Mini had been taken, and photographed the blood and the hair. They were puzzled about the blood markings inside the vehicle and on the driver's door sill, and the spattered blood on the outside of the car on the driver's side, suggesting that the victim had suffered at least two injuries, one inside the car and one outside. They took the Mini to Henley police station and reported their suspicions to Detective Inspector Insell.

The pathologist at the Royal Berkshire Hospital, where Mrs Cook's body had been transferred for a post-mortem, reported to Insell that there was a high concentration of alcohol in Mrs Cook's body and that the wounds to her skull had exposed the brain. His theory of the accident was that the woman had been thrown through the windscreen of the car and had hit her head on the tree. The detective explained that the windscreen was unbroken and mentioned the bloodstain on the road seventy-five yards from where she was found. The pathologist's view was that she could not have walked that distance after receiving so serious an injury.

Insell obtained permission for a second post-mortem and had the bloodstain scrapings sent to the forensic laboratory. He also put out a BBC broadcast describing the accident and asking for information about the dark Cortina and its driver.

Then the Detective Inspector paid a call on Raymond Cook, who on that Sunday afternoon had been to the mortuary to identify the body of his wife. Insell took PC Sherlock with him and went over the events of the accident with Cook. He asked to see the clothes Cook was wearing at the time and was told that Cook had taken them to the cleaners on the day after the accident and had asked his mother to wash his shirt. He added that he had burnt his leather gloves because, like the rest of his clothes, they were bloodstained.

Cook went on to explain that he had been married eight years and that he and his wife had recently been going out to dinner on a Thursday. On the night of the accident they had dined at the George Hotel in Pangbourne. On the way home, he said, he had felt faint and stopped the car for some fresh air. When he still felt unwell he asked his wife to drive and she agreed. After a while he heard his wife make an exclamation, looked up and was dazzled by the headlights of an oncoming car. He felt the car veer to the left and felt a bump. That was all he remembered.

Sherlock noticed that the tall but slouching Cook still spoke painfully slowly and seemed to weigh every word. The statement had taken nearly three hours.

Insell then decided to call on Mrs Cook's parents who lived next door. He learned that they were not on good terms with Cook, although at the time of the marriage they had given the couple the house as a gift. The reason for their present dislike was that Cook had deserted their daughter in the previous autumn and gone to live with a younger woman, a nurse at Borocourt Mental Hospital, where Raymond Cook had also been working. They gave the girl's name as Kim Mule, but were uncertain where she lived.

Insell reflected that what had appeared to be an inquiry into a road accident death now seemed to be rather more complicated. By the next day he had recruited a Crime Squad of six men to find out much more about the people involved and, in particular, the details of the association between Raymond Cook and a girl, he had now ascertained, who was not called Kim Mule but Kim Newell, or Valerie Dorothy Newell. He also began to feed Fleet Street crime reporters with information about the patch of blood that had been found on the road, the fact that police dogs were being used to find clues, and the police's keen interest in tracing the driver of the Cortina car who had been at the scene of the accident.

Two people came forward. One, a local man, said he had seen the car parked on the road at 9.20 P.M. and another, who had used the road at that spot at 9.30 P.M., and had not seen the car at all.

On 6 March 1967 Home Office pathologist, Dr Derek

Barrowcliff, went first to Henley police station and examined the Mini and was then taken to Rumerhedge Wood by Detective Inspector Insell. Together they searched the area of the accident and found some tiny red pieces of bone, fingernail size. Barrowcliff identified them as fragments of a skull. After he had conducted the postmortem the doctor pronounced that the head wounds of Mrs Cook pointed to murder, possibly with an instrument that was not very sharp and probably while her head was being held. There had already been two earlier postmortem examinations by pathologists at the Royal Berkshire Hospital.

The inquest arranged for the following day was abandoned. Raymond Cook was telephoned to that effect and told that the funeral, arranged for Thursday, 9 March, would have to be postponed. That same day Scotland Yard's Murder Squad was called in and Detective Superintendent Ian Forbes and Detective Sergeant Peter Hill moved into the George Hotel at Reading.

Forbes was a wily Scot who still kept his strong accent from his native Aberdeenshire, where he had begun his working life as a ploughman. He had investigated fourteen murders and solved them all, and that night he was formally assigned to the case.

He read all the statements and then looked at the physical evidence. Once he saw the red Mini he had it taken to the Yard's forensic science laboratory in Holborn. It was a shrewd move, for that car was to provide some of the most important evidence.

Meanwhile Detective Sergeant Hill held a press conference which led to banner headlines. Murder was not yet mentioned but one senior police officer was quoted: 'Foul play cannot be ruled out,' he said. That phrase, often used by the police, sometimes means they are not sure whether a crime has been committed and they are keeping their options open; sometimes it means they do not have enough evidence to make an arrest; and sometimes it means that they know they are dealing with a case of murder but that they are letting the suspect stew a little longer, keeping him without knowledge of the evidence they have uncovered. In this case it was the latter and the suspect was Raymond Cook – who now had to face the questions of the press in full cry. Crime reporters scent murder like tracker dogs but all Cook would tell them was the details of the meal with his wife at Pangbourne and then what he remembered of the car crash. After that he was vague except that he said he could remember when the car had stopped he had heard a man's voice urging him to sit still and pushing him back into his seat.

The police knew that that man was the fireman who had happened on the scene and had been directed to Cook in the passenger seat by the man who had been bending over Mrs Cook on the ground. The fireman had told the police that Cook had been difficult, falling out of the car and fighting to get out again after he had been put back into his seat. The story concentrated attention on the stranger who was presumed to be the driver of the Cortina saloon, seen near the Mini.

The fireman was a useful witness. He remembered that the Cortina was dark blue in colour, with a deluxe model grille and without wing-mirrors. And he recalled seeing the body of Mrs Cook, saying it reminded him of a woman he had once seen at a fire he had attended. That woman, it transpired, had been killed with a hatchet. He also recalled that the ignition was switched off in the Mini, as were the lights, and that the handbrake was on.

Newspaper publicity has helped solve many a murder case, and this one was no exception. The stories carried the following morning reaped rewards. That evening a house painter called Angus Macdonald told the police

that he had seen a dark blue Cortina being driven into
Reading from the Oxford direction, and that the driver
was being directed by his woman passenger. Macdonald
was on the way to visit his mother who, by an extraordinary coincidence, lived next door to Kim Newell, and she
was the woman in the Cortina. Most importantly, Angus
Macdonald remembered the index number of the Cortina,
7711 FM.

That was a neatly fitting piece of the jigsaw in place,
for Superintendent Forbes knew about Kim Newell. The
local police had found out that she was a striking blonde
who happily bestowed her favours on a number of members of the opposite sex. She and Raymond Cook had
become so friendly while they both worked at the Borocourt Mental Hospital that it led to Cook leaving his
wife, and although Cook returned later, his affair with
Kim Newell continued. He saw her most evenings and
had visited her on the Saturday morning after his wife's
death. He had telephoned her frequently since then,
using a public telephone box, possibly because he shared
a party-line with his mother-in-law who lived next door.

Kim Newell had not worked since October but Forbes
received information that Cook had been supporting her.
By now Cook was under discreet but constant police
observation, and while he attended a memorial service
for his wife at the parish church Detective Inspector Insell
went to the cleaners and collected the clothes which Cook
had sent to have the bloodstains removed. He also took a
sample of the cleaning fluid used and sent that with the
clothes to the Yard laboratory.

Then came a positive trace on the Cortina. It belonged
to a heavy plant hire company in Wrexham and when the
police went there they saw a man getting into the car
with the index number 7711 FM. That man was a Mr Eric
Jones who said, when asked if he had been driving the

car on 2 March anywhere near Reading, that he had been in London on that day. He said he had been to South Africa House, in Trafalgar Square, and also to Highgate, but nowhere near Reading. When asked which route he had taken he said that he drove down the M1 to London and returned through Birmingham. He said he had left Wrexham at seven in the morning and got back soon after midnight.

Both Cook and Newell were being plagued by visits from press reporters, and while Newell rather enjoyed the attention but was apprehensive, Cook took some slight pleasure because the police had not called on him and the pressmen were a source of information. Superintendent Forbes in fact had no intention of seeing Cook at that stage. He had played the game of cat-and-mouse with murder suspects many times before. He knew precisely what he was doing and he now had a whole dossier on the life of the Cook family.

June Cook was a Reading girl who had trained as a teacher during the war, married soon afterwards and emigrated to America with her husband in 1949. She was then twenty-four years old. The marriage broke up and she returned to England in 1958 and obtained a divorce for adultery. Less than a year after the decree she married Raymond Cook, a twenty-four-year-old engineering draughtsman she had met in Reading. June was eleven years his senior and the couple went to live in the house next to her parents. They had two sons and later she went back to teaching, leaving her sister to look after the children.

Forbes and his detectives discovered that June Cook was worth more than £10,000, which had resulted from her earnings and rents from properties she owned, and which might be motive for murder. Kim Newell was always needing money, and her lover, Raymond Cook, was the provider, but it was clear that Mrs Cook had controlled the family purse strings. As the domestic crises varied so Mrs Cook changed the disposition of her money, either in favour of or against her husband. When Cook first left home she cancelled their joint banking account which held about £3,000 and made a new will leaving her property to the children. She told the local vicar, for she was an ardent churchgoer, that her husband would return to her only if she would make adequate financial provision for him. When he did return in the January of 1967 she restored the joint bank account and made a new will leaving most of her property to her husband. In addition there was an insurance policy of £1,000 in the event of Mrs Cook's death in a motor accident. Close friends told of Mrs Cook's constant avowals that she would never divorce her husband and that she had mentioned the possibility of suicide. It had also been reported to the detectives that Kim Newell had said that she was pregnant by Raymond Cook.

To this growing and powerful circumstantial evidence was added the report of the police laboratory on the bloodstaining on the red Mini. All the blood was of the same group as June Cook's and it was heaviest on the steering column and the carpet below and also below the driver's door. There was more blood on the front passenger seat and that blood had seeped through, indicating that the passenger seat was empty at the time. It was apparent that blood had spurted from Mrs Cook's head in a number of different directions, suggesting that when she had sustained her various injuries she had been in different places, always close to the car but not inside it. It was also obvious that blows had been struck before the car collided with the tree because the impact had displaced part of the bodywork, only some of which was bloodstained.

Dr Barrowcliff, the Home Office pathologist, had studied the forensic laboratory report and was now more specific about the murder injuries. He stated that there were at least seven wounds on the front of the head, four of which were inflicted at the same time. In his view June Cook had been on her knees outside the driver's door and had been struck repeated blows from above, hitting the front of her head on the door-frame. Her neck was broken in a way consistent with having her head forced down by an assailant standing over her and grasping her hair.

The inquest opened on 17 March and was adjourned. Afterwards Detective Superintendent Forbes introduced himself to Raymond Cook there and said, 'I saw the dead body of your wife June Cook at the mortuary of the Royal Berkshire Hospital, and as a result of inquiries we have since made I am now going to take you to police headquarters where you will be charged with her murder.'

Two detectives went to see Eric Jones at Wrexham again and they were now armed with much more useful information. They knew that Kim Newell had first taken out a driving licence in Denbighshire, the county in which Jones lived, and they had traced evidence of a previous association between the two. After five hours Jones admitted he had been in Reading on 2 March because he had lost his way. He had decided to visit Kim Newell, who wanted to consult him about an abortion. Jones said he had known Kim Newell for six or seven years and had seen her in December 1966 at Chester and had met her boyfriend then, a tall man she had introduced as 'Ray'. He strenuously denied any knowledge of murder.

The two officers, Chief Inspector Wooldridge and Sergeant Hill, brought that statement back to Superintendent Forbes who then decided he would see Kim Newell. Next day she arrived at Reading police station and told her story, or part of her story. She said she had gone to school in Denbighshire and, when she left, she had worked in the bakery and confectionery trade. She left home because her father would allow her no boyfriends and at seventeen she became a student nurse and then worked as a nannie. During her first job away from home she became pregnant by Eric Jones despite their difference in age of twenty years. Later Jones aborted her. Then she got a job at Borocourt Mental Hospital and began her adulterous affair with Raymond Cook. She admitted she stayed with Cook at the Wynnstay Arms, Wrexham, but did not mention the meeting with Eric Jones.

Questioned about the events of 2 March, she said she had cashed a cheque for £10 for Cook that day. He had told her to spend £5 on a dress and he called in the afternoon to collect the change. She claimed that Cook made advances to her but her flat-mates were present and she asked him to desist. She said Cook took her aside and told her he could no longer pay the rent of her flat unless he could get a loan from the bank. She admitted he had given her some hundreds of pounds in recent months but thought he owed her that money because it was through him that she had lost her job at the hospital and had become pregnant. She added that, although Cook did not realize it, she had no intention of marrying him.

She agreed that Eric Jones had called that evening. He had asked if she was still pregnant, but when she told him she was he had said he was unable to help her. She drove with him to put him on his way home and he dropped her back at her flat at about 7.40 P.M. She had stayed in for the rest of the night and could give no information about the murder, but said she had asked Ray if he had killed his wife. 'He said he was surprised I could think like

that.' Finally, she told the detectives that she had visited
Ray every day except Wednesday, 22 March, the day
before her statement was taken.

A few days later Forbes saw Kim Newell again and this
time she mentioned that Eric Jones had met Raymond
Cook at Wrexham although there had been no mention
of the previous abortion. But, she said, Jones was adamant about not helping with her present pregnancy.
Otherwise she did not add to her story. However, another
woman closely connected with the case, Kim's sister
Janett, had already talked to her husband, Kenneth
Adams, the local dairyman. He went to see Chief Inspector Wooldridge and told him enough to prompt Wooldridge to visit his wife.

Kim Newell had told Janett that Eric Jones had killed
June Cook by hitting her with a car jack, and she went
on to say that there had been a previous conspiracy to
dispose of June Cook by running her car into the river.
Eric Jones and two other men and Sue Heslop, a flat-
mate of Kim's, had been to inspect a bridge and river
bank near Woodley airfield outside Reading. The plan
had been dropped because the men did not trust Sue
Heslop. Instead a new plot was put forward at
Rumerhedge Wood. Raymond Cook was to take his wife
out to dinner and Eric Jones was to flag the car down and
ask for a lift because his car was broken down.

Raymond Cook was to have pointed out the spot in
Rumerhedge Wood to Eric Jones on the early evening of
2 March but one simple fact upset their plans. The
Cook baby had measles and June had a hairdressing
appointment, something she insisted upon before going
out to dine. She expected her husband to be home early
to baby-sit while she went to the hairdresser, but having
been to see Kim Newell, he was late home. And so it was

that Kim Newell had to show Eric Jones the planned place of murder.

Janett Adams said that later that night, in accordance with their plan, Jones had stopped the car in which Raymond and June Cook were travelling. Jones had been wearing rubber gloves and had been allowed to enter the car. He had then hit Mrs Cook but had failed to stun her and had said, 'I'll bloody well have to kill her now.' Afterwards Jones threatened to kill Raymond Cook and his children and Kim Newell to protect himself. Kim had told her sister all the details because she feared Eric Jones might still kill her and she, Janett, would be the only person who knew the truth.

On Sunday, 16 April, Kim Newell was arrested. She had finally told the truth in a statement taking two hours and forty minutes, and soon afterwards Eric Jones made a statement admitting his part in the murder plot. Kim Newell's solicitor retained Dr Cameron for her defence and he performed the fourth post-mortem on the body of June Cook, solely to be able to testify that the injuries were unlikely to have been caused by blows inflicted by a woman. In fact his autopsy found nothing new except that the blows were more likely to have been dealt by a strong person who was more likely to have been a man than a woman. It was the first time that Dr Cameron had been called for the defence, a sure sign that he was becoming well known.

Dr Cameron's opinion was that the deceased had been subjected to considerable violence shortly before death and that the fatal head injury and fractured skull had been caused by a number of impacts by or against a hard object with considerable violence. The murder weapon was a car jack, taken from the boot of Jones's car by Cook and handed to Jones who struck the blows.

Cook, Jones and Newell were tried at Oxford Assizes,

all charged with murder. Later the charge against Newell was varied from murder to being an accessory before the fact. Jones changed his plea to guilty of murder, was sentenced to life imprisonment and gave evidence for the prosecution. He revealed that there had been more than one rehearsal for the murder and that one planned attempt had been postponed because Mrs Cook had not yet changed her will in her husband's favour. At that time her money was left to the children. Once the will was in Cook's favour the plans went ahead.

Raymond Cook, Eric Jones and Valerie Newell were all sentenced to imprisonment for life. Two months later Kim Newell gave birth to a son who was christened Paul.

Meanwhile the courts decreed that the will of Mrs June Cook leaving £10,651 to her husband could not stand because under law a murderer cannot benefit under his victim's will. The money accordingly went to their children.

5
Tragedy at the Farm

In the early hours of 14 June 1967, Dr Cameron was wakened by a telephone call asking him to attend the scene of a death by shooting at Farleigh Court Farm, near Warlingham in Surrey. Arriving there, he was shown by the police the body of Mr James Ian Gray, lying at the foot of the stairs. He had died from a gunshot wound fired from a double-barrelled gun and that gun was lying in the hallway. The wound was in the right side of the chest, three inches below the nipple, and it had taken an upward and outward direction, fracturing the right lung. Cameron deduced that the bullet had been fired from the left of the body in front and from a lower position on the stairs.

It was not a case which called for a massive and detailed police investigation, for the man who had caused the death was already in police custody. He was forty-nine-year-old George William Barr, a neighbour and close friend. The story which slowly unfolded told of a tragic sequence of events which began in all innocence on Guy Fawkes night two years previously. The evidence Dr Cameron gathered that night was to be of vital importance in a case with considerable legal complications.

Mr Barr was a manufacturer of women's blouses and Mr Gray was a farmer near Warlingham who lived at Farleigh Court Farm with his wife and family. The two families became friendly and after the night of fireworks there began a liaison between Gray and thirty-four-year-old Mrs Ethel Barr. In 1966 Mr Gray made a sudden decision to go to Australia and gave Mrs Barr some £240 so that she could join him. She did not do so, and he returned in October of that year. The affair continued with the knowledge of the two innocent parties.

In the spring of 1967, Mr Gray and Mrs Barr spent a weekend together in Scotland. When they returned Mrs Barr did not go home to her husband but went to her mother in Croydon. Mrs Audrey Gray had already left home and taken her children to live with her in a different house which her husband had provided. He also entered into a deed of maintenance for her and the children. All these events took place a few days before the night of the shooting.

On that night Mr and Mrs Barr went out to a local country club for a candlelit dinner. They had a long and detailed discussion about their relationship and its problems and, according to Mr Barr, they had resolved their differences and his wife had agreed to return home and live with him. They walked home, hand in hand, after his wife had said she no longer loved Mr Gray.

This was the moment for a happy ending to the story, but it was not to be. Later Mr Barr told police that he had seen his wife into the house and then gone to make up the boiler, and afterwards to the lavatory. He assumed his wife had gone upstairs and went to find her. He looked everywhere but she had disappeared. Thinking she must have gone back to her lover, James Gray, he got out his car, drove first towards her mother's house, then to Farleigh Court Farm. He drove through the gates but then thought better of it, turned round and went back to his own home. He asked his cousin, who was staying at the house, if she had seen his wife, and she replied she had not.

George Barr began to cry. He went to the dining-room and picked up his shotgun. His cousin told him, 'You don't need that,' but he took a handful of cartridges and loaded two barrels. After his cousin had refused to go with him, he walked out with the loaded gun and drove back to the farm. There he got out of the car, leaving the engine running.

He opened the front door and at the head of the stairs he saw James Gray, who said politely, 'Come in.' Barr asked if his wife was there and was told she was not. He said, 'I want to see for myself,' and began to mount the stairs, holding the gun across his chest, the barrel pointing to the ceiling. He was determined to get into the bedroom but Gray stood in the way and said, 'Put the bloody thing down and get out.' There was a slight struggle. Two shots rang out. The first went up through the ceiling. The second killed Gray.

Mrs Barr was not in the bedroom – she was not even in the farmhouse. The police mounted a search party and had found her lying in the woods only a hundred yards away from her home, unconscious from an overdose of sleeping tablets she had taken in an attempt to commit suicide. She was rushed to hospital and recovered next day.

George Barr was charged with murder, and in his first formal statement, he said:

'I walked up to the top of the stairs and we got together. I had the gun at the high-port [across the body with the barrel pointing upwards] and it went off into the ceiling. At the same time the gun broke in half at the narrow part of the stock. I fell down about six stairs and was holding the barrel of the gun. The deceased ran towards me with his arm up and the gun went off. I think I was lying on the stairs. Then he walked past me down the stairs holding his stomach and said, "Get a doctor, quick." Then he got to the bottom of the stairs and fell over. Then I got up to him and threw the gun up the passage and I knelt down beside him and took hold of his head. I said, "What have I done to you?" Then I dialled 999.'

Detective Superintendent Guiver of 'Z' Division, Metropolitan Police, had shown Dr Cameron the dead man lying near the foot of the stairs. The pathologist had noticed that there was extensive bloodstaining on the front of his clothing and the source of the bleeding was a hole in the middle of his chest. His spectacles were still in position. At the far end of the hall was a broken shotgun. There was extensive blood smattering extending from an upstairs bedroom on to a landing and down the staircase into the hall. The wound appeared to have taken an upward and outward direction, fracturing some of the right ribs towards the front and penetrating the right lung.

Dr Cameron gave his view that the victim, after the shooting, could have walked into the bedroom, lain briefly on the bed, and then walked back to the landing and down the stairs, where he collapsed. Cameron estimated that Gray could have lived and moved for up to five minutes before he died.

Police found that the gun, which by a strange irony Barr had bought from Gray some months before, had a defective safety catch, although Barr was unaware of the fact.

In September of 1967 George William Barr was tried at the Old Bailey for the murder of Gray. On any murder charge it is open to the jury to bring in a verdict of not guilty to murder but guilty of manslaughter. In fact the jury acquitted Barr on all charges, his defence being that both shots were fired accidentally.

But that was not the end of the litigation arising from the fatality of 13 June, for if one person kills another in circumstances which are at least a civil wrong, and there are a wife and children dependent upon the deceased, they have a right of action under what lawyers call the Fatal Accidents Act. And so the administrators of Gray's estate brought an action against Barr on behalf of the widow and children to recover damages equivalent to the dependency they would have enjoyed had Gray lived.

The civil action was remarkable and it took place more than two years after the Old Bailey jury had acquitted Barr of the murder or manslaughter of his wife's lover. A High Court judge ruled that it was a case of manslaughter. Because of that Barr was ordered to pay £6,112 damages to the dead man's widow plus the costs of the long court fight to decide the circumstances in which farmer James Gray died from gunshot wounds.

Mr Justice Geoffrey Lane's 'inescapable conclusion' – having paid proper regard to the jury's verdict – was that 'this death was the outcome of an unlawful assault involving a threat of violence by Mr Barr, a threat which he must have realized was likely to result in some injury to Mr Gray, and that is manslaughter.'

Barr claimed that the shooting occurred accidentally when he took a loaded shotgun to Gray's house with the intention of frightening him. So, he maintained, any damages he was liable for should be paid by the Prudential Assurance Company under an 'accidental injury to others' clause in a Hearth and Home policy.

The Prudential denied liability on the grounds that, despite the Old Bailey jury's verdict, Gray's death was not an 'accident' within the meaning of the policy, and Mr Justice Lane ruled that it would be contrary to public policy to allow Barr to recover by insurance. He said:

'It was urged on Mr Barr's behalf that public policy should be applied not on grounds of principle but according to the view taken of the degree of culpability or wickedness of the claimant in a particular case.

'It was submitted, therefore, that Mr Barr's actions, even assuming they were criminal, were understandable. But a husband who arms himself with a loaded shotgun, however outraged he may be, to search for his errant wife, is not easily forgiven.'

Finally Mr Justice Lane held that as the death was the outcome of an unlawful assault involving a threat of violence or of gross negligence, this amounted to manslaughter and was a crime. It was, therefore, against public policy to enforce a contract for indemnity against the consequences of a crime, and the claim against the insurers failed. After making some necessary deductions, as the law required, he awarded the widow £6,000.

The case went to the Court of Appeal but the verdict was upheld.

6

The Murder of 'The Magpie'

At 10.45 A.M. on Saturday, 1 June 1968, a chef looked out of the window of the Midway Restaurant on the road to Southend, Essex. He saw a large brown dog sniffing at the door of a green Jaguar motor car parked outside which he knew had been there for some days. The chef went to the car, looked through the windows and saw a blue tarpaulin draped over the front passenger seat. The quarter window on the driver's door was partially open and he managed to open the door. He was met with a foul smell and he lifted the corner of the tarpaulin. Underneath he saw the feet of a man's body in an advanced state of decomposition. He reported his find to the restaurant manager, who first went to look for himself and then dialled 999. The first CID officer to arrive was Detective Inspector George Harris of the Essex police and he began a full-scale murder investigation which was later to be led by Detective Superintendent Kenneth Drury of Scotland Yard's Murder Squad.

Later that afternoon coachloads of coast-bound holiday-makers who pulled up for a snack at the restaurant were surprised to see uniformed police, detectives, fingerprint men and forensic scientists at work in the sweltering sun around the green Jaguar car with its index number MCC 932. There were also several crime reporters, of whom I was one, and many newspaper photographers. One of the forensic men was Dr Cameron. He looked into the car and found under the blue tarpaulin the body of a man, curled up on the floor. The body showed changes consistent with having lain dead in a closed atmosphere for three to four days. When the tarpaulin was removed he found a blue jacket, lining uppermost, folded over the front passenger seat. It was heavily bloodstained.

Members of his team took the fingerprints of the dead man, which were sent to the Yard for identification, and then Dr Cameron had the Jaguar, with the dead man still inside, loaded on a special trailer vehicle and taken to Brentwood public mortuary, at the back of an undertaker's parlour. In the enclosed quadrangle of the undertaker's yard Dr Cameron, with the help of two policemen, removed the body of the man from the front of the car. It was a slow and difficult job and the heat was intense. The Jaguar, still on the trailer, was then driven to police headquarters at Chelmsford for further examination.

At the post-mortem Dr Cameron found two entry firearm wounds, one at the outer corner of the right eye and the other behind the right ear, 'both consistent with a near discharge of a matter of inches'. Parts of .22 calibre bullets were removed by Cameron and handed to John McCafferty, the Yard ballistics expert. McCafferty also examined swabs taken of both hands of the dead man and was able to say that he had not handled a firearm and that both bullets had been fired from the same gun.

By mid-afternoon the body was identified by a thumb impression, taken when the body was still in the car park, as Anthony John Maffia, aged thirty-eight and known as a considerable figure in criminal circles. He was later formally identified at the mortuary by his brother by the colour of his hair, a tattoo on his left forearm and a gold solitaire ring. His face was unrecognizable. His murder signalled the start of an incredible treasure hunt, for Maffia was well known as a receiver of stolen property and was nicknamed 'The Magpie'.

Both the police and the criminals were on the same trail for the Magpie's haul. There was already an indication of his riches, for police found, in various pockets of his clothing, property worth more than £700, including cash and cheques, and there were two gold 1931 mint sovereigns and many other coins. It appeared that robbery was not the immediate motive for the murder.

Mr Drury delved into Maffia's background and found out that he was a car dealer, a gold smuggler, a receiver of stolen property, particularly jewellery, rare stamps, diamonds, old coins and gold bullion. In the two years prior to his death it was alleged that more than four million pounds' worth of stolen property had passed through his hands. He was well known to be extremely selective in what he would buy and he was believed to have been connected in one way or another with some of the biggest criminal enterprises in recent times. He had been in the motor trade all his adult life and he had a vast number of associates, most of whom had a niche in the Criminal Record Office. Maffia himself had only a few convictions for crime and one of those caused a mild sensation when he helped, with another man, in 1967 to engineer the escape of Alfred Hinds while he was in the custody of two prison officers at the Law Courts in London.

In December 1951, three years after his father's remarriage, Maffia had married his sixteen-year-old stepsister, by whom he had two children. During his life with her, it was alleged, he was violent towards her which culminated in her leaving him in October 1957. He then formed an association with a young woman called Beryl Reece, with whom he had been friendly for some years, and in 1958 she went to live with him and his two children. They were still together at the time of his death, living in a detached chalet-type bungalow in Roebuck Lane, Buck-hurst Hill, Essex, which was worth £12,000.

Tony Maffia began life in East London by selling scrap car batteries. He made the rounds of car dealers and junk yards in London's East End and bought up old car batteries for pennies. He had them reconditioned and sold them at a handsome profit. Then he turned to the second-hand motor car trade and he was again successful, becoming managing director of a company buying and selling commercial vehicles. He had also been known as a financier and investment consultant in the City. He once formed the cut-price firm of London and Home Counties Insurance Company Ltd but he sold that and the sub-sequent combine crashed with debts of £250,000. From 1962 onwards Maffia appeared to have been a person of some wealth. He was also considered to be extremely mean. He was uncommunicative about his business and became known as 'The Fox' because of his business acumen and reticence about money matters. He also aspired to move into higher social circles so that he would more easily be accepted by his wealthy business associates. To that end he bought a forty-foot twin diesel six-berth cabin cruiser, *Calamara*, and became a member of the yacht marina at Wallasea Island. He also bought a fibre-glass speedboat with a large outboard engine. There was a blue tarpaulin cover for the boat which Maffia kept in his green Jaguar.

In 1967 Maffia visited Portugal with a view to buying an interest in a hotel but, when that fell through, he bought the controlling interest in a copper mine. In the following year he bought a quarter share of a £100,000 hotel in Jersey, and he had an interest in an operation that involved forged banknotes of £10 denomination. He had shown some of these notes to prospective buyers in Belgium, who suggested he had been the victim of a confidence trick and refused to trade. Maffia was furious and still in a bad temper when he returned home.

Superintendent Drury now had the history of Maffia and his lifestyle and was tolerably sure that the motive for the murder was his large hoard of property, both honestly acquired and bought as a 'fence' of stolen property. This shrewd detective already had a short list of suspects and an even larger list of criminal associates. The latter were fairly evenly divided between those who liked Maffia and those who hated him.

Superintendent Drury had been to Maffia's bungalow and talked to Beryl Reece. She had mentioned that on 27 May a man called Steve Jewell had been there and had discussed buying the bungalow and the boat. She said the two men had left in separate cars to go to the marina to see the boat and that Tony Maffia had never returned. Drury checked on Jewell and found that he had a criminal record and that he had once been in the same prison as Maffia. He made inquiries as to exactly what happened after Maffia and Jewell went off at about 11 A.M. on 27 May and he learned that Maffia and Jewell were seen together at the marina and had inspected the *Calamara*. The manager of the marina told Drury that Maffia had whispered to him that he did not think Jewell had enough money to buy the boat. Maffia had made a reversed-charge telephone call to his Leytonstone office at 1.20 P.M. saying he would be back in an hour and a half. At 1.30 P.M. Maffia and Jewell went to the Crooksea Ferry Inn, little more than a mile from the marina, where they were served by the daughter of the licensee who remembered that Maffia had a light ale and a ham sandwich and Jewell a Double Diamond and two brandies, all paid for by Maffia. At 1.55 P.M., after being seen together by three local inhabitants all of whom knew Maffia, they drove off in the Jaguar. But Maffia failed to

return to his office and some time later that day the
police were informed of his disappearance.

Meanwhile Drury's murder team had been making
inquiries all over the county of Essex. They found a fifty-
six-year-old semi-retired plasterer living on the Southend
–London road, in the village of Vange. He told police
that he had been sitting in his front window between 2.30
and 3.30 P.M. on 27 May and had seen a green Mark X
Jaguar car swerve off the road and on to the grass verge
in a layby. He had seen the driver of the car throw some
clothing from the car into the hedge, about one hundred
feet from his window. He saw the same man wipe the
interior of the passenger seat and the bottom of the front
nearside door, using his right hand. The police found that
clothing, which turned out to be a grey raglan Crombie
overcoat. In the left-hand coat pocket was a .22 live
bullet with a hollowed-out nose, a bloodstained packet of
'Puck' matches, a separate match and a Midland Bank
cheque book; in the right-hand pocket was an estate
agent's handout for Maffia's bungalow and a notice adver-
tising the sale of the *Calamara*. The coat was extensively
bloodstained, both inside and outside, and on the front
was an area of staining which proved to be similar to
the brain tissue found on the yellow material on the
transmission cover inside the car.

Another piece of evidence came from a poultry farmer
who had been driving near the marina on 27 May and
had seen a green Jaguar parked in a field just off the
road. He recalled that there was a man sitting behind the
steering wheel and another man standing outside the car
on the driver's side.

The detectives also found a man who remembered that
at 3.40 P.M. he was driving his car with his wife as a
passenger and was stopped by a man who asked for a lift
to the Moby Dick public house. He had invited the man

into the car but after a while his wife grew anxious about the passenger's behaviour – he was constantly looking out of the rear window. The driver stopped the car and asked him to leave.

On the forensic side Cameron and McCafferty had been joined by Margaret Pereira from Scotland Yard's laboratory. They were working to establish the true picture of events and they made another detailed examination of the green Jaguar. Cameron was concerned with the wounds inflicted on the dead man. Miss Pereira's role was to research the story told by the positioning of the body, the extent and grouping of the bloodstains, with blood and tissue identification and the explanation of the smears of blood. McCafferty concentrated on determining whether Maffia had been shot in the car, and, if so, in what position? And had the body been taken out of the car and later been put back into it?

Because of the distribution of the stains, smears and brain tissue, the experts were sure that Maffia had been shot from outside the car, while sitting in the driver's seat, and had toppled over towards the passenger side. He had then been covered with the tarpaulin and not taken out of the car until it reached the mortuary. The first shot entered near the right eye which forced him to collapse and he was then shot through the side of the head. The explosive force of the second shot caused a portion of the brain tissue to be forced through the first entry wound. That brain tissue had been found on a small piece of yellow material on the transmission cover near the car radio and also on the grey overcoat which had been thrown into the hedge.

Superintendent Drury learned from Maffia's co-director that Jewell and Maffia had been meeting since 1967, but on a fairly casual basis. By now the detective knew quite a lot about Stephen Leonard Jewell. He was aged forty-five, married with two sons and lived near Manchester. He had left school at fourteen and joined the Merchant Navy as a galley boy. He remained at sea for almost fourteen years, and when he left he was a ship's bosun. Then he entered the coal haulage business and for the last five years had run his own coal delivery company. He had several convictions for petty crime and it was while Maffia was serving twelve months in Stafford Prison for his part in helping Alfred Hinds to escape from police custody in the Law Courts that he met Jewell, who was serving a sentence for theft. Drury sent out a call for Stephen Jewell to be brought in to see him but, instead, Jewell contacted the police in Manchester and the Yard man flew up and collected him. On the way back Jewell told the detective that he had visited Maffia just before Christmas in 1967 and that he had expressed an interest in buying the cabin cruiser *Calamara*. He also said that there had been previous discussions about forged £10 notes which had been offered to Jewell at the rate of £32,000-worth of forged notes for £8,000 of genuine currency.

Jewell then said that he had visited Maffia at his house on 27 May 1968 when he took with him a .22 Browning automatic pistol with a plastic type butt. He said that Maffia had asked him to bring the pistol because 'he was having trouble with someone' and that Maffia gave him a box of ammunition and mentioned there was a hole in the nose of every round. Maffia told him to load the magazine of the pistol and Jewell took it with him and put it into his Vauxhall Victor Estate car. Jewell said that he had also asked about buying Maffia's house.

Maffia had agreed to show Jewell the *Calamara* and said they would each drive their cars to the Moby Dick public house and Maffia could take him on to the marina where the boat was kept. They drove together from the Moby Dick in Maffia's green Jaguar. Soon after they began the journey Maffia asked Jewell if he had brought the gun and he said he had left it in his car. Maffia drove back and Jewell collected it. They saw the *Calamara* at the marina and then drove to the Creeksea Ferry Inn and had a drink and a sandwich. Afterwards Maffia drove him back to the Moby Dick and he collected his car and drove back to Manchester.

That was Jewell's story and Superintendent Drury was not impressed. He knew it was true in part, but there were a lot of missing details. Some of those details Drury had collected from the police in Manchester.

On the evening of 27 May Jewell had talked to a steward in a local club and told him that he had been south on business, hoping to buy a boat to sell at a profit. He went on to say that while in his friend's Jaguar they had been stopped by two men driving a white Jaguar. These men had jumped out and told Jewell to get off up the road, which he did but, in the excitement, he had left his coat behind. Jewell had presumed that his friend in the south had been truly 'clobbered'.

Jewell had talked to the same steward later and said that he had received a threatening telephone call and that his contact in the south was Maffia. He then retold the story of the holdup but said it was a Hillman Minx car that had been used and not a Jaguar and that it had been four men and not two that stopped them. The next night Jewell asked the steward to contact the police and at 1.30 A.M. on Monday, 3 June Detective Constable Ronald Charlton met Jewell and, after hearing his story, took him to the police station and Superintendent Drury flew to Manchester next morning.

More details were revealed when the investigator saw Jewell again. He remembered that when sitting in Maffia's

Jaguar he had placed the loaded gun and a separate loaded magazine on the dividing arm of the two front seats, covering them with a piece of rag. At the marina, Jewell said, he took off his overcoat and placed it on the front seat over the gun. After he had driven off with Maffia from the Crooksea Ferry Inn Jewell said that three men in a silver grey metallic Zodiac saloon forced them to stop. The three men told Jewell to get out of the car and walk away for 300 yards. He said he waited for ten to fifteen minutes and then walked back to find that Maffia, the three men and the Zodiac had disappeared. He remembered that the time then was about 2 P.M. and he mentioned that he was passed by a green Land-Rover.

In addition to the disappearance of Maffia, the three men and the Zodiac saloon, Jewell noticed that his overcoat was bloodstained and was in the well of the front near side of the Jaguar instead of being between the two front seats, and that the pistol and the magazine were missing. A further ten to fifteen minutes later he drove off. After driving for about ten miles he went into a layby and threw his overcoat into the hedge. Jewell admitted leaving the Jaguar at the Midway Restaurant, after which he got two lifts back to the Moby Dick car park.

On 5 June 1968 at 5.35 P.M. Jewell was formally charged with murder and cautioned. He maintained his innocence and alleged that there had been threatening telephone calls to his wife and family from Maffia's supposed attackers, as well as a threatening letter. On 22 July the committal proceedings began at Brentwood Magistrates Court and the case was put for the Director of Public Prosecutions. The defence strongly objected to the forensic evidence of Cameron, Pereira and McCafferty, the basis of the objection being that none of the three were experts in such matters and were only conjecturing, but it proved a worthless objection made in desperation. Jewell was remanded in custody and sent for trial at the Central Criminal Court.

He appeared on 11 November 1968 in No. 1 Court at the Old Bailey before Mr Justice McKenna and pleaded not guilty. The prosecution case was presented by Mr William Howard, QC, and Mr John Hazan, and for the defence by Mr Victor Durand, QC, and Mr Felix Waley. The prosecution alleged that Jewell shot Maffia, left the body in the restaurant car park and drove home to Manchester in his own car.

Jewell, in his defence, said he first met Maffia in Stafford Prison in 1957 and, after they were both released, they kept in touch. Earlier that year he had been approached at a Salford casino by a man offering forged £10 notes for sale. He contacted Maffia and arranged to show him a specimen forged note. On 27 May he called at Maffia's house and later they left to inspect a boat at a marina near Southend. As they drove in the green Jaguar towards Southend they stopped at a layby and two men in a maroon Jaguar drew up behind. The men told Maffia he should have been at 'the site' where people were waiting.

There was a discussion and telephone calls were made before it was agreed that Maffia could go to the marina. While a call was being made Maffia opened the boot of the car and lifted out a large black-painted gold ingot. Rather than switch the ingot from Maffia's green Jaguar to the maroon Jaguar, it was decided that the men should change cars. He and Maffia drove off in the maroon car to the marina. They reached the marina and inspected the boat. As they left a nearby inn Maffia's green Jaguar arrived with at least three men inside. Maffia said, 'Oh, not those bastards again.'

Two of the men were those who had stopped them

earlier and one said to Maffia, 'Clever little bastard, aren't you? We want you in this car now and we are taking you back to London.' Maffia was pushed into the car and driven off. Jewell said he got into the maroon Jaguar with a man named Landon. On the way to Southend Landon told him of the plan to take the gold to France. Jewell added, 'In between Calais and St Malo I was to be put in the big locker, shot and thrown into the sea.'

After passing through Southend with Landon, they saw Maffia's green car on the A13 road. Landon stopped, two men left Maffia's Jaguar and approached their car. A man who got in with his clothing bloodstained said, 'That bastard "The Fox" has knifed me in the shoulder.' They drove towards London and the wounded man produced a gun, held it at Jewell's head and said to him, 'You are as bad as the other bastard.'

Jewell said he left the car at the restaurant 'absolutely terrified' and managed to get two lifts to Ilford, collect his own car and drive home to Manchester.

It was an extraordinary story and, not surprisingly, Mr Durand in his speech for the defence described Jewell as a 'pathological liar'.

Again the evidence of Dr Cameron and his team was strongly challenged by the defence, but it was accepted by the court and so effectively blocked Jewell's line of defence.

It took the all-male jury just over four hours to reach a majority verdict by ten to two to find Jewell guilty. He was sentenced to life imprisonment with no recommendation for a minimum term. An application was made for leave to appeal but it was refused.

Anthony Maffia was known as the King of the Receivers. In his will published in September 1968 he left £83,792 (duty payable £25,568) to his two children. Maffia was not only acquisitive, he was secretive. In addition to his legal estate he had a vast hoard of deed boxes, which he kept in various banks, and it was put on show so that the items could be identified. There were eighteen pieces of gold identified as one almost complete gold bar of the 140 gold bars stolen during the £750,000 gold bullion van robbery of 1 May 1967 from N. M. Rothschild and Sons, in Bowling Green Lane, London. There were thousands of pounds of mint gold sovereigns, still in their original bank wrappers, and thousands of other coins from thirty-seven different countries. There were also 1,396 faulty 3d. stamps valued at £10 a pair, numerous art treasures, Dresden china figures, diamond rings, bracelets and gems, valued altogether at about £500,000. And, apart from all that he had the proceeds of a burglary from the home of a Surrey stockbroker in December 1966, a unique collection of English coins valued at £100,000.

True to the end, the man called 'The Magpie' collected two last items – the two hollow-nosed bullets in his brain.

7

The Clue of the Cerise Dress

When Edmond Locard, the eminent French criminologist, said, 'Every contact leaves a trace,' he established one of the basic precepts of forensic science. It was never better illustrated than in the murder of twenty-year-old Mrs Claire Josephs on 7 February 1968. Professor Cameron describes it as a case of 'brilliant detective work finally clinched by indisputable forensic scientific evidence'.

Claire Jacqueline Parvin married Bernard Daniel Josephs in September 1967. At five minutes past eight on the evening of Wednesday, 7 February 1968, after approximately five months of marriage, Bernard returned home to Flat 15, Deepdene Court, at Shortlands, near Bromley, Kent, to find his bride brutally murdered in their bedroom. She was wearing, among other clothing, a cerise woollen dress. This had been a Christmas present from her husband in 1966.

About eighteen months before the marriage Claire Josephs became friends at work with a young girl who, later, married a Roger John Payne. Claire and her mother attended the wedding and the two girls remained friends, mostly by correspondence. In January 1968 Mrs Payne visited Claire at Deepdene Court and her husband, Roger Payne, was shown round the flat when he came to pick up his wife. On that occasion Claire was wearing a brown skirt and a green jumper. The significance of this will be appreciated when we come later to the scientific evidence produced in the case.

A week after the visit from the Paynes to the Josephs' flat Claire started work as a telephonist at West Wickham, about three miles away. That was on 15 Janaury 1968 and only after that date did she wear the cerise woollen dress in which she was found dead. It had been kept in a suitcase since mid-1967.

On the morning of Wednesday, 7 February 1968, Bernard Josephs and his wife had breakfast before setting off for their respective jobs. Bernard helped his wife to clear the breakfast dishes and generally tidy the flat. Claire Josephs was driven to and from work by a girlfriend and she left soon after 9 A.M. Both girls left work at 5.30 P.M. Claire was wearing the cerise dress, a blue raincoat and a chiffon scarf and was dropped off near her home at about 5.40 P.M., less than five minutes' walk away.

Police estimated that she arrived at the flat at 5.45 P.M., which was confirmed by her mother-in-law who telephoned at 5.30 P.M. but received no reply. She called again at 5.45 P.M. and spoke to Claire for about fifteen minutes, giving her instructions on how to make a lemon soufflé. That was the last occasion on which Claire Josephs is known to have been alive.

Claire Josephs' husband, Bernard, finished work in Barking at 6 P.M. and went to a nearby public house with a friend and had drinks until 7 P.M., when they were joined by the friend's fiancée and began the journey home. At 7.50 P.M. the three went to a public house in Shortlands where they bought six bottles of beer before driving Bernard Josephs to Deepdene Court. When they arrived his friend mentioned that there were no lights on in the flat and suggested that Claire might have gone to see her parents. He offered to wait and drive Mr Josephs there but his offer was declined. Bernard made his way to the flat.

He let himself in, and found the flat in darkness. He switched on the lights and put his raincoat and briefcase on the settee in the living room. Everything seemed normal, neat and tidy and undisturbed. He looked into the kitchen, walked into the hall and then into the bedroom. Switching on the light he saw his wife's legs protruding beyond the end of the bed. She was lying face downwards and slightly turned to the right. He gently lifted her head and saw a terrible wound across her neck. Transfixed with horror, he managed to get to the telephone and called his wife's parents and then his own parents. In his shock he failed to call the police or an ambulance.

His father-in-law was the first to arrive at the flat and he called the police at 8.13 P.M. The police and an ambulance arrived three minutes later, and then came the family doctor who certified that the girl was dead.

It was ten minutes later that Detective Sergeant Peck arrived and took charge of the situation, for already there had been far too many people milling about the flat, without thought of finding fingerprints or other useful clues.

Detective Chief Superintendent John Cummings arrived at 9.15 P.M. to take over control of what was to be his final and, probably, his most successful case. He noted that the flat revealed little or no evidence of disorder or disturbance and there had been no forcible entry. The dead woman's right slipper was by the wall between the kitchen and the lounge doors, an indication of it perhaps having dropped off while she ran or stumbled. Deeply experienced, he looked around the flat, searching for the points which would tell him the story of the evening's events. In the kitchen an electric mixer was still set at No. 2, plugged in but switched off at the point. In a bowl a soufflé mixture was partly made, with eggs, butter and lemons lying beside it on the right, and a recipe on the left side. This indicated to Cummings that she had been interrupted, perhaps by a telephone call or a ring at the front door. On the draining board was a cup and saucer containing coffee, while on the window sill was a matching plate containing six shortbread biscuits, obviously taken from a packet which had been broken open and was still lying on the worktop. The Chief Superintendent took the view that the person who called that night was not a personal friend, hence the more formal offer of a biscuit on a plate rather than from a packet. No weapon was found at the flat, but the next morning a 'Peerage' bread knife with a 4½-inch plastic blade with a serrated cutting edge was noticed to be missing. Despite exhaustive searches that bread knife was never found.

Dr Cameron was called in by John Cummings. The two men were old friends and since Cameron lived nearby, he was at the scene within a few minutes. It was he who said on his preliminary examination that the killing wounds were made with a serrated-edged knife. Then the two men, pathologist and detective, reconstructed the crime. They finally agreed that Claire Josephs had answered the front door to someone she knew slightly, had made them a cup of coffee in the kitchen, where she had first been attacked. She was then pushed or carried towards the bedroom and it was in that room she had been killed.

Later that night the body was removed to the local mortuary where Dr Cameron made his post-mortem examination. He found that the victim had fourteen incised wounds in the front of the neck and four stab wounds in the neck, one of which penetrated muscles through to the right base of the tongue and to the front of the spine. Over the voice box were areas of bruising and marks round the neck that were suggestive of constriction of the neck with a degree of asphyxia at or shortly before death. Marks on the right side of the mouth could have been caused by fingernails. If she had been assaulted from behind, they would be consistent with having been caused by the left hand, leaving her attacker's right hand free. The wounds in the front of her neck appeared to have been caused by a knife with a serrated edge. The marks could have been caused either by a left-handed person from in front, or a right-handed person from behind, or by a right-handed person from above the head with the body on the floor. The defence wounds on the dead woman's right hand were also consistent with having been caused by a similar serrated knife.

None of the numerous wounds in the front of the neck were fatal, but there were four stab wounds which had penetrated the neck muscles, allowing air to penetrate into the circulation with development of air embolism and subsequent haemorrhage. That was the cause of death, which Cameron estimated had taken place at 7.15 P.M. approximately. There was no evidence of sexual assault.

As there had been no forcible entry to the flat Cummings concentrated his inquiries on relatives, friends and acquaintances who could possibly have been entertained by Mrs Josephs. Neighbours were asked if there had been any door-to-door salesmen in the area, but said there had been none. The detective made a minute search of the flat. In one drawer he found a large pile of old birthday cards, letters and invitations of all kinds, many of them dating back for months. Among them was an invitation from a girlfriend called Mary inviting Claire to her wedding in 1966. The name of the man she was to marry was Roger John Payne.

Every man mentioned on the invitation cards and in the letters was traced and interviewed. Every one was checked at the Yard's criminal record office, but nothing of interest turned up until they reached the man called Roger Payne. It was discovered that he had twice been charged with sexual offences. In November 1959, at the age of seventeen, he was placed on probation for three years at Surrey Assizes for breaking into a girl's house, placing a hand over her mouth and attempting sexual intercourse with her. In April 1965 at Malden and Surbiton Magistrates Court he was sentenced to three months' imprisonment for assault occasioning actual bodily harm, when at 2.45 A.M. he entered the bedroom of a middle-aged woman. He held her by the wrists, placed his hand over her mouth and injured her as she struggled.

It had taken five days of laborious inquiries to reach the first prime suspect. Roger Payne was a twenty-six-year-old bank clerk living near Maidstone in Kent. When they saw him the detectives noticed that there were scratches on both his hands and a bruise on his forehead, which he explained by saying that he had quarrelled with his wife on Sunday, 4 February, and they had come to blows. When asked about his movements on 7 February Payne said he had been in London for a medical examination in connection with his job. He accounted for his movements on that day until he arrived home at 9.15 P.M. Before the police left they took a blood sample from Payne and took with them items of his clothing, including a hat and an overcoat.

Detective Chief Superintendent Cummings had eliminated the dead woman's husband and another possible suspect in the first twenty-four hours of the inquiry and he realized that since there were no witnesses he would need the further help of the forensic scientists. Cameron's post-mortem samples from the dead woman were taken to the Metropolitan Police forensic laboratory together with some of her clothing.

Since detectives had found no fingerprints at the scene they took the coffee cup found in the kitchen to the laboratory so that the saliva on it could be grouped. The presence of Group A was contained in the saliva, the same group as Payne. However, this could not be of any great significance since forty-two per cent of the British population are of that group. But the examination of contact between the clothing of the dead girl and Payne could begin now that the police had some of his clothes.

The dress Claire was wearing when she was murdered was made of a fluffy woollen fabric of an exceptionally bright cerise colour. Margaret Pereira, the Yard's expert on blood grouping and leading authority on fibres and textiles, found a few fibres exactly matching those of the dress on the hat and overcoat of Payne. She went on to find the cerise fibres on Payne's scarf and suit. She proved that a thin strand of thread found beneath the dead girl's thumbnail had come from his scarf. Both Payne's overcoat and suit contained a variety of colours and neither was of pure wool, and because of the number of different fibres the examination took several days. But, finally, the scientists detected on Claire's raincoat a number of fibres which could have come from Payne's overcoat and others which matched his suit. The police concluded that she was still wearing the raincoat when he had arrived.

After the clothes, Miss Pereira turned to a man's handkerchief that was found at the flat and did not belong to Bernard Josephs. It was bloodstained, and tests revealed the presence of two different groups. One was AB, MN, the same as Claire Josephs', and the other was AM which was the same as Payne's group. Neither of those two blood groups matched the blood of Bernard Josephs. Fibres were also found on that handkerchief which matched Payne's overcoat, his suit and Claire's dress.

Payne was arrested on 24 February, seventeen days after the murder. His house was thoroughly searched. Among many other things, police took possession of every item of Payne's clothing, because they still were not satisfied they had found all the evidence. During the examination of Payne's and Claire's clothing and also of the handkerchief it had become apparent that there were fibres in all those items which probably had a common source. These were rayon fibres, the majority being plain red and others in permutations of red, black, pale yellow and blue. It was thought that these fibres came from a rayon printed fabric in which the background was red. When Mr Cummings arrested Payne and searched the house he made sure that one of his aides collected all the neckties.

There were several, plus a cravat and another scarf. When Margaret Pereira saw this scarf at the laboratory she noticed it was badly frayed and was made of red printed rayon. Not only did the fibres of the scarf match those found previously but there were eight red wool fibres on the scarf which matched those of Claire's dress. One last item was a man's handkerchief of the same pattern as the one found in the flat. It was slightly larger but of a similar weave. Miss Pereira scientifically shredded that handkerchief and was able to prove that it contained 184 strands, the same number as in the handkerchief found in the flat.

Even a single human hair found on Claire's clothing matched the hair of Payne; and some dog hairs matched those of Payne's dog. Then Payne's Morris 1100 motor car was brought to the laboratory. Cummings reasoned that when the murderer left the flat he took the knife away with him to dispose of it later and the most likely place to secrete the weapon would be inside the pocket in the driver's door. That was the first part of the car to be examined, and bloodstaining was found in the bottom corner of the pocket. It was found to be of the same group as Claire Josephs', which is found in approximately one person in eighty. The inner surface of the driver's door had been washed but the human blood remained. And the car gave up one last clue. The debris on the floor was found to contain several fibres matching the nylon carpet in Claire's flat together with a few more fibres matching her dress.

Altogether the examination of Payne's clothing revealed a total of sixty-one fibres matching Claire's dress on his overcoat, twenty-two on his hat, six on his jacket and none on his trousers. The suit had been cleaned but the fibres were not lying on the surface but were embedded in the interstices of the cloth. Those fibres were brilliantly fluorescent and were easily detected by examining the garments under ultra-violet light.

Twenty rayon fibres matching Payne's scarf were found on Claire's raincoat and eight were present on the handkerchief found in the flat. There was also a single red and black rayon fibre matching the scarf under the left thumbnail of the dead woman.

It was a case in which the victim virtually caught her own killer through her hoard of old cards and invitations. This was followed by a classic investigation backed by brilliant forensic teamwork.

Roger Payne was tried for murder in May 1968 and pleaded not guilty. His defence was that he was 'not there'. He was found guilty by a majority of eleven to one after a retirement of nearly four hours and he was sentenced to life imprisonment.

The evidence of the forensic scientists had proved that Payne had been in the flat and had murdered Claire Josephs. The motive was never established, although the police were aware that the killer had a sexual problem of impotence. According to a statement he made to a third party he was able to overcome these difficulties by a sudden violent attack on a woman. He had tried it twice before and on the third occasion with these tragic results.

8

A Walk From Cricket to Murder

In the sweltering summer of 1969, the year that the American astronauts landed on the moon, the sleepy village of Paddock Wood was sweetly perfumed with new-mown hay and the scents of fruit blossom. This rural village in Kent was quiet on Sunday afternoon, 20 July, apart from a cricket match being played between a local team called the 'Mad Hatters' and the village side. At two o'clock a member of the 'Mad Hatters' team, Sean Galbally, arrived in his sports car with his girlfriend, Diana Davidson.

She sat with friends, watching the game, but then some time between 5.30 and 5.40 P.M. she became bored and left the ground to go for a walk. Her friends knew that she quickly tired of watching cricket and preferred to wander in the countryside.

Diana was an attractive twenty-one-year-old research worker at the Ministry of Defence and Development Establishment at Fort Halstead, near Sevenoaks, and lived with her family in the old-world village of Otford in the Weald of Kent. Her father was employed at the same establishment on work described as 'highly secret' and Mr Galbally also worked there. On that day Diana was wearing a very short mini-dress coloured in orange and pink stripes. Only three people noticed her leave the cricket field and they were the last people to see her alive.

When she failed to return at close of play both the cricket teams and their supporters made a search and eventually reported her missing to the local police.

Paddock Wood had a population of 4,600 and adjoins the parish of Five Oak Green where another 1,500 people lived. At the southern end of the village was the cricket ground and at the other a fruit farm known as Eastlands. The two places were linked by a main road to Maidstone.

Despite a massive police search and maximum publicity in the newspapers, not a single person reported having seen her. Detective Chief Inspector Jack Goodsall of Kent police found out as much as he could about the missing girl in the hope he might get a lead to her disappearance. He found that she was an efficient, highly intelligent girl. She had a strong interest in the country-side, wild life and wild flowers and often went for long walks alone. To her friends she was something of an enigma: sometimes remote and unsociable and at others lively and interesting. Men found her attractive but were sometimes rebuffed by her cool manner. She had two regular boy-friends who explained to the detective that she was not frigid but had strong views on social behaviour, including pre-marital intercourse. She was quite independent and confident in her dealings with the opposite sex.

During the course of the following week more than 100 policemen and 150 soldiers from a local unit, plus police dogs and their handlers and underwater frogmen, made a concentrated search of the area, but there was no trace of Diana.

During the evening of Sunday, 27 July, a retired prison officer, walking his dog, came across a naked, female body in an orchard on Eastlands Farm, less than a mile from the cricket ground. Chief Inspector Goodsall rushed to the scene and was shown the body, lying at the bottom of a ditch, face down. He noticed that the ditch was overgrown with long grass which was dry and yellowing. He sent out a call for Taffy Cameron who arrived at one o'clock in the morning and examined the body. He later wrote in his report that the body was that of a well-nourished, slim young woman, five feet one inch in height with 'considerable larval infestation' and no evidence of natural disease which could have caused or contributed to death. Neither was there evidence of sexual assault. But he did find extensive deep bruising round her neck, particularly over the left side and at the back, which he thought was consistent with massive strangulation. The girl's body was taken to Pembury Hospital for detailed examination.

There was nothing with which to identify the body, and the fingerprints of the dead girl were taken and a chart made of her teeth. However, within a few hours the body was identified as that of Diana Davidson. The fingerprints matched the prints found in Diana's bedroom and her dentist was able to identify the teeth. The hunt for a missing girl now became a hunt for a killer.

Chief Inspector Goodsall and his men searched the immediate area and soon found a fawn cardigan and a pair of open sandals, and a little further away an orange-and pink-striped dress, a pair of pants and a brassière. All the clothing was taken to the Metropolitan Police laboratory at Holborn for scientific examination. When the police had found the clothes they thought it likely that all the garments had been forcibly torn from the body. The laboratory scientists confirmed that. As well as the clothing the police had found another item near the cardigan. It was a three-foot length of braid, knotted at both ends and similar to the braid used for piping dressing-gowns. Earth and grass samples from the scene and a blood sample of the dead girl, with the scrapings from under her fingernails, also went to the laboratory.

Chief Inspector Goodsall set up an incident room at a local school about a mile and a half from Eastlands Farm.

It was manned by experienced officers who had only recently been engaged in another murder hunt, and they quickly collated all the evidence which had been gathered in the previous week. There was little doubt that Diana had been murdered on the day she disappeared, but she had not been reported seen after she left the cricket ground. The evidence pointed to a sexual murder. It would be difficult to organize the investigation, for Paddock Wood was the Mecca on summer Sundays of parties of hop-pickers from London, and to add to the problems there had been a village fête on the Saturday with an itinerant fairground staff.

A house-to-house inquiry was set up and it soon became apparent that there were a number of local domestic problems and scandals which the villagers were unhappy to talk about. Many of them asked for their anonymity to be preserved. The request was observed but the police did make stringent inquiries into anything which was in the least suspicious. The Criminal Record Office supplied lists of all sexual deviants in the area, and they too were checked as to their whereabouts on the day. They were all eliminated.

Two householders who lived off the main road, about five minutes' walk from the cricket ground, remembered seeing a girl answering to Diana's description walking in the vicinity of their houses between 5.30 P.M. and 6 P.M. on the Sunday she vanished. The detective concentrating in and around Eastlands Farm also found what turned out to be the main prosecution witness, a farm manager called Harry Cox, who lived in a cottage actually on the farm and not far from the ditch where the body was found.

This witness remembered a man calling at his house at 6 P.M. on Sunday, 20 July, 1969, and asking for directions to Charlton Lane. Although Harry Cox had lived in the district for twelve years he said he had never heard of the place, and the caller walked away. But a few minutes later the same man walked back, this time accompanied by a young woman who appeared to answer the description of the murdered girl.

That was the first positive clue, but there was no more local information forthcoming and the hunt spread wider. One team of detectives went to Bexhill-on-Sea to interview men working on the fun-fair, the same men who had been working at Paddock Wood on the weekend of the murder. And there were three reports from people who thought they had seen Diana with a man in the Paddock Wood area, though confirmation of those sightings was difficult to obtain.

Chief Inspector Goodsall decided to reconstruct the events of 20 July, and on 3 August, a week after the body was found, all the people who were at the cricket match and many members of the public who were in the area were assembled in the village. A woman police sergeant, Muriel Court, had traced the material of the dress that Diana was wearing on the fateful day to a manufacturer in Manchester, and similar material was bought and made up by Muriel Court's mother to fit Woman Police Constable Lane. At 5.30 that evening Constable Lane wore the dress and walked a timed route from the cricket ground to the orchard where the body had been found. She also wore a wig with shoulder-length dark hair, and she so strongly resembled the dead girl that many of Diana's friends present were visibly upset. The event had been well publicized and reporters from all the national press covered the reconstruction.

The result was helpful in that afterwards a number of people thought they remembered seeing Diana Davidson walking off the main road towards the entrance to Eastlands Farm, near a number of houses.

Then came a telephone call from the police forensic science laboratory saying that they had found three spots of blood on the brassière. All three spots were minute but two of them were Diana's own blood of the group O/MN. The third blood spot was classified as group O/N, and blood found on her dress was found to be of the same group. The field of suspects had suddenly narrowed – only 10.3 per cent of the population has blood of that group. It was the vital clue, the blood spot which Cameron called 'the stranger'.

Chief Inspector Goodsall decided to obtain blood samples from selected people in Paddock Wood, including some who lived on Eastlands Farm and all those without a strong alibi for the Sunday afternoon when Diana had disappeared. In the group of twenty first tested only one person had blood from O/N classification but he was quickly cleared because he had been out of the area.

In the course of the earlier house-to-house inquiry two detectives had interviewed a thirty-year-old bachelor named Roy Andrew Thomas Carter. He had moved into the area only a few months previously and was considered something of a mystery. He had been orphaned at an early age and had been raised by the local authority and then trained at a farm school in animal husbandry. He had a passionate love for animals and country life and was extremely sensitive about cruelty to animals. He would talk freely on these subjects, but always went silent when women or sex were discussed. He lived near Eastlands Farm and had recently become friendly with a middle-aged bachelor who worked locally as a railway-crossing keeper.

Carter had no real alibi for the murder on Sunday apart from saying that he had spoken to his next-door neighbours. They were away at the time and the questionnaire was marked for them to be questioned on their

return. When they did come back they denied either
seeing or speaking to Carter on that day. The officers had
also recorded that Carter was 'unshaven'. He was
included in the second group of people for blood samples,
which were obtained on 10 August. Laboratory analysis
proved his blood to be Group O/N.

Two detectives were sent to collect him and, while
talking to him in the back garden, one of them noticed a
piece of braid, similar to that found in the ditch with the
dead girl's clothing, which was being used to tether a dog
to a stake. They searched the house and found another
piece of the same braid tucked under an old mattress in
the loft.

Carter was taken to the incident room and, at first, flatly
denied the murder, but patient questioning eventually
revealed the truth. In this strangely incongruous setting
of a school, with its small desks and chairs and shelves
lined with textbooks, the thirty-year-old Carter slowly
made his statement of murder. He sat in the middle of a
table with a detective on either side. Chief Inspector
Goodsall posed the questions and Sergeant Moore wrote
down the answers.

First of all Carter said he had started to grow a beard
after he had been seen by a police officer on 3 August,
but he said he had grown a beard on other occasions. He
then said that he had met Diana, that the girl had taken
her own dress off when he had turned his back for a
moment and had invited him to have sex with her.

'What did you do on Sunday, 20 July, the day after the
Paddock Wood fête?' Mr Goodsall spoke quietly but
firmly.

Carter said he was working in his back garden and
pottered around there until 8.30 P.M. Mr Goodsall produced a length of braid and a piece of string which had
been found at the scene of the crime and said, 'You are

obviously worried about something, Mr Carter. What is it?'

There was a long pause. Carter sat with his head in his hands and he then said in a low voice, 'What will happen, sir?'

'What do you mean by that question?'

'Well, sir, I did go out and I met that girl.'

'What girl?'

'The one that was killed.'

'Where did you see her?'

'In the orchard.'

'Are you responsible for what happened to her?'

Carter nodded his head.

'I left the house about 5.30 P.M. on 20 July. I turned right and went into the off-licence. I bought some cigarettes. I come out of there. I saw the girl coming up from where the school is here. She was on the same side as where you have got the police caravan. As she passed the shop I was coming out and I saw her. She crossed over the road just before the bridge. I had already crossed over the road and was walking up behind her. I overtook her at the top of the bridge. I did not say anything to her. I called in the telephone by the 'Hop Pocket'. I called in there to phone a Mr R. Mitchell at Wateringbury for some apple-picking. I couldn't find the phone number. As I came out of the telephone box she just passed it. I walked behind her until she got by the lane next to the shop on the left-hand side. She crossed over by the corner by the lane. I crossed over just before the shop. I was just going down the lane for a walk. I was in front of her. I walked down the lane. I knocked on the door of a house. It is the first house on the right-hand side, it is white. A man came to the door. I asked him does he know anywhere where I can get some calves? He told me to go to the end of the lane and the farm was on the right-hand side. I got as far as the footpath which is overgrown. I passed another house on the left-hand side. It was black with white window frames. This was before I got to the overgrown footpath. I looked at the path. I decided to give up and turn round and come back. Coming back I passed the white cottage where I had called and I got as far as the gate where the black tank is that is on the right-hand side. I saw a girl standing in the gateway. She was the same girl which I had passed in the road. I said to her, 'Good evening, miss.' Then I said to her, 'Looks like we're going to have some good fruit this year.' She said, 'What do you know about it, you stupid bastard.' This upset me as I was polite to her. She turned to walk away towards the main lane from the gate. I grabbed her, I had her arms behind her back and my left hand over her mouth, I had her off the ground. She was very light, she was kicking, she only came up to my shoulder. I took her into the orchard and suddenly the ditch was upon us before we knew anything. We fell down into the ditch. She landed on her knees. I kept my balance and still managed to hold her. I got her hands still behind her back, holding them with my right knee. My right hand was over her mouth. I chopped her with my left hand on her left side of the neck. I was facing away from the footpath when this happened. I then ripped her dress by taking a handful at the back, then I took her brassière and pants off, the brassière was white and the pants blue. When I ripped her clothes off she was laying on her face, her head away from the path. I turned her over. I was intimate with her, I had sexual intercourse with her. I was wearing blue trousers and a "V" neck green jumper and black boots. While I was on top of her I heard someone coming down the path. I glanced up and saw him. He was by himself, he had grey hair wearing a charcoal grey suit. I crouched down in the ditch. When I was carrying her to the ditch she dropped her cardigan which was browny coloured and her shoes fell off. I got out of the ditch on the right-hand side facing up the orchard. I jumped over the ditch, picked her shoes and cardigan up, put the dress over her, the cardigan over her feet and the shoes in the bottom of the ditch. Before I left her I am positive I turned her back over on her face. I just did not want to see her face, that's all. After I covered her up I heard a car start up in the breakers' yard at the end of the lane. After the car had gone I got out of the ditch walked out the lane and turned left towards Beltring, then I turned right towards the level crossing. I walked to about 100 yards from the crossing and turned back. On the way back I stopped and looked across the fields, then I walked the end of the lane and turned towards Paddock Wood. When I got by the shops I saw a woman weeding in the garden opposite the shops. I walked straight home and got in about half past seven. I never went back there again. Since this happened I have been very sorry and very upset. It wouldn't have happened if she hadn't called me a bastard which I'm not.

'I have read the above statement and I have been told that I can correct, alter or add anything I wish. This statement is true. I have made it of my own free will.

(Signed) R. CARTER

'Witnessed (Signed) J. E. GOODSALL D/C/I 11/8/69.'

There was ample evidence to show that Carter was the killer, for he had no alibi for the day in question and his blood group was identical with the blood on the brassière and the dress. The braid found in the ditch was identical with that found in his house, originally from a dressing-gown left by a previous owner of the house. There was a transfer of fibres from the dead woman's clothes to those of Carter and vice versa. On his face were scratch marks that matched the flesh found under Diana's fingernails. The case was a triumph for forensic science, the first time that a blood spot led straight to a murderer.

Harry Cox later testified that Carter was the man who had called at his house on the day of the murder asking for directions and whom he had seen later with Diana.

At his trial Carter pleaded not guilty of murder but guilty of manslaughter. That plea was not accepted by the Crown and, after a short trial, he was found guilty of murder and sentenced to life imprisonment.

9

Death After Importuning

To be a pathologist in Central London means being called
to violent deaths which reflect the patterns of behaviour
of that section of the public which, when the law relaxes,
takes immediate advantage. Prostitutes have always been
at risk and many of them have been murdered over the
years. In the Sixties, with the relaxing of the laws regarding homosexuals, some men also became victims of brutal
killings. The year 1958 had seen the passing of the Sexual
Offences Act which legislated that 'a homosexual act
committed in private shall not be an offence, provided
that the partners consent thereto and have attained the
age of twenty-one years'.

Soon after the Act was passed there was an increase in
the murder of homosexuals. Their approach in pursuing
their sexual pleasures had become more open, in some
cases almost arrogant, and they became targets for those
who hated homosexuals, and for those who were prepared
to exploit them. Murders of homosexuals are sometimes
difficult to solve because their affairs tend to be conducted
in secret and because of the casual way in which they
sometimes meet. Often they are complete strangers to
each other, as was the situation in this case.

Colin George Saunders was a thirty-five-year-old chauffeur when he died after a vicious attack by a killer who
used two weapons, one an iron gas-ring, the other a clasp-
knife. The victim was a homosexual who had previous
convictions for importuning and gross indecency. In
October 1969 he was wandering around the concourse

of Piccadilly underground station intent on importuning again.

A nineteen-year-old unemployed man from Liverpool named Stanley Wrenn also wandered into the concourse, joining the hundreds of others who congregate there in the aimless drift of people who have nowhere to go. Saunders was used to opening a conversation with a stranger, and in this case he affected that they had met before. Within minutes he had invited Wrenn to a nearby café and, over a meal, he found out that Wrenn had nowhere to sleep and invited him to his home, a house in College Road, Bromley, Kent.

Saunders took Wrenn to his car and together they drove to Bromley to a terraced house divided into flats and rooms. Saunders lived in a double room at the front. That night they slept in a double bed and again on the next night and, according to Wrenn, 'We had sex every night – he did it to me.' Later Saunders acquired two single beds but, according to Wrenn, the older man had sex with him every night as the price of a place to sleep.

Wrenn stayed in that room for five weeks, during which the two men watched television and saw the demonstrations in America against the war in Vietnam and watched the launching of the moon-shot *Apollo*. Wrenn was a drifter who took any opportunity of a free bed and board and was a willing partner to the older man. But in mid-November he discovered that he had contracted gonorrhoea. There was no doubt in his mind that Saunders was responsible for giving him the disease since he had not had it before they met. He made up his mind to kill Saunders.

The killing was deliberate, but almost as casual as the meeting in Piccadilly were Wrenn's movements afterwards. They are best told in the statement he made after he was arrested, for there was no difficult investigation.

Stanley Wrenn read about his crime in the *Evening News*, when he was wandering about London's West End. It was on the evening of 27 November that he walked into West End Central police station, pointed to the headline in the newspaper and said, 'That's me. I did it.'

It was on the previous day that the murder had happened. Wrenn had decided to make off in the hire car that Saunders drove but, being unused to the controls, had collided with another car whose driver insisted on the police being called. Wrenn went back to the house, purported to call the police and then caught a train to London having first stolen everything which was portable. Some hours later the aggrieved driver was still waiting in the street for the police, so he went to the house and roused one of the occupants, John Anthony Knight, who let him in. The two men found the body of Saunders and called the police.

Chief Superintendent Walton and Detective Inspector Sinclair went to the house in College Road and entered the front room on the ground floor. It was a large room dominated by a grand piano on which was a photograph of three naked men all facing the same way and all of them pressed tightly together. There were two single beds in the room and one was empty. Mr Walton could see the head, neck and shoulders and right hand of a man in the other bed near the window. The head was partially concealed by a pillow and the rest of the body was covered by bedclothes and a dressing-gown. The man was obviously dead and there were multiple lacerations about his neck. There was blood on the bedsheets, the pillow, the bedhead, and there were blood splashes around the room. A gas-ring and a knife on the floor near the bed also appeared to be bloodstained.

Doctor Bain, the Divisional Surgeon, certified the man

was dead and Dr Cameron, the Home Office pathologist, was called.

The room was in chaos and the wardrobe was open, with clothes apparently thrown on to the floor as though someone had rummaged through it in a hurry. At the foot of the bed in which the dead man was found was a chauffeur's cap; on the floor between the beds was a white vest, a black rug, a broken flashbulb, a white jug, a gas-ring, a white handled knife, a tuft of hair, an ashtray full of cigarette ends and a black pottery moneybox which had been forced open. Next to the fire there was a standard lamp with a glass tumbler on its base, an ashtray with more cigarette ends, a jar of Vaseline and a tube of cream.

Mr Knight told Chief Superintendent Walton how he had found the body and said he was sure it was that of his landlord, Colin George Saunders, and at 7 P.M. that night Dr Cameron examined the body.

To the experienced Chief Superintendent there was no mystery, just a simple case of catching the killer. The name and description of Stanley Wrenn was circulated and the details given to the Press Bureau. The story was in the *Evening News* of the following day.

After Wrenn had given himself up, Chief Superintendent Walton took him to Bromley to make a statement.

'As I told you at West End Central, I did it. I did not do it until I found he had given me a disease. We found out last Thursday.

'I have not been working. I have been out looking for a job. I even went to Orpington for a job. He was moaning at me all the time. On Monday morning I got the idea I wanted to kill him, it was the only way I could get some money and get away from him. About dinner time on Tuesday I bought a knife from a fishing tackle shop not far from the hospital from a man aged forty or fifty, say for about three or four shillings. The other one at twelve shillings and sixpence was too dear. Colin [Saunders] took my key off me the day before. I was locked out on

Tuesday late afternoon, so was Tony [another man living in the house]. We used my knife to open a window and get in.

'That night we watched the telly. Colin and I went to bed about quarter to eleven. I stayed awake before I went to bed. I took a gas-ring from a cubby-hole in the television room and hid it under my bed. When I was lying awake I was listening to him, I mean Colin. I got out once or twice but I thought he was awake and I went back to bed. About five to half past five I got up. I looked out for a minute or two and hit him over the head with it [the gas ring]. I hit him over the left ear [pointing to the Chief Superintendent's left ear, a few inches above] – it was the way he was lying in bed. After the first hit he did not move, the second time I hit him he opened his eyes and looked up. He was facing the wall. I then stuck the knife into his throat. I was not sure how often I hit him. I went mad and it could be as many as thirty. I lost my senses after a few times. I stuck it in his throat and in the back of his neck. When I took it out of the back of his neck the blade was bent. There was quite a bit of blood, something came out of his mouth. I left the gas-ring on the hearth rug. I pulled the sheet over him and covered him with his dressing-gown. There was blood everywhere. I washed my hands from water in a jug and dried them on my T-shirt. I went upstairs and had a shave and a proper wash. I left the T-shirt in the room. I came down, got dressed and got the money out of his pockets and looked around. I found roughly about £12 in notes. I took the film out of his camera to sell it. I packed a case with some of his things, clean shirts. I broke a Toby jug full of tanners [sixpences] and took them. I put some things in my case. Say about quarter past nine I left the house with the suitcase, the keys and his driving licence. I started the car, the big thing. I had a terrible job starting it – it's an automatic. When I got into reverse I put my foot down and it flew on to the road and another car hit me. It was my fault. The fellow got out and said, "That's a nice thing, phone the police." I said, "I will do it." I went back to the house, pretended I called, and went back to him after ten minutes. I said the police are coming but why call them? I will settle up. A big white Mercedes came up and asked me what I was doing. I told him I knew he was from Warley Car Hire, that I was taking the car round for Colin. He got it off the road for me. He gave me the keys back and told me and Colin to come down to the office at eleven o'clock to see the manager. The other two talked together.

'I went back to the house, threw the keys on the bed. After ten minutes I left again and met the fellow in the accident at the corner. I said my mate was getting up. I am going down there, meaning the car hire office. "My mate will follow." He said I have not to go there until eleven.

'I went to Bromley North station and from there to the West End where I spent my time since. Last night I met a fellow and slept at the New Era Staff Agency. When I saw my name in the paper I decided to give myself up.'

Dr Cameron's report on Saunders's body confirmed that the injuries Saunders had sustained were in conformity with Wrenn's description of the killing.

Stanley Wrenn was a drifter. He had served for a short time in the army, in the RAMC, and been discharged. Then he worked as a paint-sprayer, shop-assistant, barman and labourer. He tried to find more work but failed and took to wandering from place to place. He had nowhere to live and took any opportunity for free bed and board.

He was put on trial at the Old Bailey on 24 March 1970 before Justice Sir Ralph Cusack, pleaded guilty to murder and was sentenced to life imprisonment. He was released from prison in June 1980 soon after his thirtieth birthday.

10

The Murderer Who Killed Himself

An attractive young woman with auburn hair and grey eyes walked out of her office in Aylesbury, Buckinghamshire, on Wednesday, 16 September 1970. She smiled a lot and, because she was good-looking, people noticed her. Her name was Nicola Brazier, she was twenty years old, unmarried and working as a secretary. The time was fifteen minutes to noon.

She left the offices of MacDonalds Sales Promotions to take some papers to the head office at Nazeing, in Essex, and drove away in her red Mini 880 TE. She had forty miles to travel.

Thirty-one hours later a family out walking in Bencroft Wood, near Hoddesdon, Hertfordshire, found her body, her hands tied behind her back. She was lying on her back close to the foot of a tree, and there was bloodstaining under both sides of her head.

The husband of the family who had found the body ran to the Woodman public house in the village of Wormley West End, telephoned the police, and Detective Chief Superintendent Ronald Harvey of Hertfordshire CID went to the scene.

Dusk was gathering as policemen ringed off the area and Mr Harvey telephoned Dr Cameron, who had just reached his home in Bromley from the London Hospital. He drove up to Hertfordshire and arrived at Worsley Woods at 11.55 P.M. Powerful arc-lights had been set up and Senior Photographer Mackintosh took a series of photographs before Dr Cameron started his examination.

Kneeling by the body Dr Cameron dictated his findings:

Body of a well-nourished young woman, five foot two inches in height, with her hands tied behind her back with cord and dressed in black leather knee boots, (right heel worn); leather waistcoat with zip at front – top six inches of zip undone; black long-sleeved polo-neck sweater – white powder and occasional grey hairs back of right sleeve; leather mini-skirt with lining with zip and leather belt (done up); pink brassière, undone at back and pulled up above breasts; yellow metal wristwatch right wrist; white metal name-tag left wrist engraved N I C O L A.

Gunshot wound through the lobe of the left ear and a vertical split laceration two inches behind the right ear consistent with exit gunshot wound; superficial cuts and abrasions at the back of the right knee; a small circular bruise at the top front of the left thigh and a similar bruise above the left knee; a small bruise on the front of the left shin; patchy brown abraded areas both sides of the pubic area and a bruise on the back and outer side of the right thigh.

The victim had been menstruating and had been sexually assaulted with extreme violence. The cause of death was a gunshot wound in the head.

Dr Cameron took a number of grey hairs from the sweater and the cord which had been used to tie the victim's hands behind her back.

John McCafferty, Scotland Yard's ballistics expert, went to the scene and was present at the post-mortem at Hertford County Hospital to examine the gunshot wound and to determine the type of weapon used. Dr Cameron handed to him two swabs taken from the area of the left ear and photographs of skin from the left side of the head. He also handed over a bullet taken from the girl's head. It was of a .32 calibre and, according to the powder burns around the wound, McCafferty considered that the gun had been fired from about eighteen inches or more away from the girl's head. He was also certain that the dead girl had never at any time handled the gun, so there could be no question of suicide.

Detective Chief Superintendent Harvey, who was leading the murder hunt, already had one good clue. A constable had found Nicola's red Mini abandoned miles away at Broxbourne railway station. The car was unlocked, and her handbag was still in it, but there was no money inside and her cheque book was missing. He suspected that the killer had dumped the car after he had murdered the girl and left the area by train.

Next day the police put the red Mini on show outside the local town hall, asking people to report if they had seen it. Meanwhile Harvey mounted a massive reconstruction of Nicola Brazier's last day alive. A policeman's wife, Lorna Camp, who was the same build and height, dressed up in similar clothes borrowed from the manufacturers, and drove Nicola's car from Aylesbury towards Nazeing, led by a police car. The cars were driven slowly and were stopped regularly so that people could see and be told the details by the police.

By these means the police established a timetable. Nicola's route had led along quiet roads until she got lost in Hoddesdon. Her first stop was for petrol at Aylesbury, and at 2 P.M. she was seen at a roundabout on the A602 outside Hertford by a lorry driver who recalled her 'because she was showing a lot of thigh'. Minutes later another lorry driver saw her driving slowly round a one-way system in Hoddesdon. He said she appeared to be looking for signposts and seemed confused. At 2.30 P.M. a motorist stopped at Tylercross at a busy road junction. He saw a young man with long hair standing under a tree, and another motorist reported that he had seen a red Mini stop and the woman driver offer the man a lift. He described the man as about six feet tall with shoulder-length grey hair.

The police search went on, but little more was forthcoming until ten weeks after the killing. Railway security men at Euston Station, searching unclaimed left-luggage, found a hold-all. Inside was a gun, a ·765 automatic pistol, a cheque book with two cheques and Nicola's wallet containing her driving licence, RAC membership and a pencil and notepad. The hold-all was new with a zip fastener made of brown canvas. The gun was stamped with the serial numbers 40084 and its holster of good-quality leather had the figures 3·3 written on the back in light blue ink. The holster was one given to children for a toy gun but the owner of the murder gun had cut the holster to fit his own.

The gun and its holster were sent to Scotland Yard to be examined for fingerprints and then the gun was passed over to John McCafferty to be test-fired. He was able to establish not only that it could fire .32 bullets but that it was without doubt the murder weapon, and Chief Superintendent Harvey set about finding its history. Weeks of meticulous work by Hertfordshire detectives liaising with Interpol traced the movements of the gun and eventually led to its last owner.

The gun was made in Belgium in 1910 and arrived in England after the 1914–18 war. In the 1950s it illicitly passed through a number of hands in Canada and in 1961 it was back in England. It was taken to Rhodesia, brought back to England in 1964 and then was taken to South Africa. Again it changed hands several times and was brought back to England in 1970. On 4 December 1970, the *Daily Mirror* published the full story of the murder and its investigation with pictures, including the gun and the holster and the hold-all. A reader remembered that he had once owned the gun and he remembered the name of the man to whom he had sold it. On that gun inquiry alone police interviewed 21,500 people.

At the Yard, meanwhile, the experts found a fingerprint on the gun, and then came another clue. When Nicola

Brazier left her home on the morning of 16 September her brother, with whom she lived, remembered that she had had three cheques, but there were only two cheques in her book when it was found. The missing cheque was found to have been used to pay for two long-playing records at Millers Music Shop in Cambridge the day after the murder. Police discovered that the purchase was made by a tall, grey-haired young man who had paid £5.4s.10d. and had written that amount on the cheque and signed it 'F. Grahame'. He had written on the back of the cheque the address '5, Essex Close, Trumpington, Cambs' which was found to be false.

One of the records the man bought was 'A Man and a Woman'.

That cheque was also sent to be examined by the fingerprint experts. Detectives took the view, and the experts agreed, that the handwriting on the cheque was not disguised in any way and they therefore began to take samples of male handwriting in the Cambridge area in the hope of finding a match. At the rate of 150 a day detectives took more than 20,000 specimens of handwriting from local men.

Slowly the investigation came together. The fingerprint branch reported that the print on the gun matched the print on the cheque. The same prints were on the leather holster.

Then someone remembered that four days after the murder the body of a man had been found decapitated on a railway line in Hertfordshire. Police thought he had committed suicide, but could not confirm it – there was certainly no indication of murder. At the time the body was not easily identifiable and Detective Constable Martin Peters was directed to take fingerprints from it. These prints had been kept. An inquest had been held at the time and the coroner had recorded an open verdict. The man had been reported missing and was identified in the normal way by police inquiries at mortuaries. He had a wife and a family; his life had been insured and the money had been paid to his widow.

That set of fingerprints provided the final clue to the killer. In February 1971 they were still unidentified but they were sent to Scotland Yard as all unidentified fingerprints are. The prints of the dead man were found to be an exact match with the prints on the gun and on the cheque. The long hunt was at an end. The man the police had been looking for was dead four days after they began the hunt.

Now the Hertfordshire police knew his identity – he was a businessman from North London – they made some further comparisons. They found his handwriting exactly matched the writing on the cheque signed 'F. Grahame' which was used to purchase the two long-playing records. A sash-cord similar to that used to tie Nicola Brazier's wrists was found in a van the dead man had owned. At the inquest on Nicola Brazier the coroner, Mr James Bolton, said that fingerprints, blood samples and handwriting were 'arrows pointing one way' to a man the police had no doubt was the killer. He also said that 'as a matter of humanity' the man should not be named.

'I have decided,' said the coroner, 'that the public interest does not require that "X" should be named. I have had to weigh, in making that decision, the misery which the naming would inevitably bring upon his family. Against that I have to consider the possible public advantage in naming.'

The police solicitor, Mr Rowland Lee, said, 'We have been satisfied for some considerable time that we have discovered the murderer of Nicola Brazier and it was decided from a very early time that the name would not be disclosed by the police. The temptation to publish the name was very great but to protect the innocent who would suffer with the guilty it was decided not to publish either now or later because no useful purpose would be served.'

The jury returned a murder verdict that left no doubt that 'X' was the killer.

Mr Bolton's view was criticized shortly after by another coroner, Mr David Paul, who said, 'If you conclude that a person has been responsible for the killing of others, whether that person be alive or dead, it is your duty to name him.' Mr Paul was addressing the jury at another inquest and he went on to say, 'Not naming the man allowed the finger of suspicion to point at many other people who may have been questioned by the police or were found dead in similar circumstances. It is no part of the jury's duty to leave that kind of question unanswered, even on humanitarian grounds.'

Finally the Director of Public Prosecutions was asked to make a ruling. He decided that the name should not be published and the case was therefore closed. However, in the police records the file has been marked 'Solved'.

11
The Masquerade

Professor Cameron has many honorary roles. In 1971 he was appointed honorary consultant in forensic medicine to the Army and in that same year it led to one of his most challenging cases that used evidence nearly seven years old.

Changi Point in Singapore, lapped by the waters of the South China Sea, is one of the most beautiful and romantic places in the world, particularly in the moonlight. On such an evening Sergeant Ian Reed of the Royal Corps of Transport drove there with his wife Dorothy, having collected her from hospital where she had been for some months suffering from tuberculosis. The couple had argued for most of the journey because she had said she was going to leave him for another man. The quarrel reached a crescendo when the Sergeant parked the car on a deserted part of the beach. He grabbed his wife by the throat and shook her, then let the body slump back on the seat. He sat there for a few minutes, upset and exhausted. When he recovered and looked at his wife he found she was dead. That was in March 1965, when Ian Reed was twenty-eight years old.

In October 1971, Dr Cameron was telephoned at the London Hospital and asked to travel to Singapore on behalf of the British Army to exhume the body of Mrs Dorothy Reed. That decision was made after the Sergeant had walked into Hounslow police station on 25 September and told the station sergeant that he wanted to confess to the murder of his wife in Singapore in 1965. Initially he was seen by Detective Superintendent Gordon Mees and

later the investigation was taken over by the Special
Investigation Branch of the Army, and was led by
Lieutenant-Colonel Kenneth Mason.

Reed had enlisted in the Army in July 1955 and after
basic training was posted to Singapore. There he met
a good-looking Eurasian dance hostess called Dorothy
Campbell at the Seven Stories night club. They went out
together several times, but the relationship cooled when
the girl admitted to being pregnant by another man.
After she had given birth and the child had been adopted
the couple met again and resumed their association. Reed
was introduced to the girl's family and met her sister
Joan, who was engaged to be married to a local man called
Ismail. The two couples frequently went out together and
in 1958 they married in the same month. Reed was posted
back to the United Kingdom and he and his wife went to
live in Essex. By 1964 they had four children and in that
year Reed was posted back to Singapore. Over the years
they had received frequent letters from Dorothy's sister
Joan, giving the news that despite the birth of three
children she was desperately unhappy because her husband was ill-treating her and was often unfaithful.

In June 1964 Sergeant Reed and his wife and family
arrived in Singapore and immediately made contact with
Joan, who suggested they should all share a house
together in the hope that her relationship with her husband Omar Ismail would improve. All went well until
Dorothy was taken ill and admitted to the British Military
Hospital, leaving Joan to look after the seven children.
After a while Reed moved to a smaller house and Joan's
husband moved elsewhere with his children. That marked
the beginning of a passionate affair between Sergeant
Reed and his sister-in-law. When the news came eventually that Dorothy was returning from hospital the two
lovers agreed that their affair would have to end.

When Reed met his wife at the hospital she told him that she wished to discuss their future together. This was a surprise to him. He had thought that if any explanation was due then he should be making it. 'On arrival at Changi,' Reed said,

'I parked the car on a quiet spot on the beach. I can't remember exactly how it all started but the point was reached when Dorothy told me she no longer loved me and had no intention of returning home. Although I tried to find out what the particular reason was she wouldn't go into any detail except to say there was another man. At this stage this was an unexpected turn of events and the immediate effect on myself was to lose control of myself and I grabbed or got hold of her around the neck and I can remember initially shaking her, but what words passed between us I can't remember. I assume it was a matter of minutes when I regained control of myself and Dorothy was slumped to one side by me in the front seat. There was just no life to her at all. Her lips were blue. I didn't know what to do at that moment. I just sat back in the car.'

Reed said that he toyed with the idea of giving himself up at Changi police station but rejected it. Instead he moved the body from the front seat of the car and put it in the boot, covering it with a sack. Back at the house, he parked the car in its usual place and found Joan in the kitchen.

'I was shaking and didn't know what to do with myself. She asked me what had happened and I told her we had had an argument and that I had choked her or strangled her or killed her anyway. I told Joan I had the body in the boot of the car and that she wasn't to go near the car. At this stage she gave a gasp and started to cry.'

Reed then claimed that he told her the whole story of the events of the evening and told her at first that he had decided to go to the police. They had a drink, and Reed

Left: The body of James Powditch was found in a Kent cornfield in 1964

Below: The body of Shona Berry, victim in the Madhouse Murder

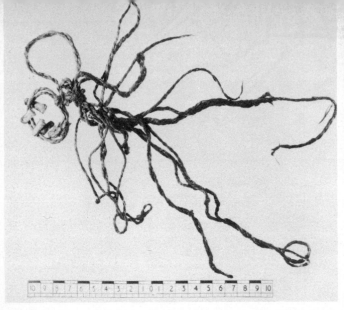

Finger bones entangled in string found near the body of Baby Lord

The jacket which identified the body of Baby Lord

Blood stains on the red Mini and a human hair

The red Mini showed little damage after the accident at
Rumerhedge Wood

The room at the top of the stairs where James Gray went looking
for his wife

Tony Maffia – 'The Magpie' – was found murdered in his Jaguar

Clues to the murder of Colin George Saunders

Police hunt for clues to the killer of Diana Davidson

The cheque cashed by the killer of Nicola Brazier

Other clues circulated in the Press at the time of the Brazier murder

Left: Dorothy Reed was killed by her husband and buried in their back garden in Singapore

Below: Professor Cameron measuring the grave of Dorothy Reed before the exhumation

The room where the shooting took place in the Barn Restaurant case, showing the cushions used to muffle the shots

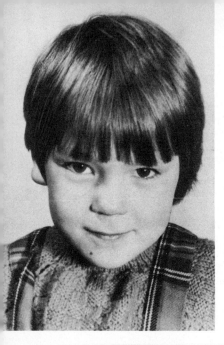

Left: Maria Colwell, brutally killed by her stepfather

Below: The burnt-out car belonging to murder victim Gordon Seddon

William Moseley, one of the
victims in the Thames Torso
murder

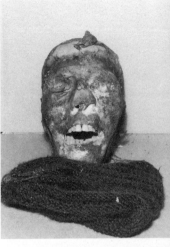

The skull of Moseley was
found wrapped in a woollen hat
in a public toilet in Islington

The body of Michael Cornwall

Above: Father Crean's body as it was found in his bath

Left: Patrick Mackay, who murdered Father Crean

George Brett *(left),* lured from his house to death with his son, ten-year-old Terry, who jumped into his father's car for the ride

Henry Mackenny, the leader of a gang of killers

John Henry Childs in whose flat in Poplar the bodies of six murder victims were reduced to ashes in a small grate

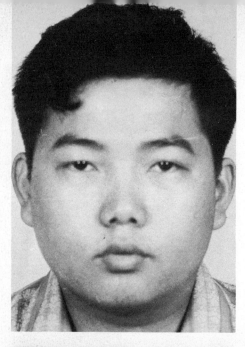

Peter Chan Woon-hing, who trafficked in drugs and was killed because he cheated over the proceeds.

His skull was later identified by Professor Cameron

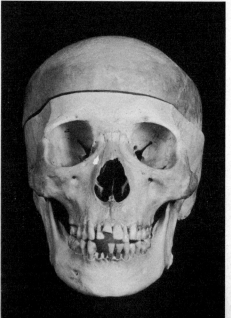

Ayers Rock, the site of the Dingo Baby Case

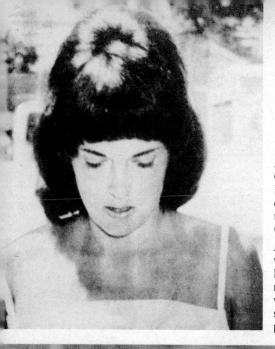

Left: Alice Lynne Chamberlain, who killed her daughter Azaria in the Dingo Baby Case

Below: Susan Barber with her husband Michael. She murdered him with a poisoned steak and kidney pie

poured her a gin and had a rum himself. They then agreed they would not tell the police, that he would get rid of the body and that they would stay that night in a hotel, taking the four young Reed children with them. Together they decided that Joan would assume the identity of Dorothy. The two sisters had looked very much alike except that Dorothy had had a prominent front eyetooth. Reed and Joan booked in as Mr and Mrs Reed and family, and so began a subterfuge that was to last for nearly seven years.

In his first statement Reed said he told Joan that he then drove the body by car back to Changi beach, took it out to sea in a rowing boat and dumped it at a point beyond the shark barriers. In fact, as he said later, he had taken the body to his house, where he had already started to dig a hole. Swiftly he enlarged it and buried the body in the back garden. Joan, however, always believed the Changi beach story.

It was fortunate that the rest of the family had not been to visit the Reeds for many months and they did not even know where Reed lived. Reed wrote to his parents in England saying that Dorothy had left him and that her sister Joan was looking after the children. From then on they lived as man and wife. They attended army functions and he always introduced Joan as Dorothy and the children always called her 'Mummy'. Then, slowly, the name 'Dorothy' faded because she told people she really preferred to be called 'Joan' because she 'liked the name so much more'. In the free and easy atmosphere of the tropics the switch of wives went unnoticed.

There was one moment of panic when Joan's husband, Ismail, became suspicious and began to haunt the neighbourhood, but they quickly moved house and the danger was averted. To improve the deception they asked a Roman Catholic priest to bless their marriage and went through the ceremony at the Church of the Blessed Sacrament in Queenstown. Reed was not a Catholic at the time but he did become one later and was baptized.

In August 1966 Reed was warned that he was to be posted to Hong Kong. He took his 'wife' and the children, using Dorothy's passport. The masquerade continued, with the whole family now attending church regularly, but there were chinks appearing in the web of deceit they had woven. Reed said:

'I think she felt she had been cheated somewhere along the line. We had got my children with us while hers were still in Singapore and she naturally wanted them with her. This was an impossible situation as it would obviously create many more difficulties and be an added complication. I told her we had made our arrangements and that no one had forced her to come to Hong Kong with me. It had all been a mutual arrangement between us. The differences between us grew and she then started to threaten to inform the police about Dorothy if I didn't do something about getting the children with us. Then she began to tell my army colleagues that I ill-treated her, that I was beating her. Whenever we had an argument she would say: "Why don't you strangle me too, you dirty murderer." She even went to my Commanding Officer and complained of my ill-treatment to her.'

At a subsequent interview Reed explained to his officer that his wife was exaggerating and he was told to try harder to make her happy. She began to telephone him at work and insist that he stopped work and come to see her, always using the threat of exposure. 'It was nerve-racking but as long as we could go to mess-parties she was happy. But as soon as the party was over and we were back home the rows would begin again. I don't want to give the impression she was a bitch to live with,' he added, 'for there were times when we were quite happy together and everything ran smoothly.'

In December 1967 Sergeant Reed was posted back to the United Kingdom and spent disembarkation leave at Gorleston-on-Sea, near his parents. Reed had prepared for this by telling them that he had married Joan, having obtained a divorce from Dorothy. But within a week she erupted in front of the parents, making accusations, although not mentioning the murder, and saying that she would 'eventually fix me'. Reed was forced to stay away from his parents and after two months moved away with his family to Heston, Middlesex. He was at that time concerned about his son Alan, who was backward at school, and Joan did not want him in the house. Reed managed to get the boy into a residential school in Bramley, Surrey, but that did not stop Joan insisting that unless he could get her children back from Singapore she would betray the guilty secret of the murder. Complications became worse when she refused to look after the children and he had to go to work and get back in time to run the household. The threats increased and he wrote to the Home Office seeking leave to travel to Singapore, with Joan posing as his wife, to adopt her children.

In August 1970 they arrived in Singapore, the scene of the murder and where the victim's body was still buried. They had worked out a plan in which Joan had to pose as four different women, using various names and disguises. Later she told the story:

'First I was to pose as a girlfriend of my Muslim husband, Ismail. As such I telephoned his sister, who was looking after the children. She told me where they were at school. For the second pose I wore a blonde wig and said I was the children's aunt. At the school they let me see the children and I took them away by bus to the city centre. The children were delighted, because, they said, they had been very unhappy. To our surprise there was no hue and cry over the "abduction". In the third pose I dressed smartly with a wig and glasses and went to see a lawyer as "Mrs Reed", saying I wanted to adopt Mrs Ismail's children. He said that Mrs Ismail would have to sign the necessary papers.

'Soon afterwards I went back to the lawyer's office as "Mrs Ismail" (myself) – without the wig and the glasses, and wearing simple Malay dress. I signed away the children. Next day I was back as Mrs Reed, the smart sergeant's wife from England. I signed again, in a different name and different writing to adopt the children.'

Sergeant Reed had to return to London at that stage and leave his 'wife' in Singapore until the entry permits were available. In November 1970 she returned with the three children and they presented themselves at Brentford Magistrates Court as Mr and Mrs Reed to make the adoption final. All went smoothly and she walked out of the court, having legally adopted her own children.

But, although Reed and his 'wife' were living comfortably in army married quarters the rows did not subside. In fact they grew worse until Reed described it as 'living on the edge of a volcano'. It was only then he had decided to tell the truth. What finally broke his nerve was that his 'wife' had discovered he was having an affair with another woman, who was married, and he was forced to admit it.

Within two weeks of Sergeant Reed making his confession Dr Cameron, accompanied by Lieutenant-Colonel Mason, flew off to Singapore to exhume the body of Dorothy Reed, buried, according to the murderer, in the back garden of a house in Teow Hock Avenue. They arrived at seven o'clock in the evening and had a conference two hours later at army headquarters. There were fourteen men in the party including Dr T. C. Chao, a forensic pathologist of Singapore who had studied under Cameron. Included in the party were photographers, a Scenes of Crime and Exhibits Officer, an expert in maps and plans and a digging party.

At 6.30 A.M. in a temperature of eighty degrees Fahrenheit the exhumation began with the marking-out of an area of the back garden measuring four feet by five feet.

The area was photographed and samples of top soil were taken from the marked area and from another part of the garden for comparison. The marked area was carefully dug out to a depth of three feet with samples of soil taken and recorded at twelve-inch intervals. At between three and four feet there was no evidence of human or animal remains. Then it was noticed that the concrete of the car-port had been extended out by two feet since the date of the burial, which made the hole that had been dug two feet adrift. Samples of soil were again taken below the concrete, digging in sideways. At 8.30 A.M. a portion of carbon material in the form of burnt clothing was discovered and further careful digging revealed a femur of human origin. Soon afterwards the skeleton and the skull were exposed. The body lay face down from the head to the knees with the legs bent backwards to the pelvis, while the arms were folded upwards to the neck.

Dr Cameron carefully removed the bones and placed them in plastic bags, and a label was written for each container. The examination of the scene was completed at 10.30 A.M., but further digging over the burial area continued for a depth of six to ten inches and the soil was riddled to find further skeletal remains, clothing or rings. On top of the skeleton were several small burnt portions of clothing while around the pelvis was material which looked like the remains of clothing with an occasional button. All these remains were taken to the local mortuary. In all, twenty-six separate items were sent by Cameron to the mortuary and he took away with him, by permission of the Singapore coroner, the skull and some loose teeth.

Dr Cameron could see that the body was consistent with that of a young, adult female. Her facial appearance was checked with a passport photograph superimposed on the skull. Later he reinserted all the teeth into the skull and another photograph was taken which again showed an accurate likeness. In his summary he reported that all his findings were consistent with the skeleton being that of Mrs Dorothy Helen Reed, alleged to have been buried at the site in 1965.

In detail Dr Cameron found that there was a depressed fracture on the left side of the skull consistent with an upward blow by or against a sharp heavy object. From the direction of the fracture this clearly could not have been produced either during the exhumation nor while the body was buried. The injury must have occurred before burial, but equally could have been inflicted while she was alive or dead. Such a fracture would certainly have knocked a live person unconscious and could have in itself led to death if no treatment was given. He found nothing inconsistent with the alleged cause of death, that is, of someone grabbing or getting hold of her round the neck and shaking her, but the exact cause of death was 'unascertainable'.

Dr Cameron left Singapore that same night on a flight at 9 P.M., for he had to take a class of students at the London Hospital on the following day. He carried with him the skull and the loose teeth carefully wrapped in a cardboard box. He was exhausted and soon after the plane took off he bought himself a glass of beer and then, weary with the long day and the heat, went to sleep. He woke at Rome, to find that the untouched beer had fallen to the floor.

At 7 A.M. on 7 October Cameron arrived at the London Hospital and handed over the skull and the teeth to Bernard Sims, Lecturer in Forensic Odontology. After his preliminary examination Mr Sims was able to establish that they were those of an adult female of about thirty years old, give or take five years.

From the arrangement of the front teeth of the upper and lower jaws, it was evident that the dead woman would have had a particular appearance when she was alive. Her front teeth in both jaws were protruding, and her 'auxiliary central incisors' were 'shovel-shaped'. These aspects, together with the other features of the skull, were consistent with someone of Asian origin.

The arrangement of her upper front teeth would also have given her a distinctive appearance. Her central incisors and upper canine teeth were prominent, with the lateral incisors slightly behind these teeth. Her auxiliary left canine tooth was completely outside the upper dental arch, and this would be a strong identifying feature. His report confirmed Dr Cameron's findings that the skull was indeed that of Dorothy Reed.

A full report of the case was sent to the Director of Public Prosecutions who had to decide where the trial of Sergeant Reed was to be held, either in Singapore or at the Old Bailey in London. There was a possibility that if the trial was held in Singapore Joan Ismail could also have been indicted for murder, and the supreme penalty for murder there was death. In the end the Director decided to hold the trial at the Old Bailey with Joan Ismail as the chief prosecution witness.

Meanwhile Sergeant Reed was being held in army custody at Chelsea Barracks. He wrote to Joan Ismail asking her to visit him officially, when he would be able to arrange for her to visit him in his cell, in private. He told her to wear a maxi-coat and boots but nothing underneath, the clothing being a sign that she felt as amorous as he did. On the arranged day she presented herself at the barracks in the afternoon and was allowed

a meeting with Reed in the Naafi with an officer present.
They talked about the children and when the time was up
Reed was taken back to his cell and she was escorted to
an army car to be taken back to her home in Hounslow.
Instead, the driver, who was a friend of Reed's, drove
her around for a while and then took her back to the
barracks where a military police sergeant took her to
Reed's cell and locked her in. Later she wrote:

'The time I spent with Ian in the cell was not all fun. First we
had a row. It was about another woman Ian had been seeing
before his arrest and I wanted to be sure he still loved me. I
was angry about this other woman at first, but suddenly Ian
grabbed me in his arms and began to kiss me passionately. You
can imagine the effect this had on me. I threw my arms around
his neck and kissed back passionately. Ian told me he was
madly in love with me and asked me if I'd wait for him no
matter what sentence he got. I said I would wait for him for
ever if he promised to marry me properly. Ian agreed. He said
he not only wanted me as his wife but he wanted to give me his
baby so we would really have something to share. And Ian
wasn't a man to waste time. The marriage would have to wait
until we knew what was going to happen to him in court. But
our love child was to be conceived there and then in the cell.
As we kissed and hugged each other Ian gently unbuttoned my
maxi-coat and let it slip off. He pushed me down on the bed
and we made love on the bunk.'

The incident was mentioned at the Old Bailey trial when
Sergeant Reed pleaded not guilty to the murder of his
wife. Mrs Ismail told the jury, 'He said he wanted to
marry me so I could stay in England. A condition of his
marrying me was that I had intercourse with him in the
cell.'

Prosecutor Mr Richard du Cann alleged the sex scene
was instigated by Reed to get Mrs Ismail to change part
of her testimony. The guardsman driver who arranged
the clandestine meeting told the court that while Mrs

Ismail was with Reed he heard a bump on the cell wall. Reed explained to him, 'I hit her. The statement that daft cow has made will put me down for life.'

And another guardsman, who was in the next cell, said Reed told him, 'If I can get her pregnant she will not be deported and give evidence against me.'

The prosecution alleged that Reed killed his wife either by strangulation or by a blow and Professor Cameron gave evidence to that. The jury decided that Reed was not guilty of murder but guilty of manslaughter. On the day he was sentenced to five years' imprisonment none of the women in his love-tangled life were around to share his final downfall.

For Dr Cameron the case was interesting because he had found a new way of making an exhumation. The soldiers who had done the digging found the spot to which they were directed had been concreted over. That had not appeared on the plans because the concrete had been laid by the person who had moved into the house after Sergeant Reed had left. Cameron, therefore, had a deep hole that had been dug alongside the position of the body so that he could stand down and view it and the remains at eye level. This method of exhumation has now become standard forensic practice.

12

Perfumed Murder

It was nearly midnight on 6 February 1972 that the screams of a woman were heard coming from a flat in Finchdale Road, Abbey Wood, in the south-east of London. It was never known if anyone responded, but, if they did, they did not report anything. The anonymity that city dwellers seek to preserve, never interfering with other people, may have been the reason. But had someone thought to investigate, or raise the alarm, they would have found a ghastly sight. For those screams were ones of terror of a mutilation which led to death.

It was not until later the next day that a neighbour noticed, at about 1 P.M., that the milk was still at the door of the third floor flat, No. 26, the home of a Mrs Margaret Richmond. The neighbour, Mrs Eileen Hunter, knew Mrs Richmond and her child and thought it strange, so she told the Housing Officer and he called an official to the flat. He brought with him a carpenter who forced his way in. They could smell smoke, which appeared to be coming from the bedroom, and looking in, they could see the mattress on the bed was burnt out. The official searched the rest of the flat until he came to the closed door of the bathroom. The door was hot to the touch, but he opened it and saw the room was full of smoke and that something was burning in the bath. He closed the door, switched off the electricity supply and called the fire brigade.

Six minutes later the men from the fire brigade arrived and doused the smouldering material, which was in fact a pile of bedclothes dumped in the bath. On closer inspection a fire officer saw an arm protruding from the material. As the smoke cleared he could see other parts of an adult human body.

PC William Kane, who was driving a police car in the vicinity, heard the fire brigade and went to the scene. When he was told of the discovery he alerted the senior CID officer of the area, Detective Chief Inspector Lynch, who arrived at the flat at 2.30.

Lynch sent for Dr Cameron and while he was waiting for him made a search of the flat. He found there were bloodstains all over the bedroom and the bathroom, and on the floor were two large carving knives and a carving fork. On the floor of the bathroom was part of a human nose and, in the main bedroom, a tooth was found on the floor, and under the bed a human eye beside a soiled sanitary towel. In the living room, on the floor near the entrance to the kitchen, a £10 Bank of England note was lying. Everything was left as it was found until the photographers came. Just before they arrived a senior uniformed officer walked in on a routine visit and spotted the £10 note. He bent down and it looked as though he was about to touch it. There was a chorus from the detectives: 'Don't touch it . . . sir.'

Neighbours revealed that the occupants of the flat were twenty-six-year-old Mrs Richmond and her son Justin Lee, aged three. They had both been seen the day before, apparently in good health.

Dr Cameron arrived with a photographer who took pictures while the pathologist began to remove articles from the bath. He found that there were two bodies in the bath, one adult and one a child's, and both were badly burned. Both bodies were taken to the London Hospital and at 7.30 P.M. Dr Cameron began his post-mortem, having first had the bodies X-rayed.

He found there was extensive burning to both bodies after death. The boy, Justin, had severe bruising of the face and neck, stab wounds of the face and multiple stab wounds of the chest and abdomen. There had also been an attempt to strangle him.

Mrs Richmond's face was almost totally destroyed by the fire and her left hand was missing. There were a number of stab wounds to her chest, her right breast had been removed, and her left eye was missing. In both cases the actual cause of death was the stab wounds.

Dr Cameron also reported:

Within the bedroom were the charred remains of the mattress and on the floor, at the side of the bed, was a human tooth and evidence of bloodstaining on the carpet, wall and door. Within the bathroom, beside the bath, were a number of top bedclothes, whilst covering the charred remains of the human bodies within the bath were smouldering blankets and sheets and other items of bed clothing, together with a mop. There were numerous empty scent bottles and, at the bottom of the bath, at the tap end, was a portion of right female breast incorporating the nipple whilst on the floor within the bathroom was an adult human nose. After the removal of the blankets it was seen that the charred remains of either a pillow or a cushion lay over the head of the adult and over what appeared to be the head of the child. The adult lay partially on its right side whilst the child lay almost on its front with its face down beside the adult head. It was noted that the bath plug was in position and there were a number of spent matches on the floor beside the bath.

Due to the condition of the body of Margaret Richmond police did not ask relatives to identify her. This was only possible with the help of Mr Bernard G. Sims, the London Hospital Odontologist, who was able to identify the teeth with the dead woman's dental chart. Margaret Richmond had separated from her husband Peter, but he was able to identify his son Justin.

Chief Inspector Lynch was tolerably certain that he

was not looking for a stranger as the murderer. The crime
did not appear to have been done by a burglar for there
had been no forced entry and nothing appeared to have
been stolen. The £10 note seemed to confirm this. This
note was examined for fingerprints and sent away for
scientific examination although, like everything else in
the flat, it was covered with a sooty deposit which made
the process of lifting a print extremely difficult.

It was vitally important for Lynch to trace the people
who had been to the flat in the days prior to the murder
and he interviewed friends and relatives. He traced a
man and a woman who had stayed the weekend with Mrs
Richmond, leaving there about 8 P.M. on Sunday, 6
February. They mentioned that Kevin Spurgeon, Margaret Richmond's boy-friend, had also stayed there.

Mr Spurgeon was on a walking holiday in the West
Country, but was traced by police and brought back to
Plumstead police station which was the headquarters of
the hunt. He agreed he was a personal friend of Margaret
Richmond and that he had stayed with her from Friday, 4
February until Sunday, 6 February. He said that they had
talked of marriage and was able to describe the clothes
she was wearing when he left. His description of the
clothes she was wearing fitted the clothing found in the
bathroom. Spurgeon was also able to describe the two
rings that Margaret Richmond was wearing on her left
hand, the hand that was missing. They were a wedding
and an engagement ring, and he was sure that she never
removed her wedding ring.

He then gave the detectives their first clue. He said
that Margaret Richmond had told him that her brother-
in-law, Jonathan Richmond, who was eighteen years old,
had tried quite recently to rape her one night in her flat.
She told him she had retired to bed on that night and that
Jonathan Richmond walked in from the living room,

completely naked, and tried to get into bed with her. She had fought him off and forced him to leave. Jonathan Richmond had keys to the flat.

Police found where Richmond lived and at a house in Westcombe Hill, Greenwich, they found his flat-mate Noel Levere. He said that he shared the flat with a person he knew as John Richmond, but who was obviously Jonathan Richmond. Levere told the police that on Sunday, 6 February, he discovered that his cheque book and £30 in three £10 notes was missing. He had not seen his flat-mate for a few days.

The Chief Inspector circulated Jonathan Richmond's description to all stations in the United Kingdom. Such messages go out on a teleprinter and are given to policemen when they parade for duty. On 8 February at 11.32 P.M. Police Constable Peter Wilson was on patrol in Salisbury, Wiltshire, and he stopped and questioned a man who was standing near the night safe of the National Westminster Bank in Castle Street. He questioned the man at length, examined the contents of the hold-all he was carrying and then realized that he was talking to Jonathan Richmond, the man wanted for murder. He took him to Salisbury police station and he was detained.

Next day detectives from London arrived and Richmond admitted the theft of the cheque book and the three £10 notes. The Detective Inspector noticed that there were scratch marks on Richmond's chest which he said were old and that he had 'got them at work'. The Inspector thought differently and took him back to London to be seen by Chief Inspector Lynch. Richmond denied any knowledge of murder, but he did say that on the night of the 6th he had been drinking in a public house in the Woolwich area, and had walked to Plumstead and slept in a telephone box for a while. Abbey Wood and the scene of the murder were only two miles away, and the telephone box only five hundred yards from the flat in Finchdale Road.

He was asked again about the scratches on his chest and he said he must have got them on Sunday, 6 February, when he fell down some steps. He admitted he had telephoned Margaret Richmond from the box in Plumstead but said he had got no reply. He also agreed that he had gone to her bedroom naked one night previously, but refused to say anything more. His explanation of the three £10 notes was that he had changed one with a friend, Mrs Webb, and had changed another in the public house and the third in Staines on Tuesday, 8 February. When he was told that the police believed that one of the notes was found lying in Margaret Richmond's flat he said, 'I don't know about that.'

The detectives were getting closer and Richmond was left in the custody of a young detective. Suddenly, at 2.15 A.M., after he had been in custody for thirty-six hours, he blurted out to the officer that he had killed Margaret and Justin Richmond. He also said that he had poured perfume all over the blankets and set light to them while the bodies were in the bath. He said he had got the perfume from the little bottles that Margaret had used for samples as an Avon representative. Only the murderer could have known that fact as the police had not given it to the press.

Margaret Richmond was a friendly person, who was sometimes lonely and had liked company. Jonathan was unemployed and without a permanent home, and he too was lonely. He had developed a passion for his sister-in-law which was not returned and, after the time he tried to get into her bed, she had told him she did not want to see him. The police were convinced that he had intended rape on the night of the murder, still smarting at having been repulsed on the previous occasion.

Jonathan Richmond was still only eighteen years old when he appeared at the Old Bailey charged with murder. Prosecuting counsel, Mr Michael Worsley, described the attack as murder in circumstances of 'almost unbelievable ferocity and savagery'. Richmond pleaded guilty and was sentenced to life imprisonment.

13

The Barn Murder

In 1972 Mr Robert Patience was fifty-four years old and the owner of the Barn Restaurant in Braintree, Essex. Patience was a short, plump man and a former wartime rear gunner in RAF bombers. He enjoyed being 'mine host' at his restaurant which he had transformed in ten years from a small roadside transport café into a popular rendezvous for East Enders. The low, white building had beamed ceilings, the walls were studded with horse-brasses and the heads of stuffed animals, and oil-lamps hung above the tables. On Sunday, 5 November, murder came to his home.

It was twenty minutes past two o'clock in the morning when Mr Patience left the restaurant, where the band was still playing, for his home fifty yards away, a modern three-bedroomed house called Sun Lido House. It was quiet and everything seemed normal. A few days later he told this story to the police:

'I let myself in. Then I noticed that the dining-room door was open, which is unusual because we don't allow the dog to go in there. I went in and was immediately confronted by the gunman – the actual fellow who did all the shooting.

'I was told to sit over the other side of the room, passing my wife and daughter, who were sitting on the settee being covered by the other gunman. My wife was in a terrible state. My daughter was trying to console her.

'The gunman said, "I want the safe key."

'I said it was over at the restaurant with the night's takings.

'He said, "I want the key." I said, "There is no point saying it is here if it is not. I am prepared to go with you to the restaurant to get you the key. You can have the money but let my wife and daughter go."

'Then he shot my wife in the head while I looked at him. She collapsed. It was terrible. I said, "She's dying. You've killed her."

'All the man said was, "She will be all right," and he let her fall off the settee on to the floor. He was a cold-blooded bastard.'

Mr Patience knew there was a key in the room but he had been playing for time. Now he found the key and threw the men two bags of money from the hall safe.

'My wife was in a terrible state. I told the gunman to get out with the money. He gave instructions to the other man to tie up my daughter and me. Then he shot my daughter through the back while she lay on the floor.

'I knew it was my turn next. There was a hell of a bang and I thought that was my lot. I felt blood running down me and I was sure I was dying. The fair-haired man who did all the talking and shooting held his gun a foot or so from the side of my head and pulled the trigger.

'Later the surgeons told me the bullet had entered my ear and by some miracle had hit a bone and bounced out again. In fact, the gunman had used two cushions, firing twice through one of them and once through the other, to deaden the sound of the shots.'

That scene had lasted exactly one hour. Only one member of the family, Mr Patience, was vaguely conscious and when he recovered a little more he managed to crawl to the telephone and call the police. Detectives and an ambulance arrived and rushed the injured people to hospital. Mrs Muriel Patience was deeply unconscious but the daughter, Beverley, and Mr Patience were less seriously injured.

The police reported the incident to all stations in the area over the radio and also informed Scotland Yard. Some hours later, when Mr Patience had recovered from his ordeal, he was able to give a description of the two men.

Three days later, fifty-one-year-old Mrs Muriel Patience died, and on the evening of 9 November 1972 Professor Cameron was called to Oldchurch Hospital to perform a post-mortem on her. He found she had suffered a gunshot wound of the head entering above the right eyebrow which had caused death. He removed the bullet, which was to be the vital clue.

Now the hunt was on for two murderers. The daughter, Beverley, a pretty twenty-year-old, was slowly recovering and under a police guard in hospital. She had had a narrow escape, for the bullet had missed a main artery by a fraction of an inch. Patiently detectives watched the two survivors and slowly managed to piece together descriptions of the wanted men so that a Photofit picture could be put together.

In the course of the hunt an informant mentioned the name of George Ince, and subsequently his name appeared in the papers as being wanted for interrogation. Soon afterwards, on 27 November, a man walked into the Old Bailey, the Central Criminal Court, and said he had heard that the police wanted to see him in connection with the murder. He was accompanied by a solicitor and later that day he was driven by police to Braintree, the headquarters of the investigation. He appeared at an identification parade and was picked out by Mr Patience and Beverley. Later he was charged with murder. His name was George Ince, of Hathaway Crescent, Manor Park, and from the onset he told the police that he was innocent.

George Ince pleaded not guilty at Chelmsford Assizes, the jury was unable to agree on a verdict and a re-trial was ordered. In that first trial Ince refused to recognize the judge and dismissed his counsel. When the judge discharged the jury he said, 'I would like to thank the members of the jury for giving me the chance of letting my case go forward in front of a truthful judge.'

Thirty-five-year-old Ince was, in fact, three times identified as the Barn murderer and twice tried for the crime. The second trial was in May 1973 at Chelmsford Crown Court before Mr Justice Eveleigh. Ince was still defended by Mr Victor Durand, QC, and in this second trial he allowed his counsel to call his vital witness, something he had refused to do in the earlier trial.

She was Mrs Doris Gray, aged forty, the wife of Charles Kray, elder brother of the notorious Kray twins, who was jailed in 1968 for his involvement in the murder of Jack 'The Hat' McVitie. The Kray twins were also in jail serving life imprisonment.

Her identity was kept from the jury on the judge's instructions after he had been told that she had changed her name to Doris Gray by deed poll in 1969 when she and Ince first became lovers. As Charlie Kray's wife she had always been known as Dolly Kray.

Mrs Doris Gray, formerly Dolly Kray, gave evidence that she had spent the night with George Ince, her lover, on the night of 4–5 November, when he was alleged to have killed Mrs Patience. She said they had spent the night at her flat in Poplar and Ince had never left her side.

The all-male jury took three hours and seven minutes to reach unanimous verdicts on all the charges against Ince. He was found not guilty of the murder of Mrs Patience, and not guilty of the attempted murder of her husband Robert and her daughter Beverley. He was found not guilty of wounding Mr Patience and his daughter and of robbing Mr Patience of £900 and credit slips.

As the verdicts were given there was clapping and shouting from the public gallery. Ince had to be pulled from the dock and, as he was hustled down the steps he shouted at police officers in the case, 'You are one hundred per cent corrupt. It is your turn now.'

The hunt for the killers went on and it was a month later that Essex police Chief Superintendent Leonard White took a telephone call from Kendal, in Westmorland in the Lake District, to say that a man held in custody there knew something about the Barn Restaurant murder. He said that a man he knew had boasted that he had done the shooting and that he still had the gun. White travelled north that night and was met by the local police who took him to the house where, hidden in a mattress on one of the beds, was an Italian pistol. It was sent straight to Scotland Yard's laboratory to be test-fired. Marks on the bullets compared exactly with those on the bullet that killed Mrs Muriel Patience, the bullet found by Professor Cameron.

The two men arrested were Nicholas Richard James de Clare Johnson, aged thirty, who was unemployed and John Brook, aged thirty, a wood machinist, both of no fixed address. They were both charged with the murder of Mrs Muriel Patience. On 16 January 1974 the third trial in the Barn Murder Case began at Chelmsford Crown Court. It lasted for twenty-four days and ended in high drama. But the investigation which led to the trial was in the classic mould of an ordinary crime in which, as so often happens, a criminal associate turns informant. In this case it was a twenty-three-year-old petty crook named Peter Hanson who was on the run from the police when he shared a room with John Brook at the Salutation Hotel in the Lake District. He claimed Brook showed him the gun and boasted that it was used in the killing of Mrs Patience at the Barn Restaurant. There was also a full confession from Brook's accomplice, Nicholas de Clare Johnson, and the irrefutable evidence of Professor

Cameron and a ballistics expert that the killing bullet came from the gun owned by Brook which was in his possession at the time.

The blue cushions, through which the bullets had been fired, had been handed back to Mr Patience after the earlier abortive trials and had been thrown away. Since they had to be produced in court the police had to search an enormous five-acre rubbish dump. Using a bulldozer and digging with spades, they searched through the mountainous household rubbish until they found the bullet-holed cushions. They also found a few items stolen from the house which had been buried in a field with a brief-case which had been used to carry away the stolen money.

In this, the third trial, there was no question of identification and the witnesses who had formerly identified George Ince as the killer admitted they had been mistaken. On the last day of the trial a telephone call warned that a bomb had been planted in the court and it was cleared for twenty minutes while the police made a search. When the court was ready to resume the two prisoners, waiting in a cell below the court, were found to be fighting. Once that was stopped both men were sentenced. Brook was given life sentences for murdering Mrs Patience and attempting to murder her husband and daughter. Johnson was found not guilty of murder but guilty of manslaughter and sentenced to ten years.

Both men lacked the criminal skill for armed robbery. When they were disturbed and could not get the safe keys, Brook shot Mrs Patience in cold blood as Johnson watched. Brook then tried to execute the other witnesses, Robert and Beverley Patience, but failed at point-blank range. Brook might have been safe even then but for his boasting and the weakness of his partner, Johnson, who told the police everything. From then on Brook and

Johnson were bitter enemies, trying to blame one another.

Brook, the cold-blooded killer with one glass eye, showed no emotion when he was sentenced. He had been a criminal for most of his life. Born in Leeds, he was first arrested when he was fifteen. He had served sentences in approved school, Borstal and prisons, mostly for shop-breaking and theft. In 1970 he was convicted for assault and occasioning actual bodily harm. A homosexual had made advances to him and Brook hit him with an iron bar, and hit him again as he fell to the ground. He had been sentenced to three years' imprisonment, which he served in Dartmoor.

At the time of the Barn murder Johnson was still serving a jail sentence in Pentonville but since he was working on the hostel scheme he was allowed out at weekends on pre-release rehabilitation leave. Brook had been with Johnson on the same scheme and while working in Braintree for a furniture company they had heard about the Barn and that Mr Patience kept several days' takings in the safe.

It was well known to criminals that Patience took a large amount of money, particularly at weekends. He himself was aware that the restaurant was a talked-about target for thieves and it was known that criminals serving jail sentences talked about the Barn as a possible source of easy money when they were laying plans for their future freedom. It was said at the trial that on the night of the murder there was £10,000 in the safe. That was the sum criminals always believed was there for the taking and the figure they frequently discussed when making their plans. The raiders had not looked inside the safe when Robert Patience opened it and only got £900.

14

Maria Colwell

Professor Cameron has always had a passionate interest in the welfare of children and a hatred of them being ill-treated. He has written many thousands of words on the subject of battered babies and is a recognized expert on that type of brutality. In January 1973 he was called to a case in Brighton, Sussex, which, when all the evidence was adduced, horrified the nation.

His initial report read as follows:

I have been involved in research on 'battered' babies since 1965, I am author of various papers on the subject and I am currently author of a textbook on the subject to be published next year. In addition to my post-mortem work I also examine living children alleged to have been victims of child abuse. The number of such child cases that I have examined, both living and dead, must number several hundreds.

At 8.10 P.M. on 11 January 1973 at Brighton Mortuary, I carried out a post-mortem examination on the body of a young girl named Maria Ann Colwell, aged seven years.

The weight of the child was 36 pounds. The average weight for a child of that age is 50 pounds. Such a loss of weight from the norm could not have occurred during the space of a few days. It would take several months. It should have been apparent to a reasonably observant person on looking at the child, either unclothed or clothed.

The bruising I found on the child's body was not all new. Some of the bruising was several days old. Bruising normally takes ten days to disappear completely. The child must have been unconscious for some hours before death. To anyone who had seen her during the 48 hours prior to her death, it must have been obvious that she had suffered serious injuries.

It was the worst bruising I have seen in the whole of my experience with battered children.

The cause of death was multiple injuries.

The Professor then made a list of the marks on the body:

The forehead showed extensive swelling and bruising, as did the bridge of the nose.

Both eyes were black and abraded (rubbing) particularly the left one.

Extensive bruising and swelling of the whole of the left side of the face and neck with a patterned abrasion of the under aspect of the left eye.

Severe bruising and swelling on the left side of the head.

A number of scratch abrasions over the neck and beneath the nose. These did not appear to be consistent with having been self-inflicted.

There was extensive bruising over the back of the neck and the nape of the neck with much swelling.

Linear abrasion over the bottom of the chest beneath the rib margin measuring approximately two inches in length, more marked towards the mid-line.

Similar linear abrasion over the upper right chest.

Areas of bruising beneath the right rib margin and 'finger-tip'-type bruising over the abdomen of varying age and also over the prominence of both sides of the pelvis, particularly on the right side.

Bruising in the lower pubic area and in the right groin.

Severe swelling and bruising of both shoulder blades and the small of the back.

Bruising over the tops of both buttocks.

Areas of bruising over the upper part of the right leg and the rim of the pelvis, particularly towards the back over the prominence of the right hip.

Multiple 'finger-tip' type bruising of varying age over the whole of the right leg, particularly at the ankle.

Fresh abrasion over the outer side of the right knee.

On the inner side of the right leg there was similar extensive bruising.

A similar pattern of bruising was noted on the inner aspect of the left leg.

Extensive bruising over the shin of the left leg and over the outer aspect of the left leg and thigh.

Extensive bruising over the back of the left hand, forearm and elbow extending up the arm.

Bruising over the whole of the right arm.

There were a number of serious internal injuries and internal bleeding and evidence of soft tissue injuries. There was also extensive deep bruising over the head, neck and face with patchy subdural staining.

The final paragraph read: 'The injuries are inconsistent with self-infliction and were inconsistent with a fall.' Professor Cameron also stated that there was no evidence of natural disease that could have caused or contributed to death at that time.

It has never been resolved what was the exact time of Maria Ann Colwell's death, but it was at 10.35 A.M. on Sunday, 7 January 1973, that her dead body was delivered to the Casualty Unit of the Royal Sussex County Hospital, Brighton. The body had been brought in a white pram covered in coal dust by Pauline Violet Kepple, the child's mother, and William Kepple, her husband.

The doctor who first examined the child found severe bruising on the body and shocking bruising of the head and particularly of both eyes. Both Kepple and his wife explained that the child had fallen down the stairs in an epileptic fit, thus sustaining the injuries. The body was in such a state that the Hospital Authority contacted Brighton police, and it was then examined by Dr Hilary Jarvis, the Police Surgeon for Brighton. He pronounced that the child had been dead for a number of hours.

Maria Colwell was born to Pauline Violet Kepple in March 1965. At that time Mrs Kepple was married to Raymond Leslie Colwell, who died four months after the birth. In August of that year Maria was taken to Mrs Doris Cooper, the sister of the dead man. The baby was in poor condition, unable to retain food, extremely thin and generally neglected. With proper care she thrived, and Mrs Cooper and her husband were prepared to bring her up as their own child.

Eighteen months later Mrs Kepple took the child away. Only a week afterwards Mrs Cooper was taken by the Child Welfare Authority to an address in Hove where Maria was found in a filthy condition, with no shoes or socks. A magistrate placed the child in the care of the East Sussex County Council, and Mrs Cooper became a foster-mother and continued to look after Maria.

In October 1967 the Children's Department gave Mrs Cooper instructions that Maria should make visits to her mother. First there were monthly visits and then the mother insisted they should become more frequent. In October 1971 Mrs Kepple successfully applied for Maria to be returned to her. At that time she and William Kepple were living together at Maresfield Road, Brighton, and the association had produced three children. They were married in the following year.

From the time Maria returned to live with her mother her general health deteriorated and she had been neglected, maltreated and kept short of food.

On Sunday, 7 January 1973, at 7.45 A.M. Mr and Mrs Kepple were seen leaving their home with a pram, but it was only at 10.35 that they arrived at the Royal Sussex County Hospital, where Kepple carried the child in to the nursing staff. When the police arrived they interrogated Mr and Mrs Kepple, who again gave the bland excuse that Maria suffered epileptic fits which caused her to fall down the stairs on several occasions and sustain the injuries.

The Kepples were taken to Brighton police station and detained. Mrs Kepple, who was obviously terrified of her husband, told lies in several statements. Eventually, however, she told the police that it was her husband who had hit the child and, in the end, he admitted striking Maria around the chest and stomach.

William Kepple, aged forty-two years, a builder's labourer, was charged with the murder of Maria Ann Colwell. At Lewes Assizes that charge was reduced to manslaughter and Kepple was sentenced to eight years' imprisonment.

The case so shocked the nation that there was an immediate public inquiry at which more than a hundred people gave evidence. What emerged was a story of muddle and sometimes incompetence by a series of public bodies. The inquiry censured two welfare departments and the National Society for the Prevention of Cruelty to Children and, in a 60,000-word report two paragraphs read:

Many of the mistakes made by individuals were either the result of, or were contributed to, by inefficient systems operating in several different fields, notably training, administration, planning, liaison and supervision.

It is at the middle and higher levels that this case has clearly shown to us that a great deal of rethinking about child care is overdue.

Professor Cameron continues to help identify the people who ill-treat children, and he advises policemen of what to look for when called to a suspect baby battering case or the sudden death of a child. He is assisted by Mr Bernard Sims and forensic photographer Ray Ruddick, both from the Department of Forensic Medicine at the London Hospital. Between them they have brought to justice many a callous brute who masquerades under the title of 'parent'.

In the opening paragraph of a long paper entitled 'The Battered Child', Professor Cameron once wrote:

One of our most cherished folk beliefs is that human nature compels parents to rear their young with solicitousness and concern, good intentions and tender loving care. Evidence to the contrary – the rather alarming frequency with which parents harm or fail to adequately care for their offspring – has forced the recognition that child abuse and neglect are well within the repertoire of human behaviour.

15

The Price of a Favour

If there are degrees of stupidity in murder one of the most outstanding in Professor Cameron's experience occurred in the country lanes around the pretty village of Mogerhanger in Bedfordshire. The setting was a black night of lashing rain early in February 1974 and the victim was a local man, Gordon Seddon, who died less than a mile from his home in the centre of the village.

At one o'clock in the morning Gordon Seddon was asleep in bed with his wife. He was awakened by a banging on the front door and put on his dressing-gown, went down and opened the door. Standing there, dripping wet, was his brother-in-law, David Lawrence Bowdler, a thirty-year-old car worker from Stourbridge in Worcestershire. Bowdler told Seddon his van had broken down and asked him to bring his car to help. Seddon agreed to lend a hand, quickly got dressed, fetched his car and the two men drove off together. Seddon never returned. Within half an hour he was the victim of a frenzied attack and lying unconscious.

The two men knew each other well. Seddon had asked Bowdler to arrange the purchase of a car from his works at an employee's discount and had promised to pay a sum of cash for the favour and the work involved. On the way to the spot where Bowdler's van was parked some harsh words were exchanged about the amount of money to be paid and the row was still raging when the two men reached the van. Seddon began to work on the engine of the van and the argument became more intense. Seddon, with his head under the bonnet looking at the engine, did not see Bowdler go to the van and pick up a chopper. He hit Seddon so many times with it that the handle broke off, and he continued to hit the unfortunate man until he fell to the ground.

Bowdler tried to lift Seddon into his car but was not strong enough. So he left him in the road and drove Seddon's car back to Bedford Road and asked Mrs Seddon for some rope. She gave him a coil of rope which was in the lounge, and he put it into the car and drove off, back to where he had left the body.

A little later Mrs Seddon was wondering what had happened and, looking out of her bedroom window, she saw her husband's car parked in nearby St John's Road, its headlights on full. She was able to see Bowdler doing something to the front of the vehicle. Then she saw him shut the lid of the boot and drive away. A few moments later she saw the car stop at the same place. Again Bowdler got out of the car, did something by the nearside front door and again drove away.

At 3.30 a.m. Bowdler once more returned to the Seddon house and told Mrs Seddon his van was stuck in the mud, saying that he would take a piece of fibre-board to help release it. He mentioned that Seddon had gone to summon the AA to help.

Bowdler went off but returned at about four o'clock and by then Mrs Seddon could see flames in the general direction of where Bowdler's vehicle had broken down. This time he said that Seddon had gone to get a tractor. Mrs Seddon noticed that Bowdler's clothing was torn and that he was wet through and covered in mud. He said to her, indicating the fire in the distance, 'It was a car.' She let him wash and tidy up, and she also loaned him a pair of her husband's trousers to replace his own.

Then Bowdler said, 'I was not going to tell you this. It was your car and not mine and there is nothing left of it but the shell.' She asked him if he should telephone the police and he did make a call, but it was not in fact to the police. Bowdler then left the house.

But someone else had telephoned the police and PC Slade went to the scene. The car, which was an Avenger, was well alight and by the time the fire brigade had extinguished the fire, only a blackened, smouldering wreck remained.

The police officer saw Bowdler at the scene and took his name and address. Again he said that Seddon had gone to borrow a tractor with which to recover his own van. PC Slade took Bowdler back to see Mrs Seddon at the house and later another officer, PC Brown, arrived. He asked Bowdler if he knew where Gordon Seddon was. Bowdler said he did not know exactly but that after attempting to free the van from the mud he had first gone to telephone the AA and later to get a tractor. At this point, 6.30 A.M., PC Brown took Bowdler to Biggleswade police station, not under arrest but to help with inquiries.

All that day evidence accumulated and was reported by various different police officers. Detective Chief Superintendent Grant, who took charge of the inquiry, was not sure what he was looking for, but his hunch was that Seddon was dead and that evidence of murder was not far away. Several people had seen the Dormobile van belonging to Bowdler and reported its whereabouts, half a mile from the Seddon home. A police officer started it with a slight adjustment to the carburetter. It was obvious, therefore, that the van had not broken down and that Seddon had been lured from his home on a false pretence.

All these snippets of evidence added up to the fact that Bowdler had told some lies during the night, in particular to Mrs Seddon. Chief Superintendent Grant had assembled a team of police officers, and he sent them to search the area, looking for Seddon and any other clues which would clear up the strange events of the night.

A postman found, in St John's Road, a wallet containing correspondence in the name of Seddon. Later, at that same spot, detectives found a large amount of blood, together with a piece of solder, a coin and some matches. Not far from the wallet and the blood was found a piece of rope. Near Bowdler's van was a broken set of top dentures, and the same officer also found part of a lower denture within a few yards. Close to the burnt-out car was found a shoe, which had belonged to Seddon, and a detective found traces of blood on the engine. In the front of Bowdler's van was the head of the chopper and part of the broken handle which fitted the head.

At 9.40 P.M. on Saturday, 9 February, Detective Chief Superintendent Grant, with Detective Inspector Wood, saw Bowdler at Biggleswade police station. After showing him the chopper and some clothing Bowdler admitted striking Seddon about the head with the axe and he then made a written statement under caution. It read:

'Early this morning I drove from Worcester to Mogerhanger. When I got there my van broke down. I went to my brother-in-law who is Gordon Seddon. He lives in Mogerhanger. He got out of bed and came with me in his car. We went to where my car was broken down. When we got to my van which was about a mile from the pub in Mogerhanger we had an argument because Gordon said he would report me because I was getting him a car from where I worked at Longbridge. We had agreed he would get me some money for getting the car. Gordon was at the engine of my van when the row took place. The engine cover is inside the van. I had a chopper in the van, that is the one you have shown me. I hit Gordon over the head with the chopper. I think I hit him a lot of times and the chopper broke. Gordon fell down to the ground. He did not speak. I kept hitting him with the broken bit of the chopper. I knew I had killed him. I can't remember too much what I done then but I remember driving Gordon's car up and down the road several times. I remember going to Gordon's house and getting a rope and a piece of board. I tried to put Gordon in his car but he was too heavy. I then tied the rope round Gordon and tied the other end to the bumper of his car. I then pulled him up the road and put him into a ditch. I will take you to the ditch and show you where Gordon is. I do remember that I threw one of Gordon's shoes into a field a little way from where my van was. I then got some petrol what was in a plastic thing in the back of Gordon's car. I used the petrol to set light to Gordon's car then I went back to his house and got cleaned up. I put my trousers at the back of a bench in Gordon's garage. When I hit Gordon I was alone with him. I remember now that at one time after I first hit Gordon he went into a ditch near my van but he got out of there and I hit him again. I hit him with something else besides the chopper. I think it was a hammer and I think it is in my van, it is a big heavy hammer. I am sorry I did this, I have some temper.'

At eleven o'clock that night Mr Grant took Bowdler and other officers to the A603 road and began to search ditches on both sides of the road. During this time Bowdler fainted, and because of his condition and the danger from fast-moving traffic he was taken back to the police station and medically examined. But before he fainted they had passed some cottages on the road where there was a white van parked with the word 'Windscreens' on the side. Bowdler had said, 'That's it, that's the windscreen van. He is near here. I know he's here, I know he's here.'

When the traffic had quietened after midnight, the Chief Superintendent and his men went to the place that Bowdler had indicated and found the body of Seddon, which was put under guard until Professor Cameron arrived. Meanwhile Dr David Paul Smyly, the local police surgeon, had been to see Bowdler at the police station where Bowdler had said to him, 'I hit him and hit him again and again. He should not have shouted at me. He said I had taken his money and I had not.'

Dr Smyly then went to see the body of Seddon lying in a ditch and pronounced that life was extinct, and at 2.30 P.M. on Sunday, 10 February, Professor Cameron took his first look at the victim. He wrote in his report:

I was shown the body of a man lying semi-prone. There was a rope around the ankles. The trousers were torn at the seat and at the back of the calves with almost avulsion of the skin of the back of the left buttock and severe friction abrasions over both buttocks, back of trunk and the backs of both calves. The upper garments were pulled upwards over the head. The left side of the head, however, was exposed showing bruising, lacerations and abrasions of the face on that side. Examination of the abrasions under a magnifying glass suggested that the body had been dragged by the feet, pulling the body feet first whilst on its back.

Then the body was removed to the mortuary at Bedford General Hospital where Cameron carried out a post-mortem. His report, in typescript, covered six foolscap pages and described the most horrifying injuries. He gave as the cause of death: 'Multiple injuries including compound fractures of the skull and face with a crushed chest.'

But perhaps the most important paragraph was the penultimate. It read: 'Evidence to suggest that after the initial head injury the deceased lived for some time in which he was able to inhale blood which had tracked down from the fractured base of the skull, there being bleeding from both ears, particularly the right.'

The watch of the dead man was found to have stopped at five minutes to two and he had left his house at fifteen minutes past one. It was more likely that he was tied to the back of his own car while still alive and dragged around the lanes until he died.

Bowdler's first statement, in which he insisted that his van had broken down and that Seddon had gone off to telephone the AA and then to find a tractor, had been disproved. Now Bowdler's wife mentioned that her husband could resort to extreme violence and although she at first denied knowing her husband was travelling to Mogerhanger on 9 February, she later changed her story and said he had some form of fixation over the car he obtained for Seddon.

It was the transaction between Bowdler and Seddon that was the main cause of the crime. Bowdler was to buy a motor car at ex-works price and Seddon was to give him a cash present for the favour. A cheque for £1,286.96p, the price of the car, had been paid to Mrs Bowdler who had, in turn, paid it to British Leyland. It was clear that there had been no dishonest appropriation of Seddon's money. That leaves only the motive as Bowdler described it in his statement: 'We had agreed he would get me some money for getting the car.' It appeared that the average payment for such a favour was about £50. But that money was never paid.

David Lawrence Bowdler was charged with murder and at Bedford Assizes was found guilty and sentenced to life imprisonment.

16

Murder on the Way to Church

It is not often that the forensic psychiatrist receives a mention in the business of crime detection. His is a quiet role, advising the detectives on the type of man they are seeking, based on a lifetime of studying the type of wounds inflicted and the methods of using the weapons. Quite early in his career Dr Cameron was faced with a difficult case of murder in which there were practically no clues and those there were pointed in no positive direction. He called in the forensic psychiatrist on his team at the London Hospital, who was able to give the vital lead.

Soon after eight o'clock on the morning of Sunday, 22 September 1974, a young woman in great distress, her clothing torn and stained with blood, staggered into the ornamental garden outside Chatham police station in Kent and fell into the arms of PC Newman, who was about to go on duty. He supported her and then helped her to lie down on the grass. He asked her what had happened and she whispered, 'I was attacked by a man,' before she became unconscious. Where the girl's clothing had been disturbed the constable could see she had a wound in her stomach. An ambulance was called and the girl was rushed to the nearby Medway District Hospital. Before she was put on to a stretcher Police Constable Norman Wright, a dog-handler, had run to the scene with the intention of finding out where the attack had taken place.

At the back of the station he saw some blood spots on the step of the gateway, which he marked with a chalk circle. Then the dog began to work and tracked along a chalk and grass path which led towards the war memorial, a monument which dominates the large area of common land between Chatham and Gillingham known as the Great Lines Common. PC Wright slipped the dog's tracking harness and together they searched a small copse and then walked along a macadam path where they found some more blood. Thirty-five yards further on there was a large patch of it. Following the blood trail, he found a woman's left shoe and soon afterwards he found the other brown shoe.

Wright stayed on the path, noted some steps on the left-hand side, and then found a number of bloodstained paper tissues. Some yards further on he saw the collar of a shirt or blouse stamped with the number '27'. That too was marked with blood. PC Wright secured all these articles in place with stones and marked their positions with chalk. Strewn around were more white paper tissues, and there were two lying in some flattened grass. The dog moved towards the monument, up a grassy bank and across another path. Suddenly she lay down, an indication that she had found an article bearing a fresh human scent. When PC Wright reached the dog he found a pair of man's sun-glasses in a case. The case was dry although the grass was very wet.

No further search was possible because a large crowd of people on a sponsored walk for charity moved across the area, obliterating all scent. PC Wright returned to the police station, and handed in the list of his twelve pieces of evidence.

The girl, who died soon after admission to hospital, was quickly identified as Susan Stevenson, an eighteen-year-old clerk who was married to a serving sailor who at that time was on board HMS *Hydra* in the Pacific. She had left her flat in Windmill Road, Gillingham, Kent, at 8.15 A.M. to walk to Rochester Cathedral where she was a bellringer and a chorister. She had walked along a footpath where she would have been clearly visible for about three-quarters of a mile until the path descends and a thick, bushy area begins, obscuring the footpath from view to all people other than those using it. It was at that point that Susan had been attacked.

Detective Chief Inspector Watson took immediate charge of the case and was able to confirm that the girl was a frequent Sunday morning visitor to the cathedral and always walked the same way. A witness, a Mr Hawks, was soon found who had been walking his dog. He had seen Susan Stevenson on the morning of the attack and had watched her gradually disappear along the Lines footpath to the point where it descends. He stated that it was then that he saw a man following her. About ten minutes later he saw a man come running back along the footpath and past him. But Mr Hawks was an elderly man and was unable to give a description of the man he had seen, and neither could he say whether the man he saw running was the same man he had seen following the girl. Inspector Watson made the reasonable assumption that Mr Hawks had seen the killer, although the witness was totally unable to give anything of a description. Watson was able to pin-point where the attack took place by the position of the dead girl's shoes, and the old cassock she had been carrying which was found in the bushes nearby. It appeared that Susan Stevenson had managed to stagger about two hundred and fifty yards along the path to the garden of the police station before she collapsed.

The time Susan left the flat was established by the residents of the ground-floor flat, Mr and Mrs Tandy, who, although they did not see her, heard her leave, and they were sure that she was alone. Apart from that, the last person to see her alive was Christopher Osenton

who, with two others, had brought her home from a
bellringing competition on the previous evening of Saturday, 21 September. He had dropped her off near her
home at 10.30 P.M.

Detective Superintendent Jack Goodsall, head of the
Kent CID, took overall charge of the case and sent for
Professor Cameron to perform a post-mortem examination. He gave the cause of death as haemorrhage due to
multiple stab wounds to the chest, abdomen and two in
the back over the shoulder blades. There were more than
thirty wounds, including defence wounds to both hands.
Many were superficial, but the deepest had penetrated to
a depth of four inches, puncturing the liver. The weapon
used, said Cameron, was probably a short, double-bladed
weapon with one edge sharper than the other. There was
also slight bruising of the vagina and of the right thigh
and in the neck region. Since there was no evidence of a
sexual assault the Professor thought that sexual inter-
ference was unlikely to have occurred, although he did
not entirely rule it out. She was fully clothed, apart from
her shoes.

The pathologist thought she had been first stabbed in
the back and that the bruising to the neck was consistent
with her having been held by an arm around her neck
from behind. He stressed the possibility that the stab
wounds to the front may have been inflicted while she
was being held from behind, or when she was on her
back on the ground, and the bruising of the vagina and
the thigh were possibly caused when the killer knelt on
her. He also said that the injuries would not have shed
much blood so the likelihood of bloodstains on the killer
was minimal.

From the outset the inquiry was linked with two previous stabbings of women in the area, one in June 1973
and the other in May 1974. In the first case a woman was

attacked by a youth in East Hoath Woods, near the village of Wigmore, and stabbed several times. She had recovered after treatment in the intensive care unit of the Medway Hospital. In the second, a woman was attacked by a young man who had a dog with him in Bredhurst Woods and an attempt was made to stab her in the back. Fortunately the knife struck the metal clip on her brassière strap and bent the blade. She received only a superficial scratch and the man had run away, dropping the knife as he went. Extensive inquiries were made in both cases and although the descriptions varied considerably it was thought that the same man had probably been responsible for both cases.

Superintendent Goodsall decided to take a close look at these two cases again to see if there were any common factors with the evidence in the murder. First a massive search of the Lines and adjoining areas for weapons or other articles was set up, a thorough house-to-house search using a questionnaire was begun and all local servicemen were to be questioned.

Special detective teams were formed to question everyone who had been in the vicinity of the Lines between 7 A.M. and 9 A.M. on the Sunday morning and also to trace all local people with previous convictions for indecency or violence towards women and account for their movements. In addition, all the witnesses in the two unsolved cases were to be traced and interviewed again and a detailed description of the dog owned by the offender in the Bredhurst Woods case was to be obtained and inquiries made to trace other similar animals.

The police asked for massive press publicity and they got it. Every item found during the search around the scene of the attack was given full coverage in the newspapers. One was a church medallion which had been worn by Susan Stevenson at the time of the attack and had almost certainly fallen off when she was first stabbed. Another was a bracelet engraved 'Trev', which was traced to its owner who told police that it had been stolen from him two days before the murder. As a result of the search, some of it with metal detectors, nine knives were found and all were examined by Professor Cameron. He reported that only three could have been the murder weapons.

But despite the search and the many 'finds' there was no real lead to the killer. Dr Cameron suggested to Superintendent Goodsall that this might be the time to use the services of his forensic psychiatrist, Dr Patrick Tooley. Goodsall agreed and the two doctors went to the mortuary where Dr Cameron made a further examination of the body and explained to Dr Tooley his reconstruction of the murder.

He said he thought it had been a sudden attack from behind, the first blows being two stab wounds in the shoulder area. The girl had then struggled with her attacker and the medallion she wore round her neck had fallen to the ground. She had run a few paces and had then been grabbed round the neck from behind. There was bruising on the front of the neck, consistent with one hand against the throat, as opposed to a strangle-hold. The girl was then forced to her knees, injuring both. Then there was stabbing to the chest from behind and above. He thought the stabbing was probably completed while she was lying flat on her back.

Dr Tooley had visited the scene and studied all the known facts. He now gave his view of the man the police were looking for. He wrote:

The man is aged between twenty and thirty-five years, possibly a psychopath with previous convictions. Generally one could expect too from his record that he had made a number of court appearances, was convicted at an early age and had possibly been in a special home; likely to be a manual worker and either unemployed or frequently changing jobs. Previous convictions could include unlawful sexual intercourse, drunkenness, robbery and assaults generally.

Father absent – mother restrictive, sexually prudish and devoted to son and spoils him. He, in turn, resents this and has a hate complex towards women. Despite that, he wants an affair with a woman but cannot make a normal approach. He does not mix socially and walks alone, in open spaces. He could be a 'peeper' but seldom resorts to indecent exposure.

That report was circulated to police who were making the house-to-house inquiries on 3 October, eleven days after the murder. It gave them something specific to look for and it also necessitated a search being made on every possible suspect in the Criminal Record Office at Scotland Yard. There were strict instructions that it was not to be given to the press.

More than 6,000 people were interviewed in the house-to-house searches and the whereabouts of all those local people was firmly established for the time of the murder. The inquiries were so intense that several hitherto unsolved crimes were cleared up. But the vital clue still eluded the detectives. Only the one male witness had seen a man on the Lines at the important time and he was unable to give a description. Police could not find any other person who had seen the same man, or indeed any man.

Superintendent Goodsall interviewed all local men with previous convictions for indecency, and all those suspected of committing that type of offence. Many were positively eliminated from the murder inquiry, but there were fifty-two whose movements on the day of the murder could not be verified. They were all taken to various Medway police stations for questioning, and samples of their blood and hair were obtained.

Press and radio appeals brought forth two further witnesses, a man and a woman, who had not come forward before because they were both married and their association was extra-marital. They were able to help identify the type of dog which had been with the assailant in Bredhurst Woods. The owner of the dog was traced and when questioned admitted the two offences. But he was not the man who killed Mrs Stevenson, although police discovered he had a sadistic streak and that he enjoyed torturing small animals.

There were numerous other strong suspects whom the police unearthed during their inquiries. A bus driver had seen a man on the day of the murder in Rochester and noticed that his left hand was cut and that there was blood on the lobe of one of his ears and on his shirt. The same man was seen by several other people but police were unable to trace him. Another man was found who had arrived home in the vicinity of the Lines at 8.30 A.M. on the day of the murder with bloodstained clothing. He explained the bloodstains by saying that his girl friend had made a suicide attempt on Friday, 20 September and he had staunched her wounds. The police were able to confirm that.

It was now six weeks since the murder and twelve more people were detained for questioning. One man called Peter Stout, a dockyard labourer who had a previous conviction for indecency, was interviewed as part of the routine check on all such persons. His alibi for the time of the murder was that at 9.30 A.M. he was still in bed, and that was supported by his room-mate. But, in fact, the room-mate could not confirm that Stout was in bed between 7 A.M. and 9.30 A.M. – only that he woke up and saw Stout sitting on his bed at the later time.

The landlady of the house where Peter Stout lived in Balmoral Road, Gillingham, which was about one mile and a half from the murder spot, was a voluntary social worker who rented her rooms to young men from poor backgrounds who were needy and, sometimes, unwanted. She told the detectives that on the morning of 22 September she heard someone leave the house soon after seven o'clock. At about nine o'clock she heard the sound of running water coming from the bathroom. That bathroom was used by Mrs Bradford herself, Peter Stout, and two other lodgers. The landlady said that Stout always went to collect the newspapers on a Sunday morning, but when she returned from church at noon there were no newspapers in the house and that she did not see Stout until the afternoon, when she noticed he had cut his hand and was wearing a bandage. Stout told her he had cut his hand while fishing. She also noticed that he looked pallid and ill and was far from being his normal fairly boisterous self. In fact, she said, he had been very quiet during the last month.

Police checked that Stout did not collect the newspapers on that day, which was contrary to his normal habit, and they were suspicious of his room-mate, a man called Colman, whom they thought was lying. Two detectives of the murder squad went to see Peter Stout again and this time he denied he had cut his hand on 22 September. He made repeated references to the Devil, saying he had to fight off temptations and blaming the Devil for telling him to steal things. He also admitted indecent assaults on women. Those admissions had no foundation in fact, and certainly could not be proved.

Stout was arrested and the police took possession of a bloodstained towel from his room. Analysis proved that the blood was his own.

The background of Peter Stout was revealing. He was aged nineteen, single and had one elder sister, two elder brothers and a younger brother. Both his parents were dead. His father had been a drunkard and a bully and was disliked by all the children, but they had all loved their mother. When Stout was fourteen he was convicted of indecently assaulting a woman and he himself had been the victim of attempted buggery when he was ten years old. This fitted exactly into the pattern of the man described by Dr Tooley and there were other things which also fitted. He was a loner who went for long walks and he did not mix well with others.

The interrogation of Peter Stout was a long-drawn-out process of admissions, half-admissions, then a complete retraction and references to the Devil and 'queer turns'.

Eventually, on 21 October, he made a statement which he signed as being the truth of what happened on that Sunday morning. It read:

'Well, I got up just before seven o'clock that morning. I got dressed in my brown trousers with studs in and I had my hooped jumper on with different coloured hoops – and that yellow mac on that I have been shown.

'I had some tissues and a handkerchief in the big pocket, then I went down to the bathroom and had a wash and went to the toilet. Then I went to the kitchen and put my yellow coat on. Then I got the knife from the drawer. When I put the knife in my pocket, I went out and turned left down Balmoral Road towards the High Street . . . I went up Windmill Road, by the hospital entrance, and saw a girl walking in front of me . . . she was about forty yards in front . . . I kept following her and started to catch her up. She looked over her shoulder a couple of times and tried walking a bit faster. I caught her up altogether and grabbed her with my left arm round her throat. Then I started stabbing her in the back. I was stabbing anywhere, and then she fell backwards towards me and I was stabbing anywhere in the front as well. She was struggling to get me off – and telling me to clear off. She wasn't screaming. When she fell backwards she went on to the ground on her back and I knelt down on one knee and started stabbing her anywhere in the front. She was waving her hands about, trying to hit me. At one time she was waving the thing she was carrying [the cassock] and trying to hit me with it. I stopped stabbing her – and tried to wipe the knife on my hand. I cut the palm of my hand. She was getting up and trying to get away from me – she struggled away down the path and I ran away . . . I didn't look back. I started to try to wipe some of the blood off my hand with the paper tissues. It didn't stop bleeding so I put the handkerchief around it. I can't remember where I put the knife. I might have dropped it.'

The statement ended with the words:

'All I can say is the Devil has got at me – and when he thinks I have my funny turns, he does some extra poking and things like that and I give in to him. I don't remember what I do when I have funny turns sometimes – they just come at any time.'

That statement agreed exactly with Dr Cameron's reconstruction of the murder and the views of Dr Patrick Tooley, the forensic psychiatrist.

The knife used to kill Susan Stevenson was never positively identified, but Dr Cameron examined a number that had been found that were capable of causing her wounds. However, the rest of the evidence was overwhelming and in March 1975 Peter Stout was tried at Maidstone Assizes, found guilty and sentenced to life imprisonment.

17

The Thames Torso

A post office worker, Mr Richard Leighton, whose hobby was ornithology, went for an early morning walk on 5 October 1974, looking for birds along the north bank of the River Thames at Rainham in Essex. At Cold Harbour Point, at the water's edge, he saw a white, pinkish object, which at first he thought was a dead sheep. On closer inspection he found it was the upper part of a male torso, minus head and arms. He reported his find to the police and so began a sensational murder investigation set against a background of torture and extreme violence.

In the next ten days four other parts of a human body, all found to be from the same person, were washed up on the foreshore of the Thames at different points over a distance of ten miles.

Commander Albert Wickstead took charge of the case and a post-mortem was made by Dr Alan Grant, the pathologist at Guy's Hospital. He reported that all the pieces originated from the same body, all severed by saw and knife. It was his opinion that all the pieces were immersed at about the same time, about five days prior to 5 October. He could find no cause of death but formed the opinion, because of the congestion of the lungs, that death was due to a head injury. Dr Grant also noted pigmented spots on the left foot and leg, an area of pallor with a sharp under margin on the leg, and vertical cuts on the chest and stomach.

Parts of the body still missing were the head, left arm, both hands, left upper leg and right lower leg, including the foot. No positive identification could be made, but detectives are adept at ferreting out facts and rumours and Commander Wickstead became tolerably sure that the murdered man was a well-known but small-time crook called William Henry Moseley, who had disappeared several days before the torso was found. In support of that theory Dr Grant took blood samples from Moseley's wife Ann and their three sons which, when they were compared with the blood of the torso, suggested a strong connection. Even so, sufficient evidence was not forthcoming for an inquest to be held and positive identification proved.

Almost a year went by while Wickstead and his men were looking for the killers. Then, on 7 September 1975 a family blackberrying in Chalkdell Wood near Hatfield, Hertfordshire, discovered an area of disturbed soil. The young son of the family, who was keen on hunting for buried treasure, called his father and together they began to dig up the earth. At a depth of fifteen inches from the surface they found a human hand.

Local police were called who cordoned off the area and Detective Chief Superintendent Harvey went to the scene. He sent for Professor Cameron, who first placed the exposed right hand in a plastic bag to preserve it and then removed the top earth from the grave to a depth of three and a half feet to expose the body of an adult male wrapped in a candlewick bedspread. The right arm was standing up straight from the shoulder.

Later the body was removed to the mortuary where the Professor made his post-mortem examination. It was dressed in brown and black French-style shoes, brown tartan socks, dark blue trousers and a white and blue patterned shirt. Over that was a dark blue battledress jacket and in the right breast pocket was the stub of a pencil. The body was in an advanced state of decomposition due to the long spell of hot, dry weather.

Professor Cameron gave the cause of death as a close proximity gunshot wound entering the right temple with the exit behind the left ear. The bullet had passed right through the skull and had not been found. There were several bruises on the body, consistent with kicks or blows before death and a mark across the right leg, possibly caused by a rope or other restraining device.

Fingerprints were taken from both hands and sent to Scotland Yard and immediately identified as those of Michael Henry Cornwall. Like Moseley, he was aged thirty-seven and they had been close friends ever since their childhood. Throughout that time their lives had been steeped in crime.

Wickstead found out that Moseley and Cornwall had been members of the same gang who based their operations in North London and he and Chief Superintendent Harvey set up a murder squad at Loughton to investigate both murders. It was an ideal plan for Wickstead, the leader, because he had been investigating gang warfare in London. There were fourteen officers from Hertfordshire and ten from the Metropolitan Police.

Wickstead went to Walthamstow's Coroner's Court and explained to the coroner for North-East London, Dr Price, the present position of the investigation and requested that Moseley's torso, which had not yet been buried, be allowed to go to the London Hospital for further examination by Professor Cameron. The coroner agreed and on 24 October a second post-mortem on Moseley was carried out by Cameron.

His findings were grave but spectacular, for they gave a lead to the type of criminals the police were hunting. Some areas of bruising were found and there was evidence of cuts and possible slash wounds in the area of the sternum (breastbone). The sternum itself was fractured. Ribs on the left-hand side of the torso were broken and this had occurred at, or near, the time of death. Professor Cameron also found evidence of torture. All the nails had been wrenched from one foot prior to death and the leg attached to that foot had been held in some sort of vice to facilitate the easy removal of the nails. There was also heat burning to the sole of the foot and marks round the body of binding with a light ligature. Cameron was convinced that the dead man had been subjected to severe torture before death, although the degree of torture was not enough to cause death. His view was that death was caused from a head wound, possibly a bullet, or a heavy blow.

Professor Cameron and his staff of experts then attended to the positive identification of the torso. The blood group had given a clear indication. Of the nine to eleven possible blood groups that were found in the family tree, the torso had proved positive in fifty per cent. In addition the upper half of the torso was X-rayed and the prints were compared with a mass radio graphic picture of Moseley which revealed eight points of similarity. And the presence of pure cholesterol gallstones was consistent with a diagnosis on Moseley while alive and under medical treatment. Cameron was satisfied beyond all reasonable doubt that the torso found in the river was that of Moseley.

That identification made legal history. It was the first time a headless body had been identified without the aid of dental charts or fingerprints.

Because of the long delay in identifying Moseley and there having been no publicity concerning his death, the news of the murders of the two men, close friends, burst on the underworld scene like a bomb. And some of the criminals began to talk. The police learned that three days before the torso was found three men had been discussing the death of Moseley at a family funeral. They were all well known in the criminal fraternity but nobody else had known of Moseley's death at that point.

Police inquiries disclosed a world of violence and criminal activity. They heard that in 1968 a man called Reginald Dudley, a fifty-four-year-old jeweller from North London, had been involved in a fight with Moseley and had tried to ram a broken bottle into his face. He failed and Moseley gave him a hiding. Dudley swore revenge because he had been made to look small in front of a large number of local villains.

It was rumoured in underworld circles that Moseley called Dudley a 'wrong 'un', or a 'grass' – an informer to the police. It was common knowledge that Dudley frequently met a Detective Chief Inspector of the Metropolitan Police who had an unsavoury reputation and was thought not to be entirely honest.

Dudley's great friend was Robert Maynard, who was aged forty and also in the jewellery trade. The two were so close they were known all over London where crooks foregather as 'Legal and General' – partners in crime. It was Dudley and Maynard with a third man who had been heard discussing Moseley's death.

On 18 October 1974 Cornwall was released from prison and returned to his North London haunts hoping to find his old friend Moseley. But Moseley had been missing for a month and there was no news of him until Cornwall heard rumours that bits of Moseley's dismembered body had been found in the Thames in Essex. Then, according to underworld informants, Cornwall embarked on his own one-man crusade to find the killers to exact his revenge. He was looking for Dudley and Maynard and they heard he was on their track. They in turn began to look for Cornwall. During the ensuing months it was said that Cornwall formed an intimate relationship with Kathleen, Dudley's daughter, and in 1975 they lived together at a flat in Thornton Heath, Surrey, a relationship which was unknown to the father.

Cornwall had many other women friends and Dudley and Maynard in their efforts to find him followed a policy of *cherchez la femme*, but Cornwall remained one step ahead of them. Then he became badly frightened and went into hiding. He was last seen on or about 22 August 1975. Rumours grew that Cornwall had been murdered and that there was a positive link between his killing and the disappearance of Moseley.

After a long and painstaking investigation Commander Wickstead arrested seven people on charges arising out of the two gangland killings and in April 1976 they were committed for trial from Epping Magistrates' Court to the Old Bailey. The trial, the longest in criminal history, lasted for seven months.

Two men, Reginald Dudley of Stapleton Hill Road, Holloway, and Robert Maynard, of Ager Road, Camden, were found guilty of murdering William Moseley and Michael Cornwall. Dudley's daughter, Kathleen, aged thirty, was given a two-year suspended sentence for conspiring to cause Cornwall grievous bodily harm, and greengrocer Charles Clarke, aged fifty-six, was jailed for four years for plots to cause both victims bodily harm. All four appealed against conviction but the verdicts were upheld by three Appeal Court judges in London in April 1979.

The other defendants were acquitted.

But that was not the end of this extraordinary case. There was just one more strange twist. On 28 July 1977, three years after the first piece of the torso had been found, a police officer was called to a public toilet in Richmond Avenue, Islington, and was shown a skull. It had originally been found in the toilet but when he arrived it was lying on the kerb, covered by a newspaper.

The skull was taken to St Pancras Mortuary and later handed to Professor Cameron at the London Hospital. On his initial examination he formed the impression that the skull could have belonged to the torso of William Moseley. The mummified, partially leatherized head was accompanied by a dark blue woollen balaclava with holes cut in areas consistent with the eyes and mouth, all wrapped in pages of the *Evening News* dated 16 June 1977 – the day the trial ended at the Old Bailey.

The head and the balaclava were extremely cold and moist to the touch and appeared to be in a state of thawing. Fractures were noted on both sides of the hyoid bone. A series of X-rays was taken and confirmed that there had been an almost intact set of natural teeth during life consistent with those of a man about forty years of age. There was chipping of an upper front tooth, which matched up with a police physical description of Moseley of 1973.

The X-ray revealed a fracture of the nose and a double fracture of the lower jaw, with the loss of a molar tooth in the left upper jaw. All the facial injuries were indicative of severe localized violence having been applied by or against the face shortly before death and could have been the cause of the bleeding within the skull box that led to death.

The cuts in the neck structure were made by an eighteen-teeth-per-inch Eclipse high-speed steel hacksaw blade and were consistent with those recorded from sections of the torso identified as that of William Moseley. Further X-ray pictures showed other identical points of comparison and unity.

At the end of his report Professor Cameron wrote:

The cause of death, in my opinion, was following severe head injuries and, taking into account the mutilation and violence described previously on the identified torso, I am in no way expressing any other opinion than previously, namely that death was due to acute head injury.

The state of the head when initially examined suggested that from the time of decapitation in 1974 it had had a number of resting places. The presence of earth and leaves indicates that at one time it would have been either on top of soil or because of the diffuse distribution of the earth it could well have been buried. The presence of a feather from a bird, a chicken or a turkey, could indicate that it had been in contact with feathered poultry either alive or dead, i.e. in a yard with poultry, a dustbin, butcher/poultry shop or a refrigerator to mention but a few places. The presence of paint suggests contact with such substances in a variety of ways. Suffice it to say such contact as described above must have been prior to the head being covered by the navy blue balaclava. The condition of the head on initial examination suggested that it had recently been removed from refrigeration in that it resembled a state of 'thawing out'. The state of mummification with leatherization of the skin could develop in varying modes of preservation.

The whole case had lasted nearly two years. There had been only mangled parts of a body found in the Thames to begin with, and then a second body which was more readily identified, followed by the skull. There were no initial clues, but Wickstead and his detectives had slowly gathered the evidence by penetrating the secrecy of the underworld.

The conspiring murderers had calculated that by dismembering Moseley's body, throwing the parts into different reaches of the Thames and removing the skull they had defeated any pathologist. They were sure the body could not be identified.

This had been a superb investigation, combining the skills of Commander Wickstead with those of Professor Cameron and his team whose identification of the torso was immaculate.

18
The Psychopath and the Priest

In the quiet village of Shorne in Kent, a few miles from Gravesend on the Thames estuary, a small cottage became the scene of a ghastly murder in March 1975. It was the home of sixty-four-year-old Father Crean, who was chaplain to St Catherine's, a small convent of Carmelite nuns who also ran an old people's home.

On the evening of 21 March Sister Thérèse, the Trinidadian Mother Superior, noticed that Father Crean had not collected his supper from the convent building so she took the tray with the food to his cottage. She found the front door locked and when she unlocked it Father Crean's dog ran in barking. She put the tray down in the kitchen, noticed the lights were on and the curtains drawn and called Father Crean. She called out again but there was no reply. However, she was not unduly worried and returned to the convent. It was nearly midnight when another nun noticed that the lights were still burning in the cottage and she went to investigate. She opened the bathroom door and saw the priest lying dead in the bath. Sister Thérèse was called and ran to the cottage. She saw the body fully dressed in a bath of blood and water and she called the police.

The duty officer at Gravesend police station went to Malt House Cottage and then telephoned his superior, Detective Inspector Kenneth Tappenden, telling him of the murder of Father Crean. Within twenty minutes he was at the house looking at the victim of a most brutal killing. The detective recognized the dead man and he also remembered an incident two years before when

Father Crean had tried to prevent the prosecution of a young local man who had stolen a cheque from him. Tappenden hastened back to the police station, despatched a message to Professor Cameron to attend, and then sent for the file on the Crean case of 1973. The man whom the priest had tried to help then was called Patrick Mackay.

Tappenden sent for Detective Sergeant Bob Brown, the man who had arrested Mackay for the theft. It was four o'clock in the morning when Brown got to Inspector Tappenden's office and teamed up with Detective Constable Mick Whitlock, who had also helped in the previous arrest. The Inspector gave them details of the case so far and told the detectives to bring in Mackay.

Cameron arrived at Malt House Cottage at 4.20 A.M. and Detective Chief Inspector Hart took him to the bathroom and showed him the body of Father Crean lying, fully clothed, in a bath of bloodstained water. Cameron's report read:

The small window in the bathroom was open and a traycloth was over the wash-hand basin. The pipe from the shower attachment appeared to have been torn off. The blood-stained water was up to the level of the overflow. There was much blood-staining of the top of the bath and all over the wall at the back of the bath and over the wall over the top of the bath with slight blood-staining over the edge of the front of the bath, but there was no evidence of water or dampness on the floor of the bathroom. No naked eye evidence of blood-stained marks on the taps of the washhand basin. The top of the head appeared to have had a towel wrapped over it. A sample was taken of the bath water and the level of the blood-stained water was marked before the plug, which did not have any attached chain, was removed to release the water. The body was removed from the bath and placed on a plastic body sheet. I remained at the scene whilst this was being carried out and whilst the body was totally wrapped within the body sheet and removed from the bathroom by police officers into the hall-way from which it was moved, in my presence, by the undertakers. In conjunction with Detective Superintendent Irvine I visited the other rooms in the house and was present when Superintendent Irvine found a box underneath the stairs in which there was a blood-stained axe. During this preliminary view of the scene I saw no evidence of a blood-stained cutting weapon. I remained at the scene until the body was removed to the mortuary.

Later the same day at 6 A.M. within the mortuary of Gravesend and North Kent Hospital, Bathstreet, Gravesend, I carried out a post-mortem examination on the body of the man previously identified to me by Detective Chief Inspector Hart as being Anthony Joseph Crean.

EXTERNAL EXAMINATION

The body was dressed in the following items of sodden, blood-stained clothing: Left wellington boot. Grey oversocks. Blue socks. Belted trousers, the zip of which was done up. Underpants. A scarf was around the neck. A green/blue blood-stained towel was over the head. Dark blue gaberdine short overcoat. Priest's black front, with a hole in the material to the left of the mid-line of the neck. Navy jacket. White shirt with cuff-links at the wrist. The shirt was done up with a stud at the back. Elastic armbands. Shortsleeved vest, done up in the front. Priest's collar with a cut to the left of the mid-line. White metal neckchain, with keys attached, around the neck. Body sheet.

In the right hand there appeared to be bloodstained brain tissue and there was dried blood in the left hand, but no rings were present on either hand and there were no 'defence' marks on either hand.

1 Bruising of the middle of the chest to the right of the mid-line.
2 Bruising to the upper chest three inches to the right of the mid-line.
3 No bruising of the right arm.
4 Bruising behind the lower left arm.
5 No bruising on the back.
6 Half-inch stab wound to the centre of the lower neck.
7 Half-inch stab wound three inches below the left ear.
8 Superficial stab wound, undercut from left to right, below the left jaw.

9 Below the left jaw there was a superficial stab wound three inches to the left of the mid-line of the chin.

10 Severe bruising of the chin, particularly on the left side, and severe bruising of the upper lip, with a lacerated abrasion to the left of the mid-line.

11 Half an inch stab wound one inch in front of the upper left ear.

12 A split laceration over the outer left eyebrow one and a half inches in length.

13 Split laceration over the outer corner of the left eye with blackening of the left eye and cheek.

14 Fracture of the nose with overlying bruising.

15 Abrasions of the neck, particularly on the left side.

16 A ragged wound to the centre of the forehead exposing brain and the underlying skull, including a semi-circular incised wound.

17 A similar compound wound of the upper left forehead.

18 There was a 'T-shaped' wound slightly to the left of the mid-line within the hair-line.

19 A 'Y-shaped' wound of the upper right forehead, extending to well within the hair-line.

20 Two semi-circular wounds to the right of the mid-line of the top of the head, the wounds three and five inches respectively above the right ear.

21 There was a fracture of the left cheek-bone (zygome).

Head and Neck

The laceration of the inner left upper lip extended to the frenum and the first left pre-molar was loosened with a fracture of the right incisor teeth, which were also loosened. There was bruising to the tongue. There was deep bruising of the inner aspect of the right collar-bone. There were extensive fractures of the skull, particularly towards the front, with severe bruising and laceration of the underlying brain, the brain having been retained for fixation and further examination.

Thorax

The lungs, which were waterlogged (oedema), showed evidence of a penetrating wound in the right upper apex with slight bleeding into the chest cavity. The heart revealed no abnormality that could have caused or contributed to death at that particular moment in time.

Abdomen

No abnormality could be detected in any of the abdominal organs, the bladder being full.

Samples taken by me and handed to Police Constable Street the Scenes of Crime Officer, included:
1) Sample of head hair   2) Items of clothing
3) Body sheet   4) Sample of urine
5) Sample of blood

Samples taken and retained by me included:
1) Skull vault   2) Brain
3) Neck structure, including lungs
4) Samples of routine organs for histological examination

SUMMARY

1 The body was that of a well-nourished man, five feet in height.
2 No evidence of natural disease that could have caused or contributed to death at that particular moment in time.
3 Evidence of extensive compound fracture of the skull, particularly towards the front, with bruising and laceration of the underlying brain; the majority of these wounds being caused by a heavy object, such as the axe I was shown at the scene, used with considerable force against the head.
4 There were multiple superficial stab wounds, only one of which penetrated any depth, the stab wounds in themselves having no bearing on the cause of death.
5 No marks on the body to indicate that the deceased had attempted to defend himself, i.e. no 'defence-type' wounds were noted.

OPINION

The cause of death in my opinion was:
1 Cerebral contusions and lacerations

2 Compound fractured skull

While Cameron was busy the two detectives, Brown and Whitlock, had started their hunt for Patrick Mackay. They had first called at the only address in their file, that of Mackay's mother at 22 Frobisher Way, Gravesend. She told them she had not seen her son since the previous year, and repeated questions elicited the same answer. Although they sensed she was lying, they had to accept her story. They searched her house and the garden but found nothing, so they drove to Scotland Yard, went to the Criminal Record Office to check Mackay's address but found there was none given on his record. The only name was that of the Reverend Black – no initials, no denomination and no address. Although most of the people of London were still asleep on that Saturday morning, the detectives began to make telephone calls. After two hours of disturbing the sleepy clergy of the city they discovered Black's address, a house in Finchley.

Thirty minutes later the Reverend Black answered his door to the detectives. He said he had not seen Patrick Mackay for months. When they told him that they were investigating a murder, Black said that he thought Mackay lived at a probation hostel on the Great North Road.

As Brown and Whitlock walked into the building shortly afterwards they heard the manager of the hostel talking on the telephone and heard him say, 'Yes, Patrick' to the person at the other end of the line. They introduced themselves and told him who they were looking for and why. The manager had in fact just been speaking to Mackay, who lived in the hostel. He had not seen Mackay for a few days since he was not compelled to stay there and he agreed to co-operate with the police by getting Mackay's whereabouts if he telephoned again and not mentioning that they had called.

The detectives searched the room Mackay used when he was in the hostel but there was nothing there which helped. Then they interviewed other men in the building and, in particular, the man who lived in the room next to Mackay. He suggested they looked on the other side of the river, in Clapham or Stockwell, because Mackay had mentioned that he had a friend there called Cowdrey. It was a lead. Two local detectives were left at the hostel in case Mackay returned and Brown and Whitlock went back to the Criminal Record Office to check on the name of Cowdrey. They drew a blank and, since they had been working for twenty hours non-stop, they decided to get some sleep.

Early next morning the Kent detectives got clearance from the Metropolitan Police to search in South London and Inspector Tappenden sent up a squad of eight policemen to help them. Sergeant Brown searched through the electoral roll and made a note of every address where anyone named Cowdrey lived. Just after 11 A.M. he briefed his men and said, 'The first house is 48, Grantham Road.'

Sergeant Brown knocked at the door and it was opened wide – wide enough for Detective Whitlock to see Patrick Mackay in the passageway behind his friend. Within seconds the detectives had him handcuffed and out in the street.

Sergeant Brown introduced himself and said, 'I arrested you in Gravesend for the theft of a cheque from Father Crean. I'd like to ask you some questions at the police station in connection with his murder.' He then cautioned Mackay and took him to nearby Tooting police station where within half an hour Mackay had confessed to the killing. He was moved to Northfleet police station where the questioning was taken over by Inspectors Hart and Tappenden. Almost immediately Mackay agreed to make a statement and Chief Inspector Hart wrote at his dictation:

Statement of Patrick David Mackay
Age: 22 years (born 25.9.52)
Occupation: Unemployed gardener
Address: 38, Great North Road, East Finchley, N.2.

'I, Patrick David Mackay, wish to make a statement. I want someone to write down what I say. I have been told that I need not say anything unless I wish to do so and what I say may be given in evidence. I went to Gravesend last Friday afternoon, 21 March 1975. I won a chicken in a raffle like I told you and took it home for my mother to cook for me. I talked with my mother but I was only at home for about fifteen minutes. I'm not at all sure about the times but I left the house about half past four. I walked to Father Crean's house at Shorne. From my own house I went along Thong Lane to a country lane that branches off from Thong Lane. I walked all along that lane past the school at Shorne, through Thorne village, past the Rose and Crown, turned left and down the hill to Father Crean's house. When I got there I saw the front door was just slightly ajar, just enough to put a finger in. I saw his car there and I saw smoke from a bonfire at the back of the house so I knew Father Crean was in. I pushed the door open and a little dog brushed past my legs and ran out of the door. It was Father Crean's dog. I had seen it when I have been there before. I don't know where the dog went but I think it might have run out of the gate. I went into the hall of the house and called, "Mr Crean. Are you there?" I wanted to talk with him over this money because things were unsettled the last I saw him. There was no reply so I knocked on the door to the left. It was locked. From there I walked to the back of the hall where there was a bike. I stood around waiting for him. From there I decided to go into the kitchen. I looked through his bedroom door to see if he was in and if he might not have been asleep – this is the bedroom on the ground floor. As he wasn't there I went upstairs and had a look round up there. Then I came back downstairs and waited in his bedroom doorway for his return. After about five minutes, this is from the time I first went into the house, I heard the front door open and then saw Mr Crean come into the hall. He didn't seem to see me. He unlocked the door to his front room.

He seemed to be standing in the doorway, doing something to his pipe, I think lighting it. I walked up to him and when I was about an arm's length away I said, "Mr Crean, it's me, Patrick Mackay." He had his back to me. He turned round and he shouted, "Oh God, I wasn't expecting to see you here." I said, "I've come to talk things over about the money I owe you." He seemed to panic a bit and started to run out of the house. This seemed to upset me a bit as I had basically come to explain things to him about this money. I grabbed hold of him by his arm, I think the right one, and we both fell on the floor in the hallway. I struggled and he struggled on the floor and he seemed to be extremely nervy. He said, "Don't hurt me." This seemed to get me even more excitable myself and then I started to strike him on the side of the head with my hand and with my fist. The next thing I knew he had broken loose from my grip and ran into the bathroom which is just off the hallway. Whilst I had been on the floor of the hallway myself I picked up an axe from a box lying just under the stairs and I began to feel even more excitable. I pulled out a knife from my pocket – no, that is wrong – that was later. He shut the bathroom door and pushed to hold it closed. I barged my side of the door and this pushed him towards the bath. He tumbled and half fell into the bath. I threw down the axe on to the floor and pushed him into the bath. He then started to annoy me even more and I kept striking at his nose with my arm and the side of my hand. I then pulled out my knife from my coat pocket and repeatedly plunged it into his neck. I then got a little more excitable and stuck it into the side of his head and then tried to plunge it into the top of his head. This bent the knife. I grabbed for the axe and with this repeatedly lashed out with it at his head. He sank into the bath. He had been in the sitting-up position with the knife, but when I first hit him with the axe he sank down into the bath. I then repeatedly got increasingly more annoyed and lashed at him with the axe. All this seemed to happen very fast. I threw the axe to the floor, ripped the plug from the wash-basin and rammed it into the bath, then turned on the taps. I had mainly the cold water tap on but I'm not sure whether I turned them off or left them at the time I left. I believe I may have turned them off. I then turned on the bathroom light, his bedroom light and his hall light. Then I stayed in the bathroom for about an hour. I was just watching him sinking and floating about in the bath and I then walked out of the house and walked round to the back of the house picking up bits and pieces of cinders from the fire, just mucking about, doodling in a sense. Then I went back in the house and into the bathroom and stayed there for about a quarter of an hour. I then thought of the chicken at my mother's house and walked out of his house altogether. I passed his car on the way out and walked to the right of the gate. This took me on to a narrow country lane which I walked up. I turned to my right and this took me back to the lane I originally used to travel down to his home. I walked along there and this took me about an hour. My throat seemed very dry and I saw a cottage. I went through a gate, knocked on the door and asked a man for a drink of water. He gave me one. I thanked him and walked home for the chicken at my mother's house. I talked to her and she gave me the chicken and I ate most of it there. I caught a bus into town, went to the pictures like I told you and caught a train to Waterloo. I threw the knife into the Thames from Hungerford Bridge on realizing I had it in my pocket. I had thrown the axe into the tool-box in the hall after I left the bathroom. The other knife I told Mr Brown about today I kept. I'm not sure whether I used this knife at the house or whether I kept it in my pocket. The only thing I want to add is it didn't seem to trouble me too much what I had done on hearing it was in the papers.

'Signed: P. Mackay'

At that time the killer, a well-built man over six feet tall, handsome in a coarse fashion, was twenty-two years old. He had watched his victim floating in the bath for an hour and sometime in that hour Father Crean had died. It was as well that the detectives had made a speedy arrest, for Patrick David Mackay was a psychopath with a terrible record of violent crime.

Shortly before the killing of Father Crean there had been a spate of muggings of elderly women in Chelsea. The officer in charge of the investigation was Detective Superintendent John Bland, the man who had arrested Frederick Sewell for the murder of Superintendent Richardson at Blackpool and who had helped to arrest the Hosein brothers who kidnapped and murdered the wife of a newspaper executive. At the scene of one of the muggings Bland had found a thumbprint on a teaspoon and he had submitted that clue to the fingerprint department at Scotland Yard. The print was identified as belonging to Patrick Mackay, who by then was being held in custody at Brixton prison charged with Father Crean's murder.

Bland went to Brixton to interview Mackay and, to his surprise, was given a confession not only to many of the muggings but also to the murders of Adele Price and Isabella Griffiths. Mrs Price was killed in her home in Lowndes Square, Belgravia, on 10 March 1975, and Mrs Griffiths at her Chelsea home in February 1974. And not only did Mackay confess but he gave a wealth of detail which left the detective with absolutely no doubt that he was telling the truth.

During his weeks on remand Mackay told his fellow prisoners of eleven killings for which he claimed to be responsible and, since none of the cases had been solved, there were relays of detectives at the prison, hoping to clear their books.

He was questioned about the murder of Heidi Mnilk, a pretty seventeen-year-old blonde from West Germany who was working as an au pair at Bromley, Kent. She was stabbed in the throat on a train leaving London Bridge and her body thrown out on the track. Mackay was put up for identification but was not picked out.

Twelve days after that murder Miss Mary Hynes, a seventy-three-year-old Irish spinster, was found dead in her flat in Kentish Town, North West London. She was savagely battered about the head with a piece of wood, her stockings stuffed in her mouth and her body covered with an eiderdown. The killer carefully locked the front door on his way out. Mackay was interviewed by Detective Chief Inspector John Harris and mentioned details that could only have been known to the killer, such as the fact that the back door had been nailed shut. Harris charged Mackay, but the case was left on the file – that is to say, it could be reopened only by the order of a judge at the Old Bailey.

In January 1974 wealthy Stephanie Britton, a fifty-seven-year-old widow, was stabbed to death at her home at Hadley Green, Hertfordshire. Her four-year-old grandson, Christopher Martin, was also murdered at the same time. An inmate of Brixton told police that Mackay had confessed to that crime, though he denied it to the police. It is interesting to note, however, that when Superintendent Bland was questioning Mackay about the killing of Isabella Griffiths in Chelsea he said that he had pinned her body to the floorboards when he stabbed her. That was not the fact in that case, but whoever killed Mrs Britton had pinned her body to the floor with a knife. Again, Mackay was not charged since there was insufficient evidence.

It was also Superintendent Bland who listened as Mackay gave him details of a down-and-out meths drinker he had killed in January 1974. Mackay said that one night, after drinking his fill of whisky, he had walked across Hungerford Bridge, which is a railway bridge with a parallel footbridge, and bumped into a vagrant who swore at him. Mackay's response was to throw him over the bridge into the Thames. But several bodies are recovered from the Thames each month and none could be associated with Mackay. There was no evidence and no charge was made.

Mackay also gave some details about the murder of a tobacconist in Rock Street, Finsbury Park, North London. The victim, sixty-two-year-old Frank Goodman, was about to close his shop on the evening of 15 June

1974, and was putting on his overcoat when a last customer entered the shop. Without warning the man attacked him with a piece of lead piping, raining fourteen blows on his head. He fell dead, and his assailant dragged the body behind the shop counter. The till was emptied and the only clue was a bloody footprint.

Under questioning Mackay remembered a great deal, but not the actual killing. But he did recall throwing away a pair of bloodstained boots at Paddington Cemetery, and when he was taken there by a detective the boots were found. Blood on the boots matched that of the dead man and Mackay was again charged but the case left on the file.

He was asked if he had murdered ninety-two-year-old spinster Sarah Rodwell at her flat in Hackney, East London, in December 1974. She was beaten to death with blows on the head and her £5 Christmas bonus was missing. He denied all knowledge and established an alibi.

Another case the police considered was that of Mrs Ivy Davies, the fifty-four-year-old owner of the Orange Tree Café at Southend-on-Sea, Essex. On the evening of 9 February 1975 she closed the café and went home to her house in nearby Holland Road where she was attacked and killed with an axe. Professor Cameron was called to that murder and reported that death was due to a single blow. There was no motive and not a single clue.

Mackay admitted that he knew the café and that he had considered robbing Mrs Davies, but swore he had not been in Southend since 1972, more than two years before the murder.

In the end Mackay was charged with the murders of Isabella Griffiths, Adele Price, Father Anthony Crean, Frank Goodman and Mary Hynes. He also admitted two robberies of old people and asked for twenty-four more to be considered.

He pleaded guilty on the grounds of diminished responsibility to the manslaughter of Mrs Isabella Griffiths, Mrs Adele Price and Father Crean. Evidence from many psychiatrists was the reason for the acceptance of the plea. Two of them agreed that Mackay had 'a gross personality disorder' and another said he had 'a severe psychopathic disorder'. And the Superintendent of Broadmoor, Dr MacGrath, who had examined Mackay, wrote, 'As a result of my examination I have serious doubts as to whether at this point Mackay is adequately motivated to the extent that he would accept or be susceptible to treatment.'

Patrick Mackay received the same sentence he would have been given if he had pleaded guilty to murder – life imprisonment.

To this day there are senior detectives who believe he committed many more murders, and they are critical of a number of mental institutions from whence Mackay had been discharged against the advice of his doctors. Indeed, a Home Office psychiatrist in 1968, when Mackay was fifteen years old, described him as a 'cold psychopathic killer'. That was long before his first murder.

The killing of Father Crean was the climax of a spectacular career of robbery, violence and murder which began when Mackay was the unhappy child of a desperately miserable home and a cold institutional upbringing, a man who lost control once his instincts were aroused, who drank too much and, whatever he did, felt no remorse. It ended when he was arrested after killing Father Crean, one of the few people who had ever befriended him. They had met by chance walking in the woods near Shorne, talked and gone to a public house for a drink. They became friendly and Mackay introduced

Crean to his mother. A few months later Mackay, short of money, broke into Father Crean's cottage and stole a £30 cheque, changed the figures to £80, and the words as well, and cashed the cheque at the local Barclays Bank.

It had been a routine investigation for the Gravesend CID, and Detective Sergeant Bob Brown had arrested Mackay. When Father Crean heard he went to the police station and pleaded that the charges be dropped. The police refused to do that, but when Mackay appeared at court he was fined £20 for breaking and entering and was given a two-year conditional discharge. He was also ordered to repay the £80 to Father Crean and promised to pay the money at the rate of £7 a week. That was in May 1973 and by March 1975 no money had been paid. Mackay arrived at the cottage to talk, he said, about the money he owed, but instead of repaying the debt, or any part of it, Mackay destroyed the man who had given him friendship.

19
The Teddy Bear Murders

The case that follows is a long and involved one, and Professor Cameron played no part in it until the police had found evidence of murder. He did not know, and the police did not know, that a spectacular and well-planned robbery would eventually lead to the detection of six callous and brutal murders. It is a story which really illustrates the cliché of the long arm of the law. One crime involving little violence was solved and then, suddenly, the pathologist found himself confronted with one of the nastiest cases in criminal history which involved him in imaginative and disgusting methods of proving the evidence.

On a sweltering morning in an English summer, 20 June 1979, a small van stopped outside a public lavatory in the High Street of the county town of Hertford. Two men dressed in blue overalls jumped out. As a third drove the van away into the traffic the two men, both carrying crash helmets, walked into the lavatory, took a cubicle each and locked the doors. Minutes later they emerged, wearing the crash helmets and the green and gold uniforms of Security Express, one of the biggest carriers of cash and high-value cargoes in Britain.

This was the first overt move in one of the most brilliantly conceived robberies ever committed, netting more than £500,000 in negotiable cash. But although the execution of the robbery was faultless the thieves had already made one mistake which was to be their undoing.

Soon after ten o'clock the two men in their uniforms sauntered away from the public lavatory and stopped outside a branch of the Midland Bank in Fore Street, only fifty yards from where they had changed clothes. There they waited in a shop doorway. At 10.35 A.M. a Security Express van pulled up and stopped outside the bank. Two guards got out, went into the bank and delivered a small parcel of money, came out and got into the van. As the second of them went to close the door a powerful man suddenly appeared in the doorway and held it open. In his other hand he held a gun. 'This is a hold-up. Get in!' he said.

Two armed robbers climbed in behind their guns and ordered the genuine three-man uniformed crew to stay quiet and obey orders. The man who appeared to be the leader wore a beard and he told the driver to take the van to a nearby bus depot and stop. There the door was wrenched open and another robber in Security Express uniform got in. He too carried a gun. One of the bandits was powerfully built and well over six feet tall, the other two were slight. Now there was a gun levelled at each member of the crew, and the man who had already established himself as leader said, 'We will shoot if we have to. Just do what you're told.'

The leader had done his homework, for he had bought his information from an employee of Security Express. He knew that the schedule for the day was at 11.15 A.M. to call at a bank in Hatfield seven miles away to collect money. He instructed the driver to proceed as scheduled.

At Hatfield the leader ordered the driver to stay in the van and left two of his men to hold him at gunpoint. He then ordered the other two guards out and walked to the bank behind them, his gun concealed under his jacket. He said, 'Do everything like normal. Give the password, collect the cash and sign for it.' Inside the bank the cashier was waiting with four bags of cash and a welcoming 'Good morning, chaps.' The password was given, the money

signed for by one of the genuine guards and with a
'Cheerio', the little procession walked slowly back to the
van. The bandits were £200,000 richer.

Then the driver was told to go to St Albans, and at
another bank the same routine was followed and four
more bags of money went into the van. There was not a
single hitch and few words were spoken except by the
gang leader who gave directions in a terse, threatening
voice. His next instruction to the driver was to go to a
transport café called the Waterloo, near Bricket Wood,
at the junction of the A405 and the M1. On the way the
leader said, 'It was a bloody disaster last time we had a
go at you. But we're better organized this time, so we're
taking you to the cleaners.' It was no idle boast, for in
the van was £524,109.

The same little nondescript van which earlier had
dropped the two men in Hertford was parked in a far
corner of the large car park of the café and the money
was transferred in seconds. The three guards were tied
up and gagged and before the bandits left the gang leader
warned, 'There is a bomb attached to the van which I can
detonate by remote control. I will let it go in forty
minutes. After that it will become harmless.' Then he
slammed the door of the security van, joined the others
in their van and was driven off.

Next stop was the car park of a big public house near
Romford, where a white BMW 320 was parked. It was a
happy party of four thieves as they drew up and jumped
out. The leader, who owned the BMW car, felt for his
keys and the laughter died away. He could not find
them although he turned out every pocket. Then he
remembered. He had left them in the overalls he had
discarded in the lavatory in Hertford. There was an angry
scene, for he had wanted to take the overalls with him
and the man who had been with him had said, 'Don't be

so fucking stupid. Whoever heard of going on a robbery with a pair of overalls over your arm?' He had allowed himself to be dissuaded.

A quick council of war reached the decision that it was too late to go back to the lavatory to collect the overalls and the keys because they knew the Security Express van would be overdue and therefore reported missing. Almost certainly the police would have been alerted and radio cars would be combing the whole of Hertfordshire. But there was one last chance. In the boot was a spare ignition key and in the van was a jemmy. The boot was forced, the key retrieved and the money loaded into the boot.

The four men, now growling in ill humour, shook hands. They had made all their arrangements for the future and there was nothing to be discussed. The leader drove off with the lid of the boot tied down with string and the others packed into the van and were driven to Hertford and dropped to go their separate ways.

The time was now one o'clock. The crew of the Security Express had waited for forty minutes then managed to free themselves and radio to headquarters that they had been hijacked. Detective Chief Superintendent Neil Dickens, head of Hertfordshire CID, was informed by radio and took over the case. He had the crew of the security van taken to Hertford police station for interrogation while the van itself was taken to the police headquarters at Welwyn Garden City and searched for clues and in the forlorn hope that at least one of the thieves had left a fingerprint. Descriptions of the hijackers given by the crew of the security van were rushed out on police radio and the national press picked it up. All that Dickens really discovered, though, was that one of the crooks was over six feet tall and the others about five feet eight, all aged between thirty and forty, and that the man who appeared to be the leader wore a beard.

The national press carried the story next morning with headlines like 'Bomb Scare Gang Get £400,000' – a police under-estimation of the sum stolen. One report said that the gang was once bottom of the bunglers' league because the police had deduced, from the descriptions, that the same gang had tried to hijack the Security Express van in September 1978 which ended in a fiasco. On that occasion the gang had fled empty-handed, leaving stolen getaway cars and gun behind. It was the throw-away remark by one of the bandits about the last time they had raided that gave the clue.

But apart from that the thieves had vanished and so had the loot.

Detective Superintendent Neil Dickens, only forty-two years of age, slim and well dressed, was no stranger to investigating serious crime, but on this job he was woefully short of leads. He had the sketchy descriptions and that was all. Minute examination of the van had yielded nothing, and the well-known police method of seeking a tip from underworld informants had failed. On Thursday and Friday teams of detectives toured the routes taken by the hijackers, calling at public houses, shops, garages, asking if anyone had seen any strangers to the area or anyone dressed in the distinctive green and gold uniform of Security Express. They drew a complete blank.

An incident room had been set up at Hertford police station and such details as were available were circulated to all police forces in the two regular publications, the *Police Gazette* and *Informations*. Scotland Yard's Central Robbery Squad, a highly specialist group with immense experience, were consulted. Since 1976 its detectives had been dealing with high-grade informants, criminals they had caught committing robbery who, facing a long term of imprisonment because of the overwhelming evidence against them, had decided to tell on their fellows. Crime reporters gave them a new name: supergrasses. But with all their knowledge and experience of the movements of the underworld, they were unable to help.

On the Saturday morning Neil Dickens gave another briefing to his squad. He told them to search the routes again and to think of places they had not searched before. 'Try the most unlikely places,' he told them. 'I don't know what you will find but I'm certain they must have stopped somewhere either to change clothes or transfer the money. Nothing is too trivial to be overlooked.'

That day came the great breakthrough. A team of police led by Detective Constable Roger Hawes prowled along the High Street in Hertford, spotted the public lavatory and went in. They inquired of the attendant if he had found anything abandoned since the previous Wednesday. He told them he had found two pairs of blue overalls, each one in a pay cubicle. He had put them aside in his office, thinking that the owners would return to collect them. The detectives took them and went through the pockets. In one was a set of car keys, two keys on a ring. They were BMW keys and both were numbered. On the ring also was a garage tab of a firm in Upminster, Essex, which the police knew specialized in BMW cars.

Superintendent Dickens sent a detective to the garage to check the keys. He discovered they would fit only a BMW 320. Patiently, he went through the list of all cars sold by the garage in recent years. The detective noted the names and addresses of the purchasers and the engine and chassis numbers of their cars. The garage proprietor explained that as a measure of security BMW issued different keys, one called the 'chauffeur's key' which would open the car door and switch on the ignition. But it would not open either the boot or the glove compartment. The other key – the 'owner's key' – would operate everything.

While the detectives still hunted for any other clues, no matter how slender, Dickens called Interpol, the international criminal police organization, for which the United Kingdom operated an office at Scotland Yard. Detective Superintendent Michael Purchase directed all Interpol inquiries at that time and it was to him that Dickens gave details of the keys and the engine and chassis numbers of all the BMW 320s sold by the Essex garage.

In the German factory the details were fed into their computer. Seconds later the card spelt it out. There was only one car in the world which could possibly have that combination of the two keys. That car, said the computer, had been sold to a garage in Essex. It named it. The computer then added the engine and chassis numbers of the car.

The man who had bought it was Philip Cohen, The Chase, Nags Head Lane, Upminster, Essex. A few fast inquiries revealed that Cohen was a wealthy greengrocer with several shops, a large, detached house in a four-acre garden, a second car, a power boat and a reputation among friends for being a big spender.

On the Sunday morning, four days after the sensational robbery, Dickens, with two of his men, called on Mr Cohen. On the way to the house through the large and well-kept grounds they saw a BMW 320 and noticed that the boot had been forced. Cohen, well dressed and clean shaven, walked into the drive and Dickens introduced himself and his party and said he was making inquiries into a robbery and perhaps Cohen could help him. Cohen saw Dickens looking at the broken lock of the boot and he explained that he had lost his car keys and had had to force the boot.

Dickens suggested that Mr Cohen might like to accompany him to the police station in Hertford to help in inquiries and, in particular, to explain how his car keys had come to be found in the pocket of a suit of overalls in a Hertford public lavatory.

The interrogation of men suspected of crime is a fine art of patience and perseverance, of remembering what is said without taking notes, of going back and forth over ground without seeming to penetrate too deeply, of cups of tea or coffee. After two days of questioning, during which he was kept in a cell, Philip Cohen said he felt he was causing embarrassment to some of his employees who had innocently helped with an alibi, because he had told them he had spent two days with his girlfriend in Brighton. He then admitted his part in the robbery.

It was then that Dickens had a sergeant take notes while he conducted the questioning. Cohen told the detectives exactly how the robbery was carried out, who had taken part and where £465,106 was buried. He explained that £59,003 of the loot had been used to pay his fellow crooks and to defray general expenses. He told of the share-out which had taken place at his house on the night of the robbery.

On the afternoon of the day of the raid he had dug a large hole in his garden, burned the wrappers of the notes, all stamped with the bank of origin, and buried the money which he had put into plastic sacks to keep it dry. He also told of burning the Security Express uniforms.

Now Dickens had the names of the robbery team.

They were Henry Jeremiah Mackenny, John Childs, aged thirty-nine, of Dolphin House, Poplar High Street, Limehouse, East London; Leonard Willsher, aged forty-six, a stallholder of Chargeable Lane, Plaistow; and Christopher Grieve, aged thirty-four of Green Lane, Ilford. Grieve was the driver of the hijacked security van and also the spy who had supplied the gang with all the information they needed.

Dickens organized a strong team of detectives, some of them armed, and the three addresses were raided after being surrounded. The three men were taken without any trouble, but there was no sign of Mackenny although a number of houses where it was thought he might be found were raided.

Cohen, Childs, Willsher and Grieve were all charged with the robbery, having all made statements admitting their guilt. They all appeared at Hertford Magistrates Court and were remanded in custody.

Cohen now felt himself able to be helpful again. When asked the whereabouts of Mackenny, the man the guards had described as 'over six feet tall', he told an amazing story of how he and Mackenny had constructed what they thought was a watertight alibi for the robbery. The alibi was elaborate and costly and it was necessary, particularly from Mackenny's point of view, because he was so easily recognizable. He is six feet four inches tall and although he crouched through the robbery to make himself less noticeable, he still felt very vulnerable.

One week before the robbery Mackenny had collected his recently widowed mistress, Mrs Gwen Andrews, and her two teenage children from their home in Barkingside and flown with them to Marseilles. It was essential for his plan that he make himself as conspicuous as possible. He had used his own passport, filled in the yellow disembarkation card in the plane during the flight and made sure that his passport was stamped as he handed it in with the card at the immigration desk at Marignane airport.

The stamp, he felt, would help to prove that he was in France when the Hertfordshire robbery took place. To back up the documentary proof he also wanted to get to know some people who would genuinely establish him in the south of France. He had £1,000 'expenses' advanced by Philip Cohen, in his pocket. He had used some of this, as had been planned, to be seen in the cafés and clubs frequented by English visitors, spending lavishly with anyone he found in the hope they would remember him.

He had booked into a small, family hotel on the coast just outside Marseilles, but he did not know that the immigration laws had been changed. It was no longer necessary for EEC passport holders to fill in police forms with all the vital statistics and hand them in with their passports to the hotel reception clerk. Mackenny had planned that such a form would add even more weight to his alibi. The other thing he did not know, or bother to find out, was that unless the authorities had some concrete reason for suspecting a traveller's motives, the yellow disembarkation cards filled in were destroyed after a few weeks. The French police and immigration were at that stage unaware that Mackenny was anything other than what he was – a tourist.

At five o'clock on Sunday morning, 17 June, he had got up, left some money with Mrs Andrews and the children, and told them to move to a caravan camp. While paying the hotel bill he told the proprietor that he was going ahead to make arrangements to make a small tour of the area. Then he caught a taxi to Marignane airport, bought a single ticket to Paris and boarded the 0720 airbus flight UP 858.

For a tall man he now faced a most difficult task – making himself as inconspicuous as possible. The core of his alibi was to be that he had remained in France, and he could not afford to be noticed travelling.

He arrived at Orly Airport at 0840, took a taxi to the Gare du Nord where he had coffee and made the second of two telephone calls to Cohen. The first had been to the house in Upminster, and now the second was to a pre-arranged number in Brighton. Cohen had driven to Brighton in the BMW 320, where his power boat *Uzima* was riding berth on pontoon 17 in the marina. The arrangement made in the telephone call to Brighton was for Mackenny to meet Cohen at the telecommunications centre in Boulogne at two o'clock and thence to be taken across the Channel in the power boat and smuggled into Newhaven to hide until the morning of the robbery and then attend the final briefing.

In Paris that Sunday morning after the telephone call Mackenny thought he had plenty of time to spare and wandered around the Gare du Nord area, window shopping and enjoying a quiet breakfast in a café near the station. But at half past ten, when he went to the information desk, he realized that he could not get to Boulogne in time. There was no plane available so he found a taxi, bargained with the driver for a trip to Boulogne and paid him double fare in advance. He was driven the 150 miles and arrived with ten minutes to spare. There he met Cohen who was accompanied by an attractive young woman.

Cohen warned him not to talk about the project in front of the woman and all three took a taxi to the yacht basin where they boarded the *Uzima*, a blue and white Fairy Seafish. The power boat roared across the Channel to Newhaven, where Mackenny walked ashore and joined Cohen and the woman in a restaurant. Then Cohen piloted *Uzima* to her normal berth at Brighton marina, said goodbye to his woman friend and drove Mackenny to Upminster. On the way he gave Mackenny the details of the robbery plan.

After the robbery Mackenny had lain low for three days and nights, hidden by Cohen in an outhouse in the grounds of the house in Upminster, and on the early

evening of Saturday, 23 June, he had begun his journey
back to Marseilles. It was the same night that Detective
Superintendent Dickens was waiting for the identification
of the keys.

He had decided to go by train and for more than an
hour he waited at Victoria, only a quarter of a mile from
Scotland Yard, for the train to Newhaven. From there he
took the ferry to Dieppe and then a train to Paris. At
Orly he caught the airbus to Marseilles and rejoined Mrs
Andrews and the children. That was on the Sunday
morning, about the same time as his partner in crime,
Philip Cohen, was disturbed by Dickens asking questions
about the car keys found in the lavatory. Mackenny was
confident. No whisper of any hue and cry had reached
him and he felt certain he had got away safely. He
relaxed, made sure he was seen regularly in a number of
cafés and restaurants, and enjoyed himself swimming,
lying in the sun and playing with the children.

After a further three days in custody, Cohen decided
to talk again. This time he said something of such gravity
that even the hardened and experienced Dickens found it
hard to believe. Cohen said that although he knew that
robbery was a serious offence he knew that two of the
team, Childs and Mackenny, had committed two murders.
He said he had no proof and that he had had nothing to
do with the killings but that he was sure he was right. It
was the first intimation of a series of the most macabre
gangland executions ever known in Scotland Yard's history. But for Cohen's carelessness in leaving his keys in a
suit of overalls, it is more than likely they would have
gone undiscovered.

The police station in Hertford, where the robbers were
held in custody, is small, as befits a semi-rural area with
little serious crime. As a result the three other men soon
got wind that Cohen was talking to the police, although

they were not sure what he had said. Like all criminals, they began to calculate their chances and decided to follow suit. First, Christopher Grieve admitted to being the driver of the van as an employee of Security Express. He claimed to have known John Childs for many months and had suggested other raids to him, supplying all the necessary information. In fact, he said, he had been what is known in the world of spies as a 'sleeper', working regularly and marking time for the right job to come along, where all the circumstances were propitious. The journey to collect money on 20 June was the one he had recommended. He had known the route, the banks to be visited and more or less the amount of money available.

Leonard Willsher told the detectives he was just a hired hand for the day. He had been chosen because he was reliable under pressure and could handle a gun.

Childs, whose sharp mind had realized that Cohen had been giving the detectives information, and probably, by that co-operation, was putting himself in an advantageous position, decided to tell his story. He admitted that he had previous convictions and that he had helped plan the robbery. He had not been seen by the guards because his role had been to drive the van – a former prison van – to drop Cohen and Mackenny at the lavatory in Hertford, then pick up the money from the Waterloo café car park and, finally, transfer it to the BMW. He said he lived in a small council flat with his wife and two children and that he worked sometimes as a driver.

Superintendent Dickens decided to seek the aid of Scotland Yard's Central Robbery Squad and called Detective Chief Inspector Tony Lundy who was in charge of a section of the Robbery Squad based at Finchley, not far from Hertfordshire. Lundy is one of the great experts on robbery in London and has been responsible for clearing up literally hundreds of major crimes. It was he who by guile and gentleness persuaded many of the men he arrested to 'grass' on their fellow criminals. In that way, in recent years, he has solved many cases of robbery. He also has an uncanny knack for getting information from lesser crooks whose criminal sights are lower but who sometimes pick up the odd piece of crucial information. Lundy drove over to Hertford, conferred with Neil Dickens and together they chatted to Cohen. They took him back over the robbery and then asked about the mention he had made of murder. He reiterated that it was only rumour but that he believed it was true that Childs and Mackenny were the people involved.

Later the two detectives saw Childs who, although visibly shaken, denied all knowledge of murder. The questioning went on for several hours and, although Childs did not shift his ground noticeably, there were one or two answers which gave the detectives food for thought.

In the end Lundy decided to write a full report because Cohen had suggested the murders had taken place in London and within the Metropolitan Police district. It was therefore his responsibility to bring it to the notice of his superiors. That night he wrote the report and took it up to the chief of the Murder Squad, Detective Chief Superintendent Arthur Howard, who consulted the senior echelons of detectives, in particular Gilbert Kelland, the Assistant Chief Constable (Crime). Kelland decided that the Yard would take over the investigation.

The man chosen for the task, although not the first 'in the frame' (the Murder Squad term for the next man available), was Detective Chief Superintendent Frank Cater, a veteran murder investigator who also had an unrivalled knowledge of London's gangs. He had worked on the Kray case, the Richardson 'Torture Trial' case in 1966 and many other investigations into organized crime.

At that time he was working on allegations of a series of assaults in the Tower Bridge area of East London, but he was called off that inquiry and into the Yard to be briefed by Gilbert Kelland. Cater chose Detective Inspector Geoffrey Foxall to be his assistant, another policeman with a profound knowledge of East London who had been working on the Murder Squad for three years. The two made an interesting-looking team: Cater, tall, lean, fair-haired, bespectacled and stern, and Foxall, broad, plump and avuncular.

The two detectives first travelled to Hertford to speak to Philip Cohen and questioned him for several days, but only for about two hours at a time. It was gentle but effective and when the Chief Superintendent left he was convinced that the story of murder was almost certainly true and that John Henry Childs was probably the key.

Cater sent Inspector Foxall to the Criminal Record Office at Scotland Yard to find the names of people who had been reported missing in recent years. At the Criminal Record Office there are more than two million files on criminals and a wealth of detail about suspected crimes. The men who work there have an encyclopaedic memory for related facts, for strange happenings and for criminal associations. Among the names they turned up were George Brett, a thirty-five-year-old haulage contractor of Upminster, Essex, and his ten-year-old son, Terry; Terence Eve, a small-time crook from Ilford; Robert Brown, a thirty-six-year-old absconder from prison, last seen in Dagenham; Frederick Sherwood, the forty-eight-year-old proprietor of a Kent nursing home, and Ronald Andrews, a thirty-nine-year-old roofing contractor of Barkingside, Essex. He took those details and those of other missing people to Cater's office at the Yard. They spent many hours in discussion and working out a strategy of investigating alleged murder in which no victims had been named and no bodies found.

While Foxall was busy tracing the names turned up in the CRO files and checking with the circumstances of their being reported missing, Chief Superintendent Cater was researching into John Henry Childs. According to Cohen, it was Childs who had first mentioned murder and had said that Henry Mackenny was the man who had killed. He found out that Childs was born Martin Emlyn Jones in a village in Wales, and had twenty-five convictions ranging from petty larceny to robbery, arson and attempted murder. At that time Childs was on remand in Brixton prison and the first interview, in a bare room furnished only with a table and chairs, did not last long. Cater explained that he was from the Yard's Murder Squad, that he was investigating allegations of several murders and that he believed that he, Childs, could assist in the investigations. Childs was happy to talk about the robbery but denied all knowledge of murder. He gave the Chief Superintendent what detectives call 'a blank' – absolutely nothing.

Cater arranged for Childs to be moved to Oxford prison, where conditions were more conducive to long interviews, and where the inmates were less likely to be Londoners and less likely to gossip about the visit from a senior detective from the Murder Squad to a man held for robbery.

One man Cohen had mentioned was Ronald Andrews, who had been reported missing from his home in Barking-side, Essex, on 13 October 1978, and whose widow, Gwendoline, had been taken to France by Mackenny to create a false alibi for the Hertfordshire robbery. The files showed that Andrews had a small criminal record and that he had died after driving his car into the River Nene, near Wisbech, in Cambridgeshire. Cater telephoned the detective inspector at Wisbech who had dealt with that case and found out that the body had never been found and that experts had decided that it had floated out to sea. He also said that when he had visited Mrs Andrews she had shown him a postcard showing a picture of the River Nene on which were written the following words: 'Dear Ron, When will I see you? I am missing you so much. Remember, remember. Love, Ann.' The postcard was addressed to Ron Andrews. The inspector travelled to London and gave the card to the Chief Superintendent.

Then Cater went to Hertford to see what Childs had had in his pockets at the time of his arrest. Only one thing was of interest – a shopping list written in the same kind of writing as the postcard. A handwriting expert at the Yard confirmed that the writing on the card and on the shopping list was by the same hand. The detective already knew that the writing was not that of Childs but he suspected Childs's wife, Tina, might have written the shopping list. Cater went to see Mrs Childs at the family home at Dolphin House, Poplar, a neat ground-floor flat where two small children were playing with their toys on the floor. The only incongruous note was an extraordinary display of weapons on the walls of the sitting-room. Cater noticed a number of axes, daggers, knives and bayonets, a crossbow, a machete, an air-rifle and some Chinese flails.

He showed the shopping list to Mrs Childs, a small dark-eyed woman, and in a quiet voice she agreed that she had written it. She also agreed that she had written the postcard at the dictation of Harry Mackenny, which he had described as 'a joke'.

Soon after that postcard had been delivered to Ronald Andrews in September 1978, he had disappeared and

Cater remembered that Cohen had mentioned that Andrews's car 'had gone into the drink in Lincoln'.

When Cater saw Childs again it was at Oxford prison. This small man, forty-four years old with untidy fair hair and scruffy beard, who wore spectacles and spoke with a cockney accent, was uncooperative and truculent at the beginning of the interview. Then Cater produced the evidence of the shopping list and the postcard. There was a long pause and Childs capitulated. He confessed that he and Mackenny had murdered Andrews, and then proceeded to tell his macabre story of six killings with a wealth of minute detail. It must rank as one of the most amazing confessions in police history and took three days.

Childs's story began in June 1972 when he was released from Chelmsford prison after serving a sentence for burglary. In jail he had met a man called Terence Pinfold and they had planned, on their release, to set up a syndicate specializing in robbery. Pinfold, who had a long criminal record, took Childs to a disused church hall in Haydon Road, Goodmayes, in East London, and had introduced him to Henry Mackenny, a giant of a man, six feet four inches tall, who had invented and patented a revolutionary underwater diving suit which was being manufactured on the premises and who lived in a bungalow next door.

The three men had a long and earnest conversation about the proposed crime syndicate but their plans were disrupted when Childs was sent back to prison on another sentence for burglary. He was released in August 1974 and returned to the church hall where he found that Pinfold had teamed up with a man called Terence Eve in making teddy bears, a craft Eve had learned when serving a sentence in Eastchurch prison in Kent.

Childs said that the diving suit business was doing badly but the soft toys were selling well. Pinfold suggested that they should get rid of 'Teddy-bear' Eve and take over his business. They never considered buying him out – they just agreed on the simple solution of murdering him. Eve was to be the first victim in the series of killings.

It was decided that Mackenny and Childs would be the executioners of Terence Eve, allowing Pinfold to be absent because as he would inherit the soft-toy business he would need an alibi. Towards the end of the year, Terence Eve delivered an order of teddy bears to Mr Robert Patience, the owner of the Barn Restaurant at Braintree, the scene of another murder (see Chapter 13). Eve returned to the church hall after midnight where the two men clubbed him to death. Childs explained that Eve did not die easily despite repeated blows from Mackenny using a piece of lead piping and Childs wielding a hammer, and in the end Mackenny strangled him.

The body was wrapped in a tarpaulin and the church hall washed and cleaned. Then the body was transported to Childs's council flat in Poplar, he having sent his wife away to relatives. Mackenny and Childs dismembered the body, using kitchen knives and a saw. They tried to further reduce the body by feeding the pieces through a butcher's mincing machine which Pinfold had provided, but the electric current was not sufficient to make the machine work properly. Mackenny tried to flush pieces of the body down the toilet but that was unsuccessful, so they decided to burn the body in the eighteen-inch-wide grate in the living room. After several days the body was reduced to ashes and charred bones, which were hammered into powder and thrown out of a moving car on the Barking bypass. The mincing machine was broken up and thrown into a canal.

Childs explained how they had lined the flat with polythene sheeting to contain the blood and had used the bath for the dismemberment.

After that killing, and the successful disposal of the body, the three men decided they could make a lucrative business of killing by contract. Some months later they collected £1,800 from a man who wanted to get rid of haulage contractor George Brett, part of the price being a sten gun with ammunition.

Childs went to Brett's home in Upminster, in disguise, with his hair darkened with black boot polish and wearing a tracksuit, posing as a jogger. Brett was out so Childs left a message saying he had some business to offer and would call back in three days' time. He returned this time wearing a bowler hat and a smart suit and driving Mackenny's car. Brett agreed to go with Childs to the church hall for a meeting and when Childs's car would not start offered to give him a tow. As they were leaving Brett's young son, Terry, jumped into his father's car for the ride.

On arrival at the church hall Childs took Brett and his son into the building and Mackenny shot Brett through the head and then again when he fell to the floor. Childs was holding the ten-year-old boy with his hand clasped over his mouth. With his other hand he gave the boy a teddy bear to hold. Mackenny put the sten gun to the boy's head and killed him with a single shot.

Both bodies were taken to another room and partly dismembered. Later at Childs's home the bodies were burned in the sitting-room and the ashes put into the canal at Stratford.

The fourth victim, Robert Brown, a former professional wrestler known as 'The Angel', was thirty-three years old and on the run from Chelmsford prison when he had the ill-luck to meet Pinfold. He had offered Brown the job of cleaning the church hall but while he was there he had seen part of the killing of Terence Eve. The conspirators decided he had become a security risk and they killed him and disposed of his body at Poplar.

Childs said that Mackenny shot Brown twice in the back of the head and once in the front. The shots did not kill him outright so Mackenny attacked him with a fireman's axe and he, Childs, stabbed him with a diver's knife. Eventually Brown was impaled on the floor with a sword and died.

The fifth man to be murdered was Frederick Sherwood, the forty-eight-year-old proprietor of a nursing home at Herne Bay, Kent. Childs claimed that he killed for a contract payment of £4,000 to be paid in instalments. Sherwood had advertised his car for sale and Childs admitted that he posed as a prospective buyer and lured Sherwood to London to collect the money from Mackenny at his bungalow, next to the church hall. There, as Sherwood counted the money for the car, Mackenny shot him and Childs hit him with a hammer. That body too was taken to the charnel house at Poplar and, eventually, scattered to the wind.

Two men were later arrested and charged with placing contracts to murder George Brett and Frederick Sherwood and both were acquitted at the Old Bailey. For that reason their names have not been given.

The last murder, which did not follow the usual pattern, was that of Ronald Andrews. Mackenny wanted Mrs Andrews for himself. Childs told Chief Superintendent Cater that he had been reluctant to help but, in return for £400 and the promise of a silencer for his own gun, he was prepared to assist.

Childs, this time posing as a private detective saying he would look for evidence of Mrs Andrews's infidelity, persuaded Ronald Andrews to visit him at the Poplar flat. Mackenny hid behind a door and, when Andrews was sitting down, shot him through the head with a revolver. Mackenny used to boast that Andrews was his 'best mate' but the friendship did not stop him that autumn in 1978 from killing him. That murder was made to look like an accident. Dressed in a frogman's suit, Mackenny drove Andrews's car to Wisbech, Cambridge-shire, crashed it through a road sign, accelerated down the river bank with enough speed to clear the exposed river mud and landed in the middle of the water channel. The car 'sank like a stone', turning over as it went under. Mackenny, an experienced driver, calmly donned flippers, waited until the car completely filled with water and swam out to safety.

Childs, who had driven up behind Mackenny, helped him climb the bank and they returned to London. The body of Ronald Andrews had been hidden under a pile of timbers at Childs's home and it was disposed of in the usual way.

Childs added a final point of refinement in the plan. He told Cater that before Mackenny drove the car into the river at the spot known as Foul Anchor, they had thrown into the car a half bottle of vodka to give the impression that the driver of the car had been intoxicated.

Cater was now faced with the monumental task of finding evidence to support these astonishing revelations. That detailed statement, taken over many hours, told without emotion and written down by the patient Inspec-tor Foxall, must rank as one of the most alarming and cold-blooded in murder history.

The investigation proved that Childs had told the truth. The detectives found evidence of shooting in the church hall and traces of blood, despite the efforts of the killers to destroy the evidence by washing everything with acid. They were able to check that the six people who had been reported missing had disappeared suddenly and had never been seen again, despite a huge police search in each case with maximum publicity.

In his statement Childs had boasted that he and his friends had found the way to the perfect murder because they had completely disposed of the bodies of their victims. And that too had to be proved, for without proof of death there can be no murder in law.

Cater called Professor Cameron, and went to see him at the London Hospital. Even Cameron, used to extraordinary tales of murder, expressed some slight surprise. The two of them went to the Poplar flat to view the scene, and when Cameron saw the size of the grate he was even more surprised that the body of a man could be reduced to ashes in so small an area and with ordinary domestic fuel. He decided on an experiment, using a dead pig weighing eleven stone, the approximate weight of a man. On the night of the experiment strict secrecy was observed so that the neighbours were not alerted. The body of the pig was carried in under cover of darkness, the curtains drawn and heavy blankets hung at the windows. Professor Cameron conducted his experiment in exactly the way that Childs had described was used to destroy the victims.

The floor was covered with polythene and the pathologist cut the pig into log-like pieces using only knives from the kitchen and a domestic saw usually used for firewood. A fire was lit and one of the team deputed to keep it fuelled. A professional fireman from the London Hospital was present in case of accidents, and for thirteen hours in the fierce heat of that small room the pig was fed to the fire. Every man there was sweating profusely but in thirteen hours the pig was totally destroyed and there was left just a pile of ash.

A photographer from the London Hospital, who took pictures throughout the experiment, was heard to observe, 'I hope my wife doesn't suggest roast pork for dinner for a while.'

Thus was one vital point of Childs's bizarre story proved, and Professor Cameron would testify that the total disposal of a human body *was* possible in an ordinary domestic grate in so short a time. Now Cater had to establish the rest of the evidence. By now he had a squad of twenty men which became known as 'Cater's Company' and he set up his headquarters at a police station at Waltham Abbey, on the Essex borders of East London. Inspector Foxall became the 'office manager', examining files of missing persons and possible contract killings going back over eight years. He checked on backgrounds, associates and possible links with other criminals and those names given by Childs.

Detectives went to see the wives and relatives of the missing people now believed to be dead. The wife of Terence Eve said that her husband had disappeared on the night before their daughter's birthday, something he would not have done voluntarily. The wife of George Brett was equally adamant that he would not have gone off with their son, Terry, of his own volition. They discovered that Frederick Sherwood, according to his wife, had just disappeared suddenly with his Rover car; and the wife of Ronald Andrews said she could suggest no reason for his disappearance for he was in good health and earning good money.

Files on the suspected murder victims were rechecked, witnesses re-examined and conferences held with detectives who had made the initial inquiries when the men were reported missing. Known associates of the missing men were questioned, visits were made to the public houses they used, the restaurants and cafés they frequented, even the garages where they bought petrol. Members of the underworld grew tired of the constant questioning and some threatened to complain. The Chief Superintendent always gave them the same answer: 'You are free to complain as often as you like. Don't let me stop you.' For this was an investigation in which a large number of people had a criminal record and, if not, they were associates of criminals.

Professor Cameron and experts from Scotland Yard's laboratory spent many days on an inch-by-inch search of the church hall factory, Mackenny's bungalow and Childs's flat. Cater was eventually satisfied that all the murders had been committed in one or other of the three places, but they never found all the bloodstains which Childs had said could be present. The acid cleaning had been too effective. They did find a bullet mark in the floor of the church hall which had been disguised with wax and stain as Childs had described, and also two other bullet marks in Mackenny's bungalow.

By now the Chief Superintendent had four prisoners but he could not find Henry Mackenny, the man known as 'Big H'. In July of 1979 he made a public appeal and issued Mackenny's photograph and description. Six weeks later Cater received information that the man he wanted was back in London and living in the East End. A massive hunt was set up which led to Ilford where, one night, Mackenny evaded capture by driving his car across two sets of red traffic lights. A few days later, on 20 September, Cater received a tip that Mackenny was staying at the home of William and Pauline Woodcraft in Morse Close, Plaistow. The last secret operation was mounted.

A team of detectives and uniformed officers, mostly armed and wearing bullet-proof vests, moved quietly into the area at midnight. Neighbours were warned to stay in their back rooms away from the road and others who were thought to be in the line of gunfire were evacuated.

Shortly after one o'clock in the morning a detective telephoned the Woodcraft house. Mrs Woodcraft answered and the detective told her that the police knew Mackenny was there, that the house was surrounded and that Mackenny was to walk out of the front door. The detective heard the message being passed and there was silence for several minutes. The house was ringed with marksmen and several guns were trained on the front door. The detective still held the telephone but nobody spoke. Then, at fifteen minutes past one o'clock the front door slowly opened and the tall figure of Henry Mackenny walked out and was promptly handcuffed.

During the course of the investigation Cater and his men found an arsenal of weapons in the loft of a house in Woodford, Essex. There was a sten gun, five revolvers, a tear-gas pistol, two rifles, four shotguns, 992 rounds of ammunition and 24 tear-gas pellets. They also found a silencer hidden in a bucket of cement in a children's school playground.

He had discovered that the gang had at one time advertised a range of activities they called 'frighteners'. For a fee they were prepared to put rats through named people's letter-boxes, beat people or even set fire to their houses. They had, at that time, literally got away with murder and they were supremely confident, particularly Childs.

In 1971 John Henry Childs had been a pathetic figure serving a sentence in Chelmsford jail for burglary. He had few friends, no interests and was insecure about most things, including his small stature, his lack of skills and his inability to steal without being caught. Occasionally he would spark with rage at a fellow inmate; once he had tried to shock other prisoners by tearing out his toe nails in front of them, using a pair of pliers. His life changed

when he met Pinfold, shrewd, self-assured and a successful villain, who had a long record of violent crime. He
had even conducted his own defence, in several trials and
won over juries with his persuasive style. Pinfold took
Childs under his wing.

Later, when they were joined by 'Big H' Mackenny,
it was he who dominated. Individually they were not
considered good class criminals by the underworld, but
together they formed a terrifying partnership. It was
Pinfold who supplied the thinking power, Mackenny the
ruthless drive and strength, and Childs would do anything
he was bidden. He was most useful as a 'front-man' for
he looked so insignificant that he was never likely to be
recognized again.

As time passed Childs became increasingly frightened
by Mackenny, probably because Mackenny was so much
taller and stronger than the others and totally ruthless.
He had spent several years in the Royal Tank Regiment
and served in Germany where he was impressed with the
nation rebuilding itself out of rubble. It became an
obsession with him that only the strong survive. He
picked up extraordinary skills, becoming an expert underwater diver, an engineer, a mechanic and electrician.
He had supported the campaign against identification in
criminal cases and marched in support of George Ince,
George Davis and others who had been charged with
offences solely on the basis of identification.

When Childs brought Sherwood to the church hall for
execution, the two men, Mackenny and Pinfold, shared a
drink to clinch the deal and then Childs handed over the
money for the car sale. Sherwood had sat down to count it
and Mackenny shot him through the head from behind.
The bullet passed through Sherwood's head, hit the table
and shattered the glass Childs was holding. Childs pulled

out his gun and he and Mackenny faced each other, Western style, both shouting accusations. Childs screamed, 'You tried to kill me.' The moment passed but the two men never really trusted each other again.

Childs had told Chief Superintendent Cater that after the murder of Ronald Andrews he had so hated Mackenny that he had planned to kill him with a bolt fired from a crossbow that hung on the wall of the sitting-room in the Poplar flat. He said he had even been out target shooting with the crossbow in Epping Forest. But Childs was arrested and the crossbow remained hanging on the wall.

In October 1980 all the evidence was assembled and the trial began at the Old Bailey. It was to last forty days and the jury was warned at the beginning that it would hear 'unpleasant and revolting' details of six murders. John Henry Childs, who had already been sentenced to life imprisonment for six murders, was the chief prosecution witness. His evidence was the most sickening I have ever heard.

There were four men in the dock, all charged with murder. At the end of the trial, after almost two days of deliberation, the jury rejected part of the Crown's case and they acquitted two men, each of whom had been accused of paying for a contract killing.

But Henry Jeremiah Mackenny, aged forty-eight, was found guilty of the murders of George Brett and his son Terry, Frederick Sherwood and Ronald Andrews. He was jailed for a recommended twenty-five years. Pinfold was jailed for life for the murder of Terence Eve. John Henry Childs, the man who turned informer, was the only member of the gang who was convicted of all six murders. He admitted them all in court.

But for the mistake of Philip Cohen in forgetting his car keys on the Hertfordshire robbery, it is doubtful if any of the murders would have ever been discovered or the killers brought to justice.

20
The Hong Kong Skull

At one time the investigator and the pathologist were almost entirely concerned with criminals operating in their own area, or certainly in their own country; but today they must be prepared to deal with criminals whose activities have been greatly increased by the speed of modern transport. There are many forms of international crime but the most prominent are the smuggling of gold or diamonds and, increasingly, the illicit traffic in narcotics.

It was in connection with the last, trafficking in heroin, that Professor Cameron was asked to identify a skull which was found on a remote beach at Castle Peak in Hong Kong. On 1 September 1979 a green canvas bag had been washed in from the sea and found by a construction worker. He noticed a foul smell coming from the bag and reported it to the police.

The bag contained a grisly mixture of a skull, a human pelvic bone and several ribs which clearly showed that the body had been hacked to pieces with no particular skill. A local pathologist decided that the remains were those of a male, aged between twenty-five and forty years old.

The local Homicide Bureau combed through hundreds of files of people who had been reported missing in recent months. The skull was photographed and the prints shown to many people, and they were also put on show outside police stations. The first breakthrough came when the wife of one of the men reported missing told police that she thought she could recognize the ear-lobes, the teeth and the nose of her missing husband, Peter Chan Woon-hing, who was twenty-nine years old.

The Chinese woman, who was called Wong Suet-hing, was seventeen and had been married for only a few months. She was shown the picture of the skull again, but this time in much better lighting, and was certain that it was that of her husband. It was lucky for the detectives that Chan Woon-hing had told his wife a great deal about his activities for she was able to reveal that he had been engaged in trafficking drugs to Europe and that he was fearful of a revenge killing because one of the gang involved believed he had been double-crossed.

The local pathologist, Dr Lam Ping Yan, reported on the contents of the green canvas bag, all of which were heavily decomposed. His report read:

A male adult human head with short black hair severed from the neck at the fourth vertebra and just below the hyoid bone of the larynx in front. The whole head was bound up in adhesive tape. The tips of the incisor teeth had been cut exposing the tooth pulps. There was a two-inch chopper wound at the back of the neck.

The following items were wrapped in a white plastic sheet: the right front of the rib-cage consisting of the inner third of the right collar bone. The breast bone had been cut vertically. The left front of the rib-cage consisting of the inner two thirds of the left collar bone. Multiple small chopper marks were seen on the collar bone.

A male adult pelvis detached from the trunk. Both lower limbs had been detached and were missing.

He gave the cause of death as unascertainable due to skeletonization and decomposition, and the fact that the flesh had been stripped from parts of the body.

Positive identification was required and Detective Inspector Li Sung took the skull to London and to Professor Cameron. He also took a photograph of Chan

Woon-hing when he was alive which had been taken in the Hon Wong studio by Lau Yu-tuen who said that he had taken it from a distance of about fourteen to sixteen feet using a flash bulb. Those details were important because the Professor had to prove identification by superimposition. The technique used is that the negative of the skull is superimposed over the positive of the face and then fitted together using the eyes, ears, nose and cheekbones as points of focus. Professor Cameron, working with his chief photographer Ray Ruddick, produced enough points of similarity for him to say that the skull belonged to the man in the photograph. He also discovered a bruise on the skull which was from a heavy blow delivered one minute to five minutes before death.

Now that the victim was positively identified as Chan Woon-hing Superintendent Stephenson and Chief Inspector Chea Phee-chuan began the investigation of one of Hong Kong's most gruesome murders. The trail was to lead to France and Holland and back to Hong Kong.

The young wife of the victim told them that Chan had been heavily involved with a drugs gang and that some weeks before his murder he had flown to Holland with a consignment of heroin which he had handed to a distributor. He waited three days for the money to be paid, as had been arranged, but was then told the whole consignment had been stolen by a rival gang. The heroin had been handed to a man called Chan Wai and, under the rules of the drug traffickers, it was his responsibility to pay compensation. But despite heavy pressure there was no money forthcoming and Chan Woon-hing resolved to go back to Hong Kong. While he was planning an expedition to return to Holland to collect his money he was asked by another smuggler, Siu Chi-Kai, to take over a second consignment of drugs and he agreed.

Siu Chi-Kai and another man bought five pounds of

heroin and recruited a courier to actually carry the drugs. She was thought to be ideal as she was unknown to the police and wanted to go to Europe to get work as a croupier or a hostess. Kong Lai-king was a pretty twenty-six-year-old girl who had worked in a bar in Kowloon as a ballroom hostess, and also worked in the Golden Majestic Escort Agency. The gang, led by Chan Woon-hing, packed the drugs in a suitcase with a false bottom and in May four members of the gang and the hostess carrying the drugs travelled to Paris. They left in two parties and arranged to meet at a hotel when the drugs had been sold in France.

Kong Lai-king walked into the customs hall and said she had nothing to declare, that she was carrying only personal belongings and some biscuits. But a French Customs Officer at Charles de Gaulle airport decided on a routine search and found the drugs in the false bottom of the suitcase. The drugs were seized and she was arrested. Kong Lai-king was later found guilty by the Tribunal of Dobigny in France and sentenced to six years' imprisonment. She appealed against her conviction but it was upheld.

The rest of the gang had seen the arrest at the airport and made their way separately to a pre-arranged meeting place in Amsterdam. Once there they made haste to find the man who had bought the earlier consignment. Chan Woon-hing, the leader of the gang, managed to collect 9,000 guilders on account and he remained in Holland to collect another 10,000 guilders. That was about the value of the previous consignment, roughly £5,000.

The rest of the gang had meanwhile returned to Hong Kong and found that the backers of the whole enterprise, the men who had financed it, were not only furious but thirsting for blood.

Siu Chi-Kai and his companion, Li Kwai-fan, who had

put up the money for the drugs, had become anxious to find out what had happened. They had sent associates to Holland who were told the drugs had been seized at Paris, but they also heard that Chan Woon-hing was in possession of a lot of money. Siu Chi-Kai refused to accept the account that the drugs had been seized by customs and decided that Chan Woon-hing had double-crossed him. He determined on revenge and approached a friend, Tam Ho-kin, asking him to recruit some associates to plan Chan's death. As Tam was unable to find any helpers, the three conspirators talked long and earnestly, planning to do the killing themselves. They then went to a fortune teller in a temple to find an auspicious day to go through a religious ceremony which would bind them together as brothers.

Chan returned to Hong Kong at the beginning of August, and 7 August was the day set for the murder. Chan was invited by his killers to a flat in On-Look Building at Yuenlong. Li Kwai-fan was told by Siu Chi-Kai to make sure that Chan did not make any noise, and when Chan struggled and shouted Siu hit him on the head with a wooden pole. He collapsed and was later found to be dead. At that point the third man, Tam, ran away. The two other killers then procured a meat-grinding machine and proceeded to dismember the body and with a chopper strip the flesh from the bones. This was fed through the grinding machine and flushed down the toilet.

As the head and the bones could not be put in the grinder they were packed into two travelling bags and dumped into the sea off Butterfly Bay. Sea currents later swept the bag containing the head to Pillar Point where it was found on the beach. The second bag was never found despite an extensive search by Royal Navy divers.

The police investigation was helped by Tam Ho-kin, who had been prepared to help lure the victim to the place of execution but refused to take part in the disposal of the body. He told the police that after the killing he was at a dinner party and saw Siu Chi-Kai and Li Kwai-fan changing the dressings on each other's injured fingers. They had had their fingertips sliced off when they were stuffing the body of the victim into the grinding machine.

Both men were charged with murder and were tried in the High Court of Hong Kong in October 1980. Professor Cameron travelled from London to give his vital evidence on the identification of the skull of the victim. He was questioned for more than two hours, mainly on the superimposition technique. That evidence was an essential part of the Crown's case and was heard for the first time in a Hong Kong court. He was also examined about the use of a meat cleaver for the chopping of the bones and the removal of flesh from the bones. In his opinion neither of these operations would have been difficult.

The court was satisfied that the skull was that of Peter Chan Woon-hing and Siu Chi-Kai was found guilty of manslaughter and jailed for eight years. Two other defendants were each sentenced to ten years for conspiracy to traffic in dangerous drugs, and a fifth defendant was acquitted.

To help prove the drug conspiracy two French police officers also gave evidence at the trial, the first time that French policemen had given evidence in Hong Kong. They brought with them the heroin which had been seized from the ballroom hostess, worth two and a half million dollars in Hong Kong. On the day the killers and the traffickers went to Stanley Prison those drugs disappeared in smoke when they were burned by the police.

21

The Dingo Baby Case

The death of Azaria Chamberlain, which became known all over the world as the Dingo Baby Case, was to become of acute interest to Professor Cameron and his department. He and his staff had followed the case in the newspapers and, like all professionals in the world of forensic science, had pondered and tried to evaluate the extraordinary evidence which had been given at the Coroner's Court in Alice Springs and which ended with Azaria's parents, Michael and Lindy Chamberlain, being exonerated from all blame in her death. On 27 May 1981 Dr Kenneth Brown, the scientist whose evidence at the inquest had been virtually dismissed by Coroner Barritt, arrived at the London Hospital. He had been on the staff there some years before, and he knew exactly where to find Professor Cameron. Brown explained that he was concerned about the way his evidence had been received and wanted to check out his techniques with the Professor.

Dr Brown handed over the clothing of the dead child, and Cameron and his team of experts went to work, using a doll on which to fit the clothing and the skull of a dingo dog to make the experiments for a video film. Using the latest scientific methods, the Professor produced a picture of what he thought had happened and sent his report to Mr Peter McAulay, the Northern Territory chief police commissioner.

In mid-September Professor Cameron flew to Brisbane in complete secrecy. He travelled as plain James Malcolm Cameron and met the Chief Minister, Paul Everingham, and Northern Territory Solicitor-General, Brian Martin.

The Professor stayed for a few days and presented his lengthy report, including the video. It was enough to convince them that the investigation in Australia had not been as thorough as it should have been.

Four days later, on 19 September, Paul Everingham ordered the police to reopen their investigations.

It is rare for Professor Cameron to write up one of his own cases and those he does have a different and fascinating background that is of great interest to the medical profession. The circumstances in this case are unique, for he and his team produced evidence that had not been revealed by any of the experts who had worked on the case. He was able to prove that a human hand had committed the murder of the baby and that a wild dog was not responsible for the death.

This story is written in the Professor's own words and is taken from an address he gave to the Medico Legal Society in April 1984.

Mr President, fellow members and honoured guests, it is indeed a privilege and an honour to be invited for the third time to lecture to this Society. I will do my best to describe the dingo case from all aspects and then finally put to you the evidence which persuaded the Northern Territory Authorities to reopen the case after the first coroner's inquest. It is not my position, as a witness of the Court, to say whether my evidence is correct or not and I will leave it to you to decide as to whether the court was right in finding Mrs Chamberlain and her husband guilty. It is a fascinating case and one in which, even to this day, many are not convinced as to whether they have heard either the end of it or the truth.

Azaria Chantal Loren Chamberlain was born in Mount Isa Maternity Hospital, Queensland, Australia, on 11 June 1980 to a young pastor and his wife, members of the

Seventh Day Adventist Church. At birth the child was said to weigh approximately 6½ lbs and was 18–19 inches in length – in other words, she was a normal-sized female infant.

Blond-haired thirty-six-year-old Michael Chamberlain and his attractive wife, Alice Lynne, usually known as Lindy, had two other sons, Aiden aged six and Reagan, four years of age. The Chamberlain family had been predominantly male and Azaria, which apparently means 'Blessed of God', was described by the Chamberlains as 'a wonderful gift'. When the new infant was approximately nine weeks of age the parents decided to take the family for a holiday and on Wednesday, 13 August 1980, they packed their camping gear into their yellow Torana hatchback and set off for Ayers Rock. They spent the first night en route and the next two nights at Alice Springs.

Ayers Rock is a tiring 250-mile drive in a south-westerly direction from Alice Springs through clouds of fine red dust. This mammoth landmark, resting in a desert like a huge beast at rest, is a tourist attraction in the very centre of Australia.

For those of you who cannot appreciate the size of Australia, if you were to take it off the map and put it over America on the same scale, apart from the Great Lakes, the whole of America would be covered. If we were to put the same country over Europe, from Southern Scotland to North Africa and even right across to Russia would be covered by the continent of Australia.

As far as Ayers Rock is concerned, more than 500 million years of geological erosion have carved deep folds in the surface of this monolith which is approximately 1,600 feet high, nine kilometres in circumference, and was first seen by a white man in 1873.

This awesome geological freak in the heart of Australia

is the source of many myths of Aboriginal folklore, yet today luxury coaches, campers and light aircraft bring tourists by the thousand almost all the year round. They touch it, they climb it, they photograph it, or simply watch it changing moods – purple at dawn, blood-red at sunset, and silvery black in the rainfall.

On arrival at the campsite, Michael and Lindy Chamberlain, with some help from their boys, did not take long to set up their light green and orange four-man pup tent which had a ridged top, a low wall and a built-in ground sheet. The entrance to the tent was through a flap with a zip front and a barbecue area was approximately twenty metres distant. The back of the tent looked on to Sunrise Hill covered in shrubland.

Despite the cramped conditions, packed head to toe, the Chamberlains slept well on their first night. At 10 A.M. on Sunday, the next day, they set off on a day's exploration around the Rock. Michael Chamberlain apparently decided to climb to the top and, being athletic and fit, made the summit with relative ease, leaving his wife and children at the base of the Rock. On his descent, he offered to take the boys with him, leaving his wife Lindy and baby Azaria behind. The temperature at that time was approximately 120 degrees Fahrenheit. They visited a number of tourist attraction points around the base of the Rock on their descent, including a fertility cave, where, surprisingly, later in the investigation, a bloodstain was found which was consistent with having arisen from a person with a similar blood group as Lindy Chamberlain, a blood group that approximately ten per cent of the white population of Australia have. That evidence had no bearing whatsoever in the case. There are a lot of red herrings in the case.

After spending the first day of their holiday pottering around and taking photographs – Michael Chamberlain was a very keen photographer – they returned to the camping area, where the boys were ready for bed. After Reagan had fallen asleep, Lindy Chamberlain pulled up the zipper in the tent flap and took baby Azaria and Aiden to the barbecue site where Azaria was wrapped in clothing and could not be properly seen. She subsequently put Azaria into a bassinet, or carry-cot, in the right-hand rear of the back of the tent, wrapped in six blankets like a cocoon, with the blankets coming up to within half an inch of the crown of her head.

Lindy Chamberlain looked around for a tin opener because Aiden wanted baked beans. She did not zip the flap up again as she knew her son would be going to bed as soon as the supper was over. The time at this stage would be approximately 8 P.M. She was still holding the tin opener at the barbecue site when her husband, as he later recalled, heard a short, sharp cry. Thinking that it had arisen from the tent, he asked Lindy if the baby had settled. This she thought was so, but decided to check and started to walk back to the tent, hurrying the last couple of metres.

According to the story, she saw a dingo reversing out through the flaps of the tent and could see its shoulders and thought it was shaking its head as if it had something in its mouth. Blankets apparently were scattered and she gave the now well-known cry, 'The dingo has got my baby.'

The Rock, and its surroundings, is a territory in which a number of dingos live. These wild desert dogs probably came with the Aboriginals from the Asian continent when the great land masses were joined thousands of years ago before the white explorers arrived in Australia. A dingo is a tawny-coloured dog with a distinctive bushy tail, not unlike a small German shepherd dog. There are apparently very few pure dingos in Australia today as there has been much cross breeding between the dingo and the cross-bred Aboriginal wild dog. The largest dingo is now said to stand at 22 inches to 23 inches in height.

The dingo is alleged to have run round behind the tent into the scrubland and disappeared into the night. The temperature of the night was considerably lower than during the day. This was noted particularly by Pastor Chamberlain who apparently was frustrated because he did not have his car keys to switch on the desert light fitted to his car. One of the first professional witnesses at the scene was Nurse Bobby Downes (now Elston), a pretty brunette from the local clinic. Police rangers and black trackers joined the campsite in the search, but as the night wore on the temperature dropped even lower and it was decided by the police that the Chamberlains should be taken to a motel for the night.

Whilst a sergeant drove Mrs Chamberlain and the two boys, Nurse Downes unpitched the tent, placed it in the rear of the hatchback and drove with Mr Chamberlain to the local motel.

This sensation story, leaked out to the press, of a baby snatched by a dingo at Ayers Rock, was almost too bizarre to be true and although the staff at the motel were rather loath to allow the Chamberlains to be bothered with unwelcome intrusions by the press, Mr Chamberlain was prepared to talk to the papers and television stations. The next day Michael Chamberlain went back to the Rock and using black and white film took further photographs of a tent in a similar position with the Rock in the background together with the young boys.

Naturally, the Chamberlains did not want to stay at the Rock and they made preparations to leave the following Tuesday.

At the time of Azaria's disappearance, well-dressed

Lindy Chamberlain described the child's weight as being approximately 10 lbs and she was 23 inches in length, which would be normal for a child of that age. She described the child's clothing in detail and, with the exclusion of a matinée jacket, all were found subsequently.

Police and rangers maintained a vigil at the Rock and their purpose was to shoot dingos on sight. The exact numbers that were seen or shot vary considerably, but there was no evidence of human flesh found in any of the animals.

For those of you who are unaware of the teaching and beliefs of the Seventh Day Adventist Church it would be appropriate to say that it is a staunch Protestant body which believes that the scriptures provide an unerring rule of faith and that Christ's return is imminent. It advocates a life of strict temperance – no alcohol or tobacco and abstinence whenever possible from tea, coffee and meat. Michael Chamberlain, an ordained pastor of the church, married his wife when she was aged twenty-two in 1970, and they moved to Mount Isa in Western Queensland where they followed the teaching and beliefs of their church.

Many people who watched the Chamberlains in the two to three days after the disappearance of their young daughter believed that they found great strength in their religious beliefs. They did not stay in their motel room, locking themselves away in their misery, but instead spoke quite openly to searchers, campers, and to the police as well as to members of the media, and appeared to accept the death of Azaria with no hope at all of the child being found alive.

After taking photographs they amazingly bought souvenirs of the Rock as gifts to relatives on their return home.

Eight days after Azaria's disappearance a tourist from Victoria, Wallace Goodwin, walking through the scrub on the west side of Ayers Rock, noted close to a large boulder a heaped collection of child's clothing. Realizing the importance of the find he hastened back to the police station and a senior constable later took a photograph of the clothing after laying it out. Some of the important features noted were that the singlet was inside out and that the bootees were fastened up and were still inside the legs of the suit. No evidence of human remains was found within the clothing apart from bloodstains which were principally around the collar of the jumpsuit and on the vest.

Naturally, such a story gripped the imagination not only of the locals but also the nation as a whole. It was felt, obviously, that this was not a straightforward case of a dingo 'grabbing' a baby from a tent and dropping the child where the clothing had been found.

Numerous theories abounded and were bandied about during the time the Chamberlains tried to resume a normal life. Not long after the discovery of the clothing the police naturally called upon the Chamberlains to go over the circumstances of the night when their child disappeared and to inform them also that a coroner's inquest would probably be held in late October or December. Stories naturally then began to circulate, as they always do in local communities, one of the most unpleasant of which being that the child had fallen from a supermarket trolley at five weeks old and, as a result of becoming a spastic, had to be sacrificed.

It was a fact that the child had been involved in an incident in a supermarket when aged five weeks and had been examined at the local hospital. The whole case naturally was a source of gossip, rumour, and unfair comment, with numerous anonymous letters and telephone calls.

In the time preceding the coroner's inquest a number of experiments were carried out with animals dressed in human clothing similar to that in which baby Azaria had been dressed, including a young goat, or kid, which had been humanely killed and thrown into a dingo pen at Adelaide Zoo to be recorded on video.

The date for the first coroner's inquest was set for 15 December 1980 when fifty-four-year-old Dennis Barritt, the coroner for Alice Springs, a former Victorian police detective of seventeen years' experience and a barrister of thirteen years' experience, presided. During Coroner Barritt's inquest forensic evidence revealed that the damage to the clothing, the absence of saliva, the absence of dog or dingo hairs, and the absence of pulled threads or other fragments, suggested that the deceased was removed from her clothing by a person rather than a dog or dingo.

It was further suggested by the deputy crown solicitor that damage to the clothing was more consistent with that caused by a person rather than a dog or a dingo, and in addition the site where the clothing was found was several kilometres from where Azaria disappeared, suggesting that the clothes had been placed on site where found rather than dragged there by a dog or a dingo. The coroner confirmed that the child was dead and that the manner in which the clothing was found would indicate at some stage that there had been human intervention in the disposal of the body.

Friday, 19 December 1980, was to be the last full day of the inquest before adjournment until 19 February 1981. To all appearances the inquest had served more to deepen the mystery of Azaria's disappearance and raise more questions than there were answers. During the adjournment the Chamberlains kept themselves very much to themselves in that they now left Mount Isa and had moved to Avondale College, a Seventh Day Adventist Centre near Newcastle, New South Wales, where Michael Chamberlain was studying for a Master of Arts degree. The Chamberlains were represented by Mr Phillip Rice, QC and his instructing solicitor, Peter Dean. Mr Ashley Macknay, the deputy crown solicitor, with his junior Michael O'Loughlin, assisted the coroner.

The scientific evidence at this inquiry was given principally by Dr Andrew Scott, formerly of the Metropolitan Police Laboratory, and then head of the oral biology section of the Institute of Medical and Veterinary Science at Adelaide.

He stated that he had found no dingo hair or saliva on Azaria's clothing and that the blood on the clothes was the same group and type as Azaria's. By taking the blood group of the Chamberlains and comparing the blood on the clothing, he had found it was consistent with having come from a child of the union of both. He also confirmed that the blood found near the fertility cave was of the same type as that of Mrs Chamberlain and which is present in approximately ten per cent of the white population. He concluded that the baby singlet found with the jumpsuit had been folded.

The witness responsible for the experiment in Adelaide Zoo was Dr Kenneth Aylesbury Brown, a forensic dentist of the oral biology department of the University of Adelaide, and himself a Seventh Day Adventist, who had been previously attached to the Department of Forensic Medicine at the London Hospital Medical College whilst a Churchill fellow for further study under the aegis of Mr Bernard Sims and myself. Much of the research work that he talked about left itself wide open to criticism.

After closing addresses by Mr Rice and Mr Macknay,

there was the summarization of the evidence before an historic television coverage the following day, Friday, 20 February. This was one of the rare occasions that a television crew was allowed to enter a coroner's court and televise a coroner summing up a case.

Coroner Barritt, wearing his dark-rimmed spectacles and dressed in a patterned shirt and tie, with his eyes cast down on his thirteen-page prepared statement, spoke slowly and nervously and gave a thorough recap of all the evidence that had been presented to him.

He further indicated that in an attempt to remove the baby from the tent a dingo would have caused severe crush injuries to the base of the skull and neck, and lacerations to the throat and neck, with such injuries resulting in swift death. After death he found that the body of Azaria had been taken from the possession of the dingo and disposed of by an unknown method by a person or persons unknown.

In a virtual monotone the coroner continued with his summing up and, as well as criticizing the forensic dentist, he hit out at the Northern Territory police force forensic science section. He extended his deepest sympathy to the Chamberlain family, informing them that he had taken the unusual step of permitting the proceedings to be televised in the hope that by direct and accurate communication innuendoes, suspicion and gossip might finally cease.

He also made the remark that if anybody were to reopen the case he hoped that they would rot in hell.

In due course Dr Kenneth Brown from Adelaide visited the London Hospital Medical College where he requested a second opinion. Following examination of all the material, the general opinion was that:

The garments came from a child of a blood group consistent with being that of a sibling of the union of one Michael

Chamberlain and one Lindy Chamberlain. That is to say that the blood group would be consistent with the blood of one, Azaria Chamberlain.

There were no marks on the clothing to suggest involvement with any member of the canine family, or drag marks, and total absence of saliva. This was the original finding of Dr Scott of Adelaide at the first coroner's inquest.

The vest or singlet presented blood stain distribution which confirmed that the singlet had been on the correct way round when the bleeding occurred and then turned inside out on removal from the body.

All the jumpsuit studs had been done up to the neck at the time the bleeding occurred; the top two studs had been undone prior to the jumpsuit coming into contact with the reddish sand, and only undone further for the removal of the bootees.

Examination of the bloodstained jumpsuit revealed what appeared to be the handprint of a small right hand of an adult. The hand, contaminated with wet blood of the same blood group as that found elsewhere on the suit, held the body within the jumpsuit and at the same time the body was gripped by a similarly wet blood-contaminated left hand grasping the upper right shoulder of the body contained within the jumpsuit. Over the left shoulder-blade region was a further vertical bloodstained handprint. There was no evidence to suggest the hands came from two individuals but would be consistent with one individual holding the jumpsuit whilst the body was within this item of clothing and whilst the blood was flowing.

The distribution of the blood on the jumpsuit, and for that matter on the singlet, would suggest that the blood flowed on to the collar, from above, around the front of the neck in particular, and at the one time and not from two separate areas or from rivulets of blood, which would have been anticipated were an animal involved or if there had been a head injury.

These stains were demonstrated more clearly in ultraviolet fluorescent photography by Mr Ruddick, chief photographer, the London Hospital, and further demonstrated in a colour video film with the superimposition of the hand of a young woman using a suitably dressed doll.

One was satisfied at this stage beyond all reasonable doubt that there was little if any evidence of the involvement with a member of the canine family.

There was evidence, however, to suggest that a human being

with bloodstained hands of the same blood group as the blood from the infant, held the jumpsuit whilst the blood was still flowing on to the clothing. That is to say, the blood flowed around the neck, possibly pooling at the back, but not from isolated points. The blood was foetal in type and the bloodstained handprints were stained with blood of the same type.

The finding of the clothing in a relatively neat pile would suggest that it had been placed there, not by an animal, but by a human, provided they were placed there after the clothing was dry. There was no reason to assume that they would have been tampered with by any animals, particularly with evidence that other items of clothing, including tampons, remained undisturbed in the region of the area examined.

The sand staining on the garment and the finding of the clothes would suggest that after the blood had dried, the top two studs of the jumpsuit were undone, and the clothing in that state, with the body still within it, came into contact with the sand, as there was no evidence to suggest an uneven distribution of the sand on the clothing. This would have occurred had the clothing been put into contact with the sand when folded.

In the absence of a body, one must assume an unascertainable cause of death. Having said that, however, from the presence of bleeding on to the jumpsuit, from the amount of bleeding and from the recorded temperature of the surroundings, it would be reasonable to assume that she met her death by unnatural causes, and that the mode of death had been caused by a cutting instrument across the neck, cutting the vital blood vessels and structures of the neck. Such an instrument could never have been wielded by an animal other than a human animal.

In mid-September 1981 I flew to Brisbane incognito, where I met not only the commissioner for the Northern Territory, but also the Chief Minister, Paul Everingham, and the Northern Territory Solicitor-General, Brian Martin. I presented a rather lengthy report which, with other items, was sufficient for Mr Paul Everingham on 19 September 1981 officially to order the police to reopen their investigations.

The yellow Torana hatchback of the Chamberlains

was submitted for further scientific examinations. On 20 November 1981 Mr Justice Toohey, a Supreme Court judge, sitting in Darwin, ordered a new inquest after hearing evidence from the police. Coroner Barritt's findings at the first inquest were quashed and a second inquest was opened.

Investigations were carried out between the first and second inquest under Detective Chief Superintendent Neil Plumb. The new inquest was held at Alice Springs on 14 December 1981, with Mr J. Galvin, the Northern Territories' chief magistrate, presiding as coroner. Mr 'Des' Sturgess, a Queensland barrister, was appointed to assist the coroner and his assistant was Mr Michael O'Loughlin of Alice Springs Crown Law Department. Mr Phil Rice, the QC who had represented the Chamberlains at the original inquest, was assisted by Mr Andrew Kirkham, a Melbourne magistrate, together with Mr Peter Dean, the Chamberlains' original solicitor.

At this inquest, Mrs Kuhl, a forensic biologist from New South Wales, described bloodstains found in the Chamberlains' car as being what she considered as foetal blood in babies of six months and under. Laboratory examination of a pair of scissors found in the car demonstrated blood of foetal origin on the cutting edge, in the hinge area, and around the handle. She described areas in the car where foetal blood had been found which involved the front seat supports and the carpet.

She concluded that the blood would have been at least twelve months old by the time she examined it in September 1981. She had also found foetal blood in the inside of a yellow container that had held an imitation chamois leather. She also found positive evidence of foetal blood on the under side of the glove box and on the centre console. She described what she meant by foetal blood, namely, that of foetal haemoglobin with the oxygen-carrying capacity in the blood beginning to decrease when the presence of adult haemoglobin began to be seen and this occurred anything up to six months of age. There were, of course, certain rare medical conditions in which this was seen but very rarely in Australia. Such a trait would have been seen in the parents of the child, but was not. She agreed that the blood in the car was that of a child under six months.

The court was adjourned to Ayers Rock where I and my two colleagues, Bernard Sims, senior lecturer in forensic odontology at the London Hospital Medical College, and Mr Ray Ruddick, chief photographer at the London Hospital, touched down at Ayers Rock at 9 A.M. to the delight of the assembled media.

It was quoted that, of the crowd attending the hearing in the 35°C heat, it was not difficult to pick out the man the press were endearingly referring to as the 'pommy witness'. Although the pale complexion did not give me away, the straw hat, dark sunglasses, turned-up jeans and a tourist camera did, and I can assure you that sweat poured down my face as I trudged through the low desert scrub. I am not ashamed to admit that, if I noted a shady spot, I went for it, a fact not missed by the Australian press.

By 9 A.M. for the Monday session a crowd was pressing on the door of No. 1 court. The court was packed half an hour later, with a crowd of hopeful people still standing at the door. A screen had been set up in front of the empty jury boxes with a projector facing it, and when the counsel agreed that the public could sit in the jury boxes because of the pressure of space, these were immediately filled.

At this stage, I entered for the first time an Australian court. The evidence which I gave was demonstrated by video and by transparencies, together with straightforward one-to-one colour and black and white photographs. Following my evidence, Ray Ruddick confirmed the ultra-violet photography and he was followed into the witness box by Professor Malcolm Chaikin, Dean of the Faculty of Applied Science, and the head of the School of Textile Technology, the University of New South Wales. He had been involved in textile research for thirty years and talked of the constituents of the jumpsuit with a number of exhibits to supplement his evidence.

Mr Sims was subsequently called and confirmed that in his opinion there was no evidence upon the clothing to involve a member of the canine family either by teeth marks or the presence of saliva 'as one would expect'. All mammals, he pointed out, secreted saliva and there were three glands which produced this fluid. Basically, the function of the saliva was to act as an antiseptic because it covered and coated the gums and without it bacteria could get into the gums. Saliva also lubricated and without it an animal could not swallow.

Bernard Sims's testimony apparently gave the impression of a forensic lecture and his presentation intrigued the court. He further spoke of the enzymatic effect of saliva in digestion and pointed out that the dog, being a hunting animal, could not perspire through its fur and would have to perspire through its mouth. This is why a dog always has its mouth open, it being the only mechanism a dog has for maintaining heat control and fluid balance.

The case was finally adjourned until 1 February 1982, and when the inquest resumed submissions were made by Mr Sturgess and Mr Rice. It was Coroner Galvin's view that although the evidence was largely circumstantial, a properly instructed jury could arrive at a verdict and he committed Mrs Chamberlain for trial on a charge of murdering baby Azaria, and her husband to be charged with being an accessory after the fact of murder. They were granted bail of $5,000 (Australian) each. As a result both the Chamberlains were committed for trial at Darwin beginning on 13 September 1982.

It is interesting in that were this case to have occurred in Britain there would have been no such committal. She would have been charged with infanticide. But in the Northern Territory there is no such charge as infanticide – it was murder or nothing – and, if and when found guilty, sentence was mandatory.

This trial aroused remarkable interest, not only in Australia, but also abroad. At least four books on the case were being prepared before it even began. So many persons wanted seats that the overspill had to follow the proceedings on a closed-circuit television. The chief prosecutor on this case was Mr Ian Barker, QC.

On Monday, 13 September 1982, at 8 A.M. within Darwin Supreme Court, Lindy Chamberlain, now seven months pregnant with her fourth child, sat impassively in the dock as Mr Barker spoke. The jury had been chosen – three women and nine men – and to the charges both the Chamberlains answered, 'Not guilty, your honour.' The case was held in front of a Supreme Court judge, James Henry Muirhead. Unlike Coroner Barritt, the ex-detective, and Coroner Galvin, Justice Muirhead displayed a warm sense of humour, setting the jury at ease almost immediately by drawing their attention to the television cameras which were put there purely for the convenience of the press to avoid overcrowding. Mr John Phillips, QC, representing the Chamberlains, was supported by the previous team for the defence, namely, Mr Kirkham and Mr Peter Dean.

At this inquest Professor Malcolm Chaikin, who at the second inquest had described the make-up of the material of Azaria's clothing, said that after examining the jumpsuit he had concluded that the four areas of damage were caused by sharp scissors and that a dingo's tooth could not have caused the damage on the collar, sleeve or back. He went on to describe his experiments using a dingo's tooth mounted on a machine and thrust into clothing containing a freshly killed rabbit. Alike on the singlet and jumpsuit which were under tension, a tooth could not rupture the material even when the fabric-covered tooth penetrated the carcass to a depth of one centimetre.

Fibre tufts found in the Chamberlain's car were similar to those which fell when he cut his experimental jumpsuit. He also made a comparison with tufts found in Michael Chamberlain's camera bag, saying these were similar in size, weight and shape to those produced in the experiments. After examining Azaria's torn napkin, said the professor, he concluded that several indentations and one tear in it were caused by 'a slightly pointed object'. The textile expert then told the court about his examination of the camera bag which belonged to Michael Chamberlain. In this he discovered, among other fibres, six baby hairs which were identifiable from dog hairs because of their different characteristics.

Mrs Joy Kuhl, the forensic biologist from the crime laboratory of the New South Wales Health Commission, was the thirty-fifth prosecution witness to be called and spent a considerable time in the witness box describing foetal haemoglobin. As one would expect, equally eminent forensic experts were called by the defence, which gave totally conflicting evidence in support of the 'dingo theory'.

The judge, in his summing up, warned the jury to treat the evidence given by the defending experts with caution. The jury were out for six and a half hours at the end of a trial which had lasted seven weeks. Their verdict was unanimous. Lindy Chamberlain was guilty of murdering her baby daughter, and her husband, the pastor, of being an accessory after the fact.

Lindy Chamberlain was sentenced first. To her Mr Justice Muirhead said, 'There is only one sentence I can pass upon you. That sentence is, you will be imprisoned with hard labour for life.' She was then thirty-five years old and about to deliver a child within a matter of days. Her husband, who had spent the night free on bail, stood in the dock next day awaiting sentence in his turn. Surprisingly, in view of the sentence passed on his wife, Pastor Chamberlain was given a suspended sentence of 18 months' hard labour and was placed on a three-year good behaviour bond of $500 (Australian). Not once did Lindy Chamberlain waver from her story that she saw a dingo rush out from the tent a second before she discovered that her baby was missing.

The prosecution admitted to being unable to state precisely how the child had been killed since no body or murder weapon had been found, nor any motive for the murder, or to assert that Azaria was anything but a perfectly normal, healthy child. Mrs Chamberlain was released on bail three weeks later after the birth in a prison hospital, of her fourth child, Kahlia, pending the result of her appeal against conviction.

On 29 April 1983 three Federal Court judges in Sydney dismissed the appeal and ordered her to be returned to prison to resume her sentence of life imprisonment with hard labour. After subsequent appeal to the High Court in Canberra, her final appeal was turned down by a three to two majority, thus exhausting all avenues of appeal in an Australian legal case, there now being no leave to appeal to the Privy Council.

I must acknowledge not only the excellent support

given to me by Mr B. G. Sims and Mr R. F. Ruddick, together with Dr Graeme J. A. I. Snodgrass, consultant paediatrician at the London Hospital, but also to the numerous past and present senior CID officers and forensic pathologists who attended private seminars prior to our going 'down under'.

One must congratulate not only counsel for the prosecution but also compliment the thoroughness of the solicitors for the Chamberlains.

Finally I should like to thank Commissioner Peter McAuley and Detective Chief Superintendent Plumb for accepting the evidence as sufficient to reopen a most intriguing case in Australian legal history.

Thank you.

THE CHAIRMAN   The word 'fascinating' is the correct one. Professor Cameron has been good enough to say that he will answer questions and hear comments from anybody.

MR LEONARD CAPLAN   What was it that led to the prosecution naming the wife as the supposed murderer, rather than the husband?

PROFESSOR CAMERON   This was a problem which we as prosecution witnesses did not need to worry about, but I do know that a number of legal views were expressed or cast doubt, like you do, on the veracity of differentiating the charges.

A MEMBER   Professor Cameron, the two boys were never questioned?

PROFESSOR CAMERON   The two boys were questioned and, from what I am led to believe, when interviewed, they gave identical statements and, when re-interviewed and breaking off the interview half way and starting again, they went and had a playback and carried straight through. They never changed in any way whatsoever, but naturally, they could not be interviewed too often. In fact no blood samples were taken from the two children at all because it was considered totally unnecessary in view of there being no challenge to the clothing being that of baby Azaria.

THE CHAIRMAN   Are there any accounts of dingos attacking human beings, particularly babies?

PROFESSOR CAMERON   There are a number of cases in Australia, particularly in the Aboriginal legends, of dingos attacking livestock and, it is alleged, children, but there is no factual proof whatsoever of dingos attacking such objects, unless they already be dead. They go mainly for insects and small mammals.

THE CHAIRMAN   And do they eat carrion?

PROFESSOR CAMERON   Not often. I have no definite proof. There were a number of dingo experts called both for the prosecution and for the defence and there seemed to be considerable diversion of views as to whether they were four-legged animals or eight-legged octopi and their views changed from day to day.

THE SECRETARY   Professor, I thought you were saying that it looked as if the body had been buried in the babygrow and then the babygrow had been dug up again.

PROFESSOR CAMERON   No. When one examined the babygrow there were no bloodstains whatever on the babygrow or on the carry-cot. There was very little blood on any of the six blankets in which the child was wrapped like a cocoon. There were a couple of drops of blood on a couple of parkas that were found inside the tent and also on Mrs Chamberlain's trousers, which were only detected after they had come back from the cleaners. As to the clothing and the jumpsuit, it was my view that this had been buried in sand or in the red sandstone adjacent to Ayers Rock whilst something was inside it, because there were no crease-marks in the clothing and it was uniformly stained with sand as if it had been buried in sand and not as if the clothing had been buried empty.

MR EVANS   What was the defence explanation for the bloodstains on the mother's trousers and the bloodstains in the car?

PROFESSOR CAMERON   There is an expert here who knows more about what the defence's view would be as regards the bloodstaining, but, as far as we were led to believe, the Chamberlains' view was that the blood on the car was not that of Azaria. They did offer the explanation initially that, being Seventh Day Adventists, they were very good Samaritans, and if they knocked an animal down and they picked him up and threw him in the back of the car this would cause the blood contamination. That was one story.

The second was that, as was pointed out, it was a child's blood; it was then suggested that their two boys frequently fought in the car and this was coming from them. Then when it was pointed out or suggested by Mr Barker, on Mrs Kuhl's evidence, that this was a child under six months, no explanation was given. There is, and there always will be, considerable disquiet by many forensic biologists as to the presence or absence of foetal haemoglobin in the bloodstain of that age and as to categorically as stated in this case.

MR ERIC NEWHAM (Oxford)   I had the privilege to attend a conference in Australia where this subject was discussed and the only point that I would like to make, sir, is that this was, in our view, a wonderful determination by pathologists' forensic evidence to show without question that the defence put up would not stand up and I think that, because of the weird background, some of us might think that there might be something in the defence.

The point that I would like to make is that I am quite certain, in talking not only to the forensic scientists on the spot but also to lawyers there, that there is no question whatever that the right decision has been made. I think there is a danger – do not you, sir? – that because something is peculiar and weird, therefore we do not believe the obvious scientific evidence; but the scientific evidence here, as I understand it, is absolutely clear.

MR WOOLF (solicitor)   There was a suggestion early on in your very interesting talk, sir, that the child suffered some sort of mishap earlier on in its life and that possibly its death may have been sacrifice on somebody's part. I was wondering whether there was any theory to that effect advanced at the trial and whether you had any thoughts on the subject.

PROFESSOR CAMERON   There was never any suggestion made either by the prosecution or by the defence that this child had suffered any brain damage as a result of an injury that we knew it had received when it was aged five weeks, when in a supermarket it fell out of a trolley, voluntarily apparently, and landed on its head. Those of us who have a rather low threshold of suspicion in dealing with child deaths would have liked to have read more fully the history of the examination of that child. The notes are rather sparse, to say the least, and the child had not received any X-ray and, therefore, one can only assume that the clinicians who examined it when it was taken into hospital were correct in saying that there was no damage at all. Suffice it to say that it played no part in the prosecution case to suggest that this child had any injury which caused its death or could in any way be attributed to its death as you would get, say, in a battered child.

MR GRAHAM DOWN   You tell us that in Australia there is no such crime as infanticide.

PROFESSOR CAMERON   In the Northern Territory.

MR GRAHAM DOWN   In the Northern Territory. But in

practice is it the custom in Australia for a woman in these circumstances to serve a lesser sentence than had she murdered somebody older?

PROFESSOR CAMERON I cannot completely answer your question because I have not got that experience. Suffice it to say that all I know is that the Northern Territory is the only State with no infanticide law and that, as far as I am led to believe, any person so charged would be charged with murder and sentence is mandatory.

DR JULIUS GRANT Is there any theory as to the where-abouts of the body? Presumably there must have been a very complete search of the neighbourhood and the mother could not really have got very far in the time available – I am not sure how many hours were available – and in an area like that disturbance in the sand should be fairly conspicuous.

PROFESSOR CAMERON I think that, because of brevity, I had to omit a number of points of evidence. Whilst Mr Chamberlain drove with Nurse Downes back to the motel, Mrs Downes did note that he had his photographic bag immediately in front of his seat and she asked him whether she could take it to give him more room and he said, 'No, I am a keen photographer, I always keep my camera there.' It was only subsequently, as a result of Mrs Kuhl's examination of the carpet on the driver's side of the hatchback, that they found that the carpet had been washed but there was still, I believe, a rectangular mark immediately in front of the driver's seat which was allegedly bloodstained and which would marry in perfectly with this photographic bag. Examination of the photo-graphic bag further confirmed that there were washed bloodstains. Examination of the contents of the bag did reveal multiple or nineteen white loops, as the material you would get when you cut a towelling with white loops, which satisfied the textile expert that this was consistent with the cutting with the scissors of a jumpsuit, and together in that bag were found head hairs which were similar to those found on the vest.

That evidence, although not played on or given in evidence, although not pointed out or used by the defence or challenged by the defence, suggested that there was a possibility that the child, whilst bleeding, was placed in this photographic bag and removed to the motel. But again, this is supposition. We have no proof and certainly I have no proof whatsoever.

MR C. ROTHMAN   I know a little about the Seventh Day Adventist Church. They are either Christian Jews or Jewish Christians and the idea of homicide is repugnant to them. Were any psychiatric interviews carried out on the Chamberlains before the trial and, if so, do we know anything at all about the state of their minds?

PROFESSOR CAMERON   As far as I am led to believe, there were no psychiatrists, for the prosecution asked to interview them and I think they were the only specialists that were not called by the defence in this case. We did have a psychologist who could interpret the behaviour of dingos but not the behaviour of individuals.

MR BAYNES COPE   Was there any significance in the amount of wrapping up of that child at 8 o'clock in the evening of the day when the temperature reached 110 degrees Fahrenheit? It seems an awful lot of wrapping up, to an ignorant bachelor.

PROFESSOR CAMERON   I think that only when you have been to Ayers Rock do you realize that, although the temperature can be anything up to 35°C during the day, it gets very near zero at midnight. It would be getting very cold at 8 or 9 o'clock at night and it would be not unreasonable for a caring mother to wrap a child in such a number of items of clothing.

There were some remarks passed as to when the child

was last seen. The last sighting of that child was at 3 o'clock in the afternoon, when the child was actually being photographed. It was seen at 7.30 at the barbecue, but it was wrapped up totally, apart from the top of its head, and there were remarks passed by a witness that they saw the legs moving, but it is not difficult even with a body in total rigor, to make the legs move if you have it in your arms, and therefore there is no definite proof one way or another as to whether this child was alive or not at 8 o'clock.

THE CHAIRMAN   I am afraid that our time has run out and it only remains for me to thank the Professor very much for a fascinating talk. It is a problem that probably will never be solved because it is all on theories and nobody knows. But we have been given a great insight into it and we are very grateful to you, sir, for giving us that insight.

Mrs Chamberlain is approaching her fourth Christmas in jail since that steaming hot day in Darwin when twelve jurors agreed beyond reasonable doubt that she had cut the throat of her ten-week-old baby daughter Azaria.

At that time there were lawyers who maintained, in private, that she should never have been convicted. The controversy continues and has become noisier than ever. Lawyers for the 'Free Lindy' movement say extensive new evidence about the case will prove that a dingo took the baby, as Mrs Chamberlain has always claimed.

Lindy Chamberlain is serving her life sentence for murder in Darwin jail, where she works in the laundry. In court, during the trial, she was always neatly dressed and composed. In jail she is said to be popular with the other prisoners, helping them to mend their clothes and even, sometimes, offering legal advice.

Since the trial Mrs Chamberlain has had another baby called Kahlia, who is being cared for by the Seventh Day

Adventist Church, to which both parents belonged. It teaches that Christ will come again and, on that day, the righteous dead will rise again and be united with Christ in heaven. Michael Chamberlain, the husband, was a pastor in the Church until recently, when he resigned. He continues to campaign on television, arguing his and his wife's innocence.

22
Poison Pie

Murder by poisoning was not uncommon in the early years of this century, and food and drink were sometimes the means by which a victim was killed. Major Armstrong served arsenic-flavoured scones for tea, Dr Lamson spiced Dundee cakes with aconite and Richard Brinkley served stout flavoured with cyanide. They, and others, were hanged, and as a direct result of their crimes a strict control of poisons was imposed. Thereafter poisoning went out of favour as a means of murder.

But in 1982 this pitiless method was used again, this time in the town of Westcliff-on-Sea, in Essex, a quiet suburb of Southend. At No. 29 Osborne Road lived Michael and Susan Barber in the terraced house they had taken after their marriage in 1970. Susan had already had a six-month-old daughter then and there were rumours that, although Michael believed the child to be his, it was, in fact, the child of a previous lover.

The couple had their share of quarrels and twice she had left him but returned after a few days. Despite that, they had two more children. The marriage was far from stable and Michael was seven years older than Susan. Before 1970 he had been in trouble with the police for taking cars and for traffic offences, but in 1972 he was in worse trouble, for indecently assaulting his six-year-old niece, the daughter of Susan's sister. And yet, despite these lapses, he was quite popular in the neighbourhood and was considered a hard worker who liked his game of darts and a pint of beer.

Michael Barber was captain of a local public house

darts team and one of his players was Richard Collins, a young man who lived with his wife only three doors away from the Barbers. Richard was naïve and some people thought him rather stupid, but he was tall, young and strong and well-liked. He was liked particularly by Susan Barber, and in time he was to become putty in the hands of this well-built, experienced married woman who thirsted for excitement.

By 1981 the friendship between Susan Barber and Richard Collins had developed to a point where they went to bed together every morning after Michael went to work at a factory at five o'clock. The affair went on for some time and there were other occasions when the couple met.

When Michael was not drinking and playing darts he liked to go fishing, and on Saturday, 23 May 1981, he left his house at four o'clock in the morning to go fishing with a friend in the Thames estuary. Susan had carefully told Richard of the plans and, as Michael drove away, Richard was let into the house. Unfortunately the weather had changed and a strong wind had blown up. The sea fishing trip was cancelled, and Michael returned at five o'clock to find a terrified Richard Collins naked in the bedroom, trying desperately to pull on his clothes. In the matrimonial bed was Susan, also naked. Michael Barber punched Richard in the face and then turned and punched his wife on the ear. Collins fled and stayed away from Osborne Road for some weeks, living with his brother in another part of the town.

The blow to Susan's ear had caused painful bruising and a few days later she had to go to the doctor. Michael went with her. The doctor asked questions and learned the truth about their personal problems. After a discussion, Susan told him that she was prepared to try to preserve the marriage. The couple returned home together but within days they were not on speaking terms and were writing notes to each other, using a trusted friend as a 'postman'.

Michael Barber worked at a cigarette factory and on 4 June he developed a severe headache. It grew steadily worse and he had to attend the factory clinic to get some tablets to ease the pain. He suffered the same pains next day and was given more tablets. Then he noticed that he also had occasional attacks of stomach ache and felt sick. He mentioned this to some of his pub friends but did not go to the doctor. A week later he felt really ill. His throat was inflamed and he had a splitting headache. His wife called the doctor who prescribed an antibiotic and a linctus, but his condition continued to deteriorate and the doctor sent him to Southend General Hospital by ambulance.

Michael Barber grew progressively worse and within three days he was moved into intensive care, placed on a ventilator and sedated. Tests suggested he was suffering from a rare disease, Goodpastures Syndrome, but, in spite of treatment, his condition declined and on 17 June he was removed to the Hammersmith Hospital where specialist treatment is available for kidney diseases.

Susan had been visiting her husband at Southend Hospital and she was informed that he was seriously ill with only a poor chance of survival, a piece of news that, apparently, she took quite calmly. Meanwhile the doctors at Hammersmith were unable to diagnose what Barber was suffering from until the question of paraquat poisoning was raised by the registrar in respiratory medicine. The consultant physician gave instructions that blood and urine samples were to be sent to the national Poisons Reference Centre at New Cross Hospital for analysis. He later understood the analysis to have proved negative.

Susan visited her husband twice at Hammersmith, once

accompanied by Richard Collins, although he stayed outside while she went to the ward. She had given him the details of the situation and he knew that Michael was dangerously ill and that his recovery was unlikely.

On Saturday, 27 June 1980, Michael Barber died and his wife was telephoned with the news. The death certificate gave the cause of death as cardiac arrest, renal (kidney) failure and bilateral pneumonia. A post-mortem examination was fixed for the following Tuesday.

Professor David Evans supervised the post-mortem which was carried out by Dr O'Brien. The major organs of the body were removed and, after samples had been taken for special examination, the organs were placed in a bucket and labelled with the name of the deceased and the post-mortem number. The bucket was filled with formalin, a preserving fluid, and placed in an ante-room at the mortuary. No firm conclusions were reached, although the pathologists still thought that the findings suggested paraquat poisoning.

On 3 July 1981 the body of Michael Barber was cremated at Southend Crematorium. His wife and his family were there and so, separately, was Richard Collins. He was crying throughout and was still crying when the mourners went back to Osborne Road where Susan served food and drinks. On that night Richard moved in to live with her.

For six weeks Susan was deliriously happy but after that Richard began to worry. She had met another man on their regular visits to the public house and she let him know that he would be welcome at the house. Soon afterwards the new man moved in and Richard was ordered out.

At Hammersmith Hospital the doctors had examined the histology slides of the organ samples taken from Michael Barber. The conclusion of these microscopic findings suggested there had been ingested toxin, most probably paraquat. It was decided to hold a clinical conference into the whole history of the case.

Susan Barber was still enjoying the good life, and in October 1981 she reaped the financial benefits of her husband's death. She received £15,000 in death benefit, plus a refund of pension contributions of £800 and £300 per annum for each of her three children.

The money gave Susan a new chance to expand her social life, and another regular at the pub went to live at Osborne Road. Since all the lovers either played in the darts team or were acquaintances there were sometimes harsh words exchanged. When Susan told her latest lover that Richard Collins owed her £60 he decided to act as a debt collector and demanded the money. Collins refused to pay and was assaulted, an offence for which the latest paramour went to jail.

But the drinking parties went on. Susan bought herself a CB radio and became well known on the Southend airwaves. She met yet another man, known to the police through black magic rituals and drug offences. Video and blue movie shows were held at the house and the new friend took up residence.

Then towards the end of January 1982, the doctors and experts at the Hammersmith Hospital finalized their clinical material in the case of Michael Barber. Their view was that his death looked like paraquat poisoning, although it was pointed out that paraquat was said to have been excluded in the original test. However, when the file was examined again, there was no note regarding any examination having been made by the National Poisons Unit. A check with the unit concerned revealed that no samples taken from Michael Barber had ever been sent for analysis.

In the next few days the team of Hammersmith Hospital

worked at great speed. Serum samples were found and sent to the Poisons Unit at New Cross Hospital. Samples of tissue from the major organs, still lying in the bucket in the mortuary eight months later, were sent to Imperial Chemicals Industries Ltd., the manufacturers of paraquat. The results were soon returned to the hospital. Paraquat had been found in both the serum and the tissue.

On 15 February 1982 the circumstances of the death of Michael Barber were reported to the Hammersmith Coroner in a letter written by a consultant at the Royal Post Graduate Medical School, Hammersmith Hospital. That letter was forwarded to the Southend Coroner who sent it on to the Southend police. It read:

Dear Sir,
   Re: Michael Barber, 29 Osborne Road,
     Westcliff-on-Sea, Essex.
I am writing to you having spoken to your officer on the telephone today, about Michael Barber, of 29 Osborne Road, Westcliff-on-Sea, Essex, who was a patient under my care on the renal unit at Hammersmith Hospital and who died in hospital on 27 June 1981. The cause of death was combined acute respiratory and renal failure thought to be due to an infection and was not reported to you. However, we now have unequivocal proof that it was in fact due to paraquat poisoning and this is my reason for writing to you at this stage.

Detective Chief Inspector John Clarion of the Essex police took charge of the investigation. He found he was faced with some difficulties because of the delays and errors that had been made. The whole history of Michael Barber's illness had to be gone into and everybody concerned, doctors, nurses, analysts, laboratory technicians and porters, had to be interviewed and all the scientific tests made yet again.

Professor Cameron was called in to look at all the evidence and make a forensic judgement of the histology samples. He gave his opinion of the cause of death as paraquat poisoning. The police found a mass of evidence. Richard Collins quickly admitted that he had been told by Susan Barber of her intention to murder her husband. He was able to recall a suggestion made by her to cut the brake pipes on her husband's car. He remembered being present when the two of them returned home from Hammersmith Hospital when Susan, having been asked by the medical staff about poison, poured the contents of her husband's medicine bottle down the kitchen sink.

It now transpired that the naïve Collins had told a number of people what Susan had done. It was after he had been supplanted by another lover, and at the time local people had thought he was hurt at being dismissed from the love nest at Osborne Road and paid scant attention.

Susan told the police that she resented her husband finding her with Collins on the day of the fishing trip and had no intention of trying to go on with the marriage. She admitted that one evening she had put some Gromoxone (a weed-killer) in her husband's dinner and had watched him eat it. She remembered it was steak and kidney pie. When nothing happened immediately she gave him another dose, and, soon afterwards, when he had been prescribed medicine for his sore throat, she gave him some more – in the medicine. She had found the Gromoxone in the garden shed, where her husband had put it after bringing it home from some work he had done with a landscape gardening firm.

On Monday, 5 April 1982, Susan Barber and Richard Collins were arrested and charged with conspiracy to murder. In the following November they appeared at Chelmsford Crown Court before Mr Justice Woolfe. Collins, on whose behalf strong evidence of good character was given, was sentenced to two years' imprisonment.

Susan Barber maintained that she had had no intention of killing her husband but 'just wanted him to suffer as she had suffered'. In sentencing her to life imprisonment for the murder of her husband Mr Justice Woolfe said, 'I cannot think of a more evil way of disposing of a human being.'

Postscript
The Pathologist and the Shroud

Professor Cameron has spent much of his time over the years interpreting clues to murder apart from those found on the body. That is why he was asked to examine the Turin Shroud, the length of old cloth preserved in Turin Cathedral, in an effort to solve the mystery of whether or not it is the shroud worn by Jesus Christ after he was crucified.

He had previously examined many medico-legal incidents in the Bible and taken part in discussions to determine from the clues the cause of death and the identification of the victim.

This last chapter was written by Professor Cameron for the British Society for the Turin Shroud and first published in the book entitled Face to Face with the Turin Shroud, *by Peter Jennings.*

The Gospel record nowhere implies that the shroud in which Jesus Christ was wrapped after his crucifixion revealed an image of his body, let alone his numerous wounds. The task of reconstructing the chain of events that link the Turin Shroud to Calvary is by no means easy. The Gospels recall how Christ was scourged, crowned with thorns, forced to walk perhaps some six hundred yards bearing the cross-beam of the cross, during which time he may have had numerous falls to the ground. Thereafter he was subsequently nailed to the cross and later his side was pierced with a lance by a Roman sentinel.

I have been asked to comment on the image as a

pathologist. Colour photographs of the Shroud indicate
the body to be a sepia with a touch of yellow ochre hue,
which appears so faintly when viewed that it can only be
visible to the naked eye in certain conditions. The darker
brownish marks in the body represent trickles of blood
and/or serum issuing from the wounds. The outline of the
figure stands out well in the black and white photographs
taken by Giuseppe Enrie, in 1931. The cloth itself por-
trays a naked male corpse with hands crossed, and around
the chin, supporting the lower jaw, is a sudarium – a
napkin or handkerchief which passes across the beard
and behind the hair. The position of the body as depicted
on the Shroud is consistent with that of a crucified body
in a state of post-mortem rigor (that is, muscle-stiffening
after death whilst still on the cross), which would naturally
set it in the position into which the body would slip after
death.

I agree entirely with my colleague, Dr Derek Barrowcliff, Home Office Pathologist and Medico-Legal Expert
from Warwickshire, when he states that bodies do bleed
after death for a period of time, but the Shroud does not
show any smudging of the rivulets from the marks of the
scourging, nor from the abrasions, particularly on the left
knee. Blood, however, that has flowed during life and
clotted on the skin may somehow have been transferred
to the cloth. It is not unknown for clots to undergo what
is known as fibrinolysis as a result of enzymatic or
bacterial action and they could possibly be absorbed by
linen; that is to say the blood would break down into
numerous components and would be extremely difficult
to differentiate.

The multiple puncture marks with attendant rivulets of
blood over the scalp, extending from the centre of the
forehead towards the front round to the level of the ears
at the back of the head, would suggest a clump of thorny

twigs being pressed down upon the head, rather than a circlet, which artists frequently symbolize as a 'crown of thorns'.

The image of the face is indicative of one who has suffered death by crucifixion and is not alive, for the linen cloth would act like a plastic membrane and would be sucked into the mouth and nostrils were the victim alive, as happens in tragic cases when a plastic bag is placed over the head of a child or adult resulting in death.

Reviewing the face, one can see several swellings and bruises over the facial areas, particularly the left cheek and forehead, under the right eye and across the nose, which could well be broken. The lower lip also gives the impression of having been swollen, injuries consistent with the face having come into contact with firm or hard surfaces during life; that is to say, with the victim either being struck in the face or falling on the face whilst carrying the beam of a cross. The eyes appear to be closed and sunken, suggestive that eye changes after death had occurred. There is no indication to suggest that any metallic coin or object had been placed over the eyes to keep them closed. The arms are bent and across the lower abdomen; this would, in my opinion, have been done forcibly in order to break the rigor or muscle-stiffening of the shoulder-girdle – a not unusual problem when dealing with death from any cause, in order to get the body into a straight position. The track of the blood rivulets from the nail-marks on the wrists indicate fluctuation in the degree of sagging of the body on the cross during life. This varied from 55 to 65 degrees approximately.

Anatomical experiments carried out in 1940 stated that, in order to support the victim in crucifixion, the nails would need to have been driven into the wrists (carpal bones) and not the palms of the hands (between the meta-carpal bones) as has been depicted by artists throughout the ages. This mode of positioning of the nails in the wrists could damage the median nerve, causing the thumb to bend over the palm for, as can be seen from the image depicted on the Shroud, the thumbs are not seen. The image of the hands suggests the fingers to be somewhat shrivelled, indicative, in my opinion, of either deprivation of blood or post-mortem change.

The lance entering the chest cavity on the right side of the body in the fifth interspace, that is to say between the fifth and sixth ribs in an upward, inward direction, would penetrate the right lung, causing it to collapse, with resulting pneumothorax (i.e. air under pressure in the chest cavity) and subsequent bleeding from the lungs into the chest cavity, and further penetration for some eight to nine inches (i.e. the length of the blade of a Roman lance) could well penetrate the principal chamber on the right side of the heart. Such a wound is frequently seen in domestic murder in the present day, resulting in almost immediate death resulting from bleeding into the chest cavity. A spear wound is visible in the Shroud itself just to the left of a triangular patch sewn on by the Poor Clares after the fire at Chambéry in 1532.

Examination of the upper back of the trunk reveals deep bruising of the shoulder blades, indicating the angle at which the cross-beam of the cross might have been carried, but within this bruising there are marks of scourging. I agree entirely with Dr Bucklin's view that the scourge marks on the body would be consistent with a flagrum. Had the victim been a Roman citizen, he would have been beaten with rods, not whipped with the flagrum, and, secondly, the inflicters of this punishment were not of the Jewish faith as their law forbade more than forty lashes.

I am also in total agreement with the views expressed by Dr Robert Bucklin and Dr Barbet that the nail fixing the feet passed between the metatarsal bones, that is to say the long bones of the foot, and not through the heel bone.

The image on the Shroud indicates to me that its owner – whoever he may have been – died on the cross, and was in a state of rigor when placed in it. Even after the most extensive scientific and forensic tests, it is my belief that we shall only be able to prove the fact that the Turin Shroud *might* be the burial cloth of Jesus Christ, not that it actually is.

Index

Index

True crime – now available in paperback from Grafton Books

Crime fiction – now available in paperback from Grafton Books

Isaac Asimov
Banquets of the Black Widowers   £2.50 ☐

Colin Wilson
The Schoolgirl Murder Case   £1.95 ☐

Agatha Christie
The Secret Adversary   £1.95 ☐
The Murder on the Links   £1.95 ☐
The Mysterious Affair at Styles   £1.95 ☐
The Man in the Brown Suit   £1.95 ☐
The Secret of.Chimneys   £1.95 ☐
Poirot Investigates   £1.95 ☐

John Bowen
The McGuffin   £1.95 ☐

To order direct from the publisher just tick the titles you want
and fill in the order form.

GF2681

The best of crime fiction now available in paperback from Grafton Books

John Hutten

Accidental Crimes	£1.95	☐
29 Herriott Street	£1.95	☐

Dan Kavanagh

Duffy	£1.50	☐
Fiddle City	£1.50	☐

Joseph Hansen

Troublemaker	£2.50	☐
Fade Out	£2.50	☐
Gravedigger	£1.95	☐
Skinflick	£1.95	☐
The Man Everybody was Afraid of	£1.95	☐
Nightwork	£1.95	☐

Stephen Knight

Requiem at Rogano	£2.50	☐

Rod Miller

The Animal Letter	£2.50	☐

To order direct from the publisher just tick the titles you want and fill in the order form.

GF3081

Crime fiction – now available in paperback from Grafton Books

James Hadley Chase

One Bright Summer Morning	£1.95	☐
Tiger by the Tail	£1.95	☐
Strictly for Cash	£1.50	☐
What's Better than Money?	£1.50	☐
Just the Way it Is	£1.95	☐
You're Dead Without Money	£1.50	☐
Coffin From Hong Kong	£1.95	☐
Like a Hole in the Head	£1.50	☐
There's a Hippie on the Highway	£1.95	☐
This Way for a Shroud	£1.95	☐
Just a Matter of Time	£1.95	☐
Not My Thing	£1.95	☐
Hit Them Where It Hurts	£1.95	☐

Georgette Heyer

Penhallow	£1.95	☐
Duplicate Death	£1.95	☐
Envious Casca	£1.95	☐
Death in the Stocks	£1.95	☐
Behold, Here's Poison	£1.95	☐
They Found Him Dead	£1.95	☐
The Unfinished Clue	£1.95	☐
Detection Unlimited	£1.95	☐
Why Shoot a Butler?	£2.50	☐

To order direct from the publisher just tick the titles you want and fill in the order form.

GF2781

True war – now available in paperback from Grafton Books

Alexander Baron		
From the City, From the Plough	£1.95	☐
C S Forester		
Hunting the Bismarck	£1.50	☐
Ka-Tzetnik		
House of Dolls	£2.50	☐
Olga Lengyel		
Five Chimneys	£1.95	☐
Dr Miklos Nyiszli		
Auschwitz	£1.95	☐
Alexander McKee		
Dresden 1945 (illustrated)	£2.50	☐
F Spencer-Chapman		
The Jungle is Neutral [illustrated]	£2.50	☐
Bryan Perrett		
Lightning War: A History of Blitzkrieg (illustrated)	£2.95	☐
Leonce Péillard		
Sink the Tirpitz!	£1.95	☐
Richard Pape		
Boldness Be My Friend (illustrated)	£2.50	☐
Baron Burkhard von Mullenheim-Rechberg		
Battleship Bismarck (illustrated)	£3.50	☐
Livia E Bitton Jackson		
Elli: Coming of Age in the Holocaust	£2.50	☐
Charles Whiting		
Siegfried: The Nazis' Last Stand (illustrated)	£2.50	☐
First Blood: The Battle of the Kasserine Pass 1943 (illustrated)	£2.50	☐

To order direct from the publisher just tick the titles you want and fill in the order form.

All these books are available at your local bookshop or newsagent, or can be ordered direct from the publisher.

To order direct from the publishers just tick the titles you want and fill in the form below.

Name _____

Address _____

_____

Send to:
Grafton Cash Sales
PO Box 11, Falmouth, Cornwall TR10 9EN.

Please enclose remittance to the value of the cover price plus:

UK 60p for the first book, 25p for the second book plus 15p per copy for each additional book ordered to a maximum charge of £1.90.

BFPO 60p for the first book, 25p for the second book plus 15p per copy for the next 7 books, thereafter 9p per book.

Overseas including Eire £1.25 for the first book, 75p for second book and 28p for each additional book.

Grafton Books reserve the right to show new retail prices on covers, which may differ from those previously advertised in the text or elsewhere.